Finding Your Granite

Security, Audit and Leadership Series

**Series Editor: Dan Swanson, Dan Swanson and Associates, Ltd.,
Winnipeg, Manitoba, Canada.**

The *Security, Audit and Leadership Series* publishes leading-edge books on critical subjects facing security and audit executives as well as business leaders. Key topics addressed include Leadership, Cybersecurity, Security Leadership, Privacy, Strategic Risk Management, Auditing IT, Audit Management and Leadership

For more information about this series, please visit: https://www.routledge.com/ Internal-Audit-and-IT-Audit/book-series/CRCINTAUDITA

Finding Your Granite

My Four Cornerstones of
Personal Leadership

Douglas P. Pflug

CRC Press
Taylor & Francis Group
Boca Raton London

CRC Press is an imprint of the
Taylor & Francis Group, an **informa** business

First edition published 2022
by CRC Press
6000 Broken Sound Parkway NW, Suite 300, Boca Raton, FL 33487–2742

and by CRC Press
2 Park Square, Milton Park, Abingdon, Oxon, OX14 4RN

Library of Congress Cataloging-in-Publication Data
[Insert LoC Data here when available]

ISBN: 978-1-032-03410-2 (hbk)
ISBN: 978-1-032-03411-9 (pbk)
ISBN: 978-1-003-18718-9 (ebk)

DOI: 10.1201/9781003187189

Typeset in Times
by Apex CoVantage, LLC

Contents

Endorsements

REVIEW #1

Finding Your Granite: My Four Cornerstones of Personal Leadership is a moving and powerful memoir. The author, Doug Pflug, grew up in a small town in Southern Western Ontario, where from a very early age, had to overcome unimaginable obstacles. Doug decided to attend university to escape the confines of small-town life, where his stint as a standout athlete led him to discover his real calling as a law enforcement officer. This memoir chronicles his internal struggle to understand his version of his life and to have the courage to step forward from his past. It offers a glimpse into a way of life that most of us will never experience, as well as an inspiring story about one man's capacity to rise up and excel. Read this book now!

Dr. Gary Marshall: DBA—Leadership
www.linkedin.com/in/dr-gary-marshall-dba-1a57b2aa

REVIEW #2

Doug's story brought back many of the struggles I faced during my time with the Canadian Forces and post-service. It is a story that many veterans and public safety members share, and I am truly inspired by Doug and his ability to put that fight into words and his willingness and courage to share it with others. A key underlying principle to leadership displayed is that not all outstanding leaders are born but are created. Leadership is a journey that a select few navigate with the grace and humility that is showed in this book. A must-read for LEOs and public safety professionals.

Adam Kinakin: Founder, International Law Enforcement Training Network
https://podcast.ilet.network/show/tactical-breakdown/

REVIEW #3

Reflecting on his life and career, Doug recounts the many events and people that shaped him. From a serious childhood illness, through school, his involvement in sports, coaching, and a successful police career—he learned from the good and from the bad along that journey. He presents his personal learnings and advice on resiliency and leadership from the heart, and additionally offers challenges to make the reader a better person and leader. A down-to-earth and enjoyable read!"

Chris D. Lewis: OPP Commissioner (Ret.) and author of "Never Stop on a Hill"

REVIEW #4

Webster's dictionary symbolizes "granite" as possessing "unyielding firmness or endurance". Doug Pflug provides a blueprint for life based of real-life experiences from birth and how he utilized many of his life moments to create a legacy driven by the ideals of firmness and endurance". We all have life history and Doug tells his story like we are at a backyard barbecue—relaxed and sincere—in hopes we can identify with something that can help us as we create our own legacy.

James "Jim" Barker: Canadian Football League GM, VP and Coach: Four-time Grey Cup Champion. XFL Coach and Champion. TSN CFL Analyst. https://en.wikipedia.org/wiki/Jim_Barker

REVIEW #5

Doug and I met early in my career. He helped me set a base for hockey's physical demands. Never would I have guessed he was battling the demands of his job. Doug is an incredibly positive person, always presents himself with a smile and a joy to be around. When I asked him to assist me in presenting the Stanley Cup in Guelph, he jumped right onboard. Incredibly happy he has come out on top of his PTSI and helped others with the same battles.

Rich Peverley: 7-year NHL veteran and Stanley Cup Champion with the Boston Bruins https://g.co/kgs/cxbwE9

REVIEW #6

From life struggles, obstacles, adversity and the darkness that Doug reveals. It is a testimony to who Doug is as a person and a mentor. Doug discusses and shares the events that he encountered as a young man that many people would not discuss. This says everything about him as a leader. A leader is not just someone who shows only their best and positive side, a leader is someone we can relate too. Doug is someone we can relate too because we all have our own personal battles that we do not share. We all need help and Doug discusses that countless times that we need to help each other and pick each other up. It's not a sign of weakness but a sign of strength. Amazing read and listen, Thank you Doug for being an inspiration to many including myself.

Johnny Augustine: 2-year CFL veteran and Grey Cup Champion Winnipeg Blue Bombers https://g.co/kgs/my1yxV

REVIEW #7

Something happens when someone writes so openly and honestly about their life experiences, no matter how hard it is. . . . The world breaks open, people lean forward and everyone who has ever had to deal with tough situations feels less alone. To me, Doug's display of that level of vulnerability is a display of amazing inner strength and a sign of a true leader. I knew Doug in high school as a cool, football player who was a pretty big deal. Now I know him as a leader/author . . . and he's even a bigger deal!

Naomi Sneickus: Canadian Actress and Comedic Icon "Mr. D" on CBC https://g.co/kgs/QCH1qx

REVIEW #8

Doug beckons us forward into our own self-discovery through the humble grace of his own story. Through humour and vulnerability, Doug ushers us into an opportunity for a perspective shift; encouraging us to embrace life's triumphs and tribulations as a crucible for transformation instead of destruction. His servant leadership motivates us to consider that our messes are perhaps a gate to explore a higher purpose. Doug inspires us to climb into the crucible of change instead of running for the hills and even if we have run for the hills . . . and felt that we've missed it . . . that it's never too late because every setback is just a setup for true success".

Sheila Good: International Speaker, Coach, Author and Creator of Born to Influence. Www.Bossladybizcoach.com

Introduction

Doctors told Paul and Joan Pflug to say goodbye to their newborn son as he underwent life-saving surgery in 1966 at six days old.

Although the first surgery was considered a success, he again fell ill at three years old. He was hospitalized so the doctors could start treatment for what they believed to be childhood leukemia.

One can only imagine the stress this young couple in their early 20s faced while dealing with their sick little boy. This was the 1960s, so many medical advancements that are known today had yet to be discovered. It is difficult to imagine the paralyzing fear and devastation that these two incredibly young parents had experienced with the suffering and possible death of their baby.

Miraculously, Doug survived. Since that time, he has displayed incredible physical, emotional, and spiritual resilience. He has grown stronger because of these two near-death medical conditions, as well as many other experiences through life. During his early school years, students and teachers marginalized and bullied him, calling him names like "Fatty Pflug" and "welfare trash".

In high school, he became a target for two teachers for reasons only known to them. In his senior year of high school, he experienced further trauma when a dear friend he had faithfully protected from school bullies tragically lost his life in the 1985 Air India bombing.

After graduation, he went to the University of Guelph, where he played varsity football and wrestled. On the academic front, he pursued his education in hopes of one day being a police officer so he could "serve and protect".

In 1989 he secured that dream and joined the Guelph Police Service.

In 2006, he experienced a life-altering Post Traumatic Stress Injury (PTSI) after being unsuccessful in saving a two-year-old little girl who had drowned in the bathtub. This event forced him to face his accumulated past personal and professional traumas and demons. Being aware that the self-realization and acceptance that he longed for could not be done alone, he sought out a PTSI counsellor named Mary Margaret. She collaborated diligently with him and helped him face his past. Through this incredibly caring and supportive environment, Doug could rediscover himself and be reacquainted with his service heart.

Doug now uses these experiences and life lessons learned along the way during his 35 years of accumulated time as a police officer, elite strength and conditioning coach with Wrestle Canada, the Guelph Storm Hockey Club and Special Olympics Canada, and training/ mentoring athletes in the NHL, AHL, NCAA, OHL, National and Provincial Levels to #RiseUpAndExcel.

Doug now coaches and mentors thousands, using the framework of his stress management and resiliency model, "Who Was I, Who Am I and Who Do I Want to Be?" and "I Can, I Must, I Will".

He holds his Executive Leadership, High-Performance Leadership, Change Leadership, and Managing for Execution certificates, all from Cornell University, Ithaca, New York. He combines this with his life experience and knowledge as an Executive Leadership Coach and Mentor.

Doug is also a full-time instructor in the Leadership Unit of the Ontario Police College and to date has taught over 4,000 recruits and 200 senior students.

On July 1, 2020, Doug was named one of Canada's "123 Exceptional Canadians" by the Governor-General of Canada's Office. They awarded him the Queen's Sovereign Medal for Volunteerism. In 2012, they awarded him the Queen's Diamond Jubilee Medal for his service to the community in both his police and personal capacity. In 2010, they awarded him the Governor-General of Canada Police Exemplary Medal for outstanding law enforcement contributions.

He lives in Guelph with his wife and best friend, Michelle, and his daughters, Reighan and Alexis.

This is an enlightening story of personal, physical, and emotional chaos. It demonstrates the building of resiliency, personal and professional growth, and triumph. It is a tale that Doug hopes will help others deal with their own experiences by using his tools to #RiseUpAndExcel.

"I am because of you"

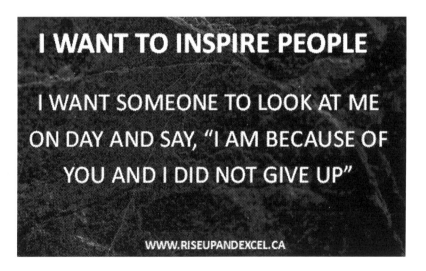

Life is how we remember it, bearing in mind that my perception is my reality in the same way it is for you.

This book is a form of my memoirs and not written in a classic form. It is a series of both positive and negative stories. These stories were relayed through my eyes, and my hope is that your takeaways are the lessons I learned through the great leaders that I have worked with over many spheres of influence. I am so fortunate to have been involved with some incredible great men and women that have led me or I have led.

*****

I dedicate this book to my loving and supportive wife, Michelle, my amazing daughters, Reighan and Alexis, and my incredible family and friends who always stood by me, helped pick me up when down, pushed, and assisted me to #RiseUpAndExcel.

Thank you all for believing in me. I am because of you.

Lastly, to all those frontline workers who work tirelessly to make our communities and citizens safer, thank you.

I am eternally indebted to your selfless dedication and service.

—Doug

Pflug Family Coat of Arms

The shield is split into two, which usually shows a marriage. Each family's items are represented on each half of the shield

Main colours:

Azure or Blue: Loyalty and truth

Gules or Red: Military fortitude and magnanimity

Mullet (star): usually five pointed; however, in Fred heraldry, the mullet is a six-pointed star. It usually is the rowel of a spur. The mullet is also the mark of distinction of the third son. See cadence. It is also said to denote some divine quality bestowed from above.

Eagle: A noble device signifying a person of action, ever more occupied in high and weighty affairs, and one of lofty spirit, ingenious, speedy in apprehension, and judicious in a matter of ambiguity; real courage, freedom, and immortality. It proudly served as an emblem of the might and unity of empire for Babylon, the Caesars, Charlemagne, and many Holy Roman and Byzantine emperors and Russian Czars, Aztecs, and Napoleon. The heraldic Eagle appeared in Persian and Egyptian battle ensigns and on Roman legions' flags. The Romans called the Eagle the "bird of Jove" and carried it on their standards into battle. If a legion lost its Eagle, it was in disgrace until the Eagle could be recovered. The Roman custom was to let an Eagle fly from the funeral pyre of a deceased emperor, bearing the god's soul to heaven after a period of earthly incarnation as the emperor. Early Christians honoured the Eagle as a symbol of hope, strength, and resurrection. The latter is based on the early belief that the Eagle, unlike other birds, periodically renewed its plumage and youth by flying near the sun and then plunging into the water. The majestic Eagle was central to many mythologies and sacred writings of humanity.

AUTHOR'S NOTE

The events in this book are real. I have tried to recount the stories to the best of my memory and from my personal perspective. Sometimes my memories fade, so I have reached out to others who were there in attempts to be as accurate as possible.

As I relay my story to you and explain how I adapted and overcame trauma with resiliency tools I've developed over the years, I will not specifically name the personnel deemed "negative" in this book, as I did not seek their permission for this project.

My goal in this book was not to criticize or point fingers of blame. It was to highlight and frame the context of the adversity I faced in my life, celebrate the opportunity of the experience, learn from it, and look for the Next Opportunity. This book is about how I was knocked to my knees and, then, what made me get up. This is also about the wonderful people in my personal and professional lives.

This book highlights exceptional people that I have had the pleasure of learning from or those I have guided in their path towards personal and professional successes. This story is about me and how it can positively inspire the "we" who read with the common theme of, "do the right thing because it was the right thing to do". I will say their names as I hold them in extremely high esteem. I am because they invested in me.

At the end of this book, I have created my "Doug Pflug's Influential Leadership Wall of Honour" where many of these names will also be listed for all to see and celebrate outstanding leadership. These incredible people supported me when I faced good and evil. They brought me hope, love, calm and took the time to teach me valuable lessons and overcome evil and excellence in both casual and emergent situations. They taught me that in the darkness and despair, there is always light. That light is not an external source; it is in all of us—we just need to find our own switch.

If you are looking for a traditional self-help book, I would suggest you put mine down as it will not fulfill your needs. This book guides personal wellness based on my real-life journey. I hope to educate, entertain, and inspire you to create your own plan by evaluating "who you were, who you are, and who you wish to be" to achieve personal and professional successes. At the end of this book I have provided you with several exercises for you to complete and help you reflect, research, plan, and move towards the personal and professional successes of your desires.

This is my story, compiled of many lessons learned from incredible triumph and devastating losses. Through these experiences that I share with you, I hope to enable you to find your inner light as I have found mine, and you will achieve the personal and professional success you desire.

This task will not be an easy one, and it may take quite a while and sometimes test your mettle. In the end, I have followed this quote on excellence my entire life,

> I firmly believe that any man's finest hour, the greatest fulfillment of all that he holds dear, is that moment when he has worked his heart out in a good cause and lies exhausted on the field of battle—victorious. [1]
>
> —Vince Lombardi

As I move forward, I would like to thank everyone who took the time to listen to me, find out who I was, invest their time and experience in me, and then help guide and support me. Leadership and resilience are both nature and nurture. Having loving and supportive parents and a great circle of positive influences around me in my life has magnified my abilities and helped me be resilient to many of the physical, emotional, and spiritual adversities that I have experienced.

I have always believed that conflict builds character, and as I relay some of that conflict to you, I want you to know that I always tried to look at it through a positive lens. I tried to look at the situation as an important opportunity to gain experience and personal growth. My credibility for this story was born through these periods of personal development.

Now is the time to roll up your sleeves, tie up your shoes, firmly plant both feet on the floor, brace yourself, and begin *your* process and journey towards your being able to www.RiseUpandExcel.ca.

I am truly honoured to be your tour guide through my journey and hope that I can help you plan and fuel yours.

Thank you because had it not been for your efforts, I would not have grown to be the man you know today. You know who you are.

ALL PROCEEDS FROM THE SALE OF THIS BOOK WILL GO TO WWW.V-EH.CA

I wanted to thank you for buying this book.

I will donate all profits for the sale of this book to our dear friends at Veterans and Everyday heroes www.v-eh.ca.

The V-EH! community was created to help supply whatever we can to those veterans and emergency services members. This could look like helping financially towards a service dog funding a goal, discounts for services, rides to appointments, financial help for services, and acts of kindness.

We will tailor our support to the needs of those V-EH!s out there who could use some kindness.

To date, V-EH! Veterans and Everyday Heroes have brought in $40,000 in funds raised to provide our

members with service dogs. This Initiative in partnership with www.searchlightservice-dogs.com/ is saving the lives of everyday heroes.

Searchlight Service Dogs is a Canadian Registered Not-for-Profit Charitable Organization, operating in Ontario. Our principal aim is to supply the highest quality Service Dogs to our clients. We came into existence in 2019, but the idea and concept of Searchlight Service Dogs has been in the works since 2017.

We understand the outstanding benefits a Service Dog can have in helping people regain portions of their lives affected by PTSI and other mental health conditions. We have made it our goal to supply those suffering from mental health injuries/illnesses the ability to function better in their day-to-day lives.

Because of the severe lack of professionally trained Psychiatric Services Dogs, we became increasingly interested in getting involved. As we do not receive any government funding, we rely on generous donations from individuals and corporations to keep working and helping people.

Although there is no cost for our Service Dogs, we collect an application fee for enrollment in our programs and we expect funds raised by potential clients in order to cover the costs involved in the raising and training process and other operational expenses.

Preface

I attended the University of Guelph from 1985 to 1989. I joined the Guelph Police Service shortly after as a Constable in August 1989. Guelph is one hour west of Toronto and ten minutes north of the 401. The city has a population of 87,000[1] people, and there is a mix of manufacturing and agriculture. Each fall 15,000 students move into the city to attend the University of Guelph.

They assigned me to work on A Platoon, which had some incredibly talented officers. Sadly, our Staff Sergeant loved to play mind games to exercise positional power and control over us. This confused me. I thought policing would mirror the high-end atmosphere of "Team First" that I had experienced playing on the varsity university football and wrestling teams. We had extraordinary leaders and the type of people I would follow into battle because of mutual respect, understanding, core values, and purpose.

Early in my career, this police leader asked me if I thought I was better than him because I went to university and played two sports. This shocked me, so I responded with the fact that I had not even finished my degree. I was eight courses short when I was hired by the Guelph Police Force. He then bragged that he had a "real BA [Bachelor of Arts]" and sarcastically said, "I've been to Aylmer", and walked away. Shortly after that, he targeted me for reasons only known to him and successfully played mind games with me.

I was working a 5:00 p.m. to 3:00 a.m. late-afternoon shift in October 1994 very early in my career when I was dispatched to a report that a prankster had left a bloody mannequin in a pile of leaves in the gutter on Walnut Drive, in Guelph. I thought little of it at the time; I believed it was devil's night, so I thought I'd put the mannequin in my trunk and drive it to our property storage. I thought that it was just a simple found property call.

When I arrived at the location, it devastated me to discover that the mannequin was actually a deceased little blond-haired boy who was run over by a car. He was believed to be playing in the pile of leaves and hidden. I could do nothing because it was clear that he was deceased, so I called the discovery into the dispatch. I stayed with his mangled little body as they processed the scene, trying to offer some semblance of compassion and humanity.

After several hours, a veteran officer asked me to help pick his little body and place it onto the stretcher. As I lifted his upper body, big alligator-style tears filled my eyes and dropped on his little face.

We have to remember back in the late 1980s. The common thread was that "real men don't cry, and if I did, this would be a direct indication of my lack of strength, masculinity, or professionalism; I was not cut out to be a cop.

I quickly wiped the tears away and walked away from the scene to the command vehicle to shield myself from the other officers. As I stood there and tried to compose myself, I remember feeling two powerful hands on my shoulders. I felt myself spun around and pushed up against a nearby vehicle. The officer pointed his finger in my face and said,

'Suck it up, stop acting like a baby; we didn't hire you to cry like a baby; we hired you to act and fight like a man". He laughed and walked away.

As I now reflect on that day, I think back to his words. I am 6'1", 240 lbs on an athletic frame, while he was an average build of 5'10", 175 lbs. I could have easily been that officer who beat him up, but that was not who I was as a person or as a police officer.

I did not sleep well that night. This was the first deceased body I had ever seen. I was lost, devastated, and confused. I had no one to explain, rationalize, or care about how I was doing, and I felt alone.

The next day I attended lineup; I sat at the back of the room trying to disappear with my feelings of anxiety. I was overwhelmingly fearful of what the senior officer or the tyrannical police leader would say. The lineup was business as usual. The Staff Sergeant read a few briefings and assigned us our patrol zones.

I quickly got up, and as I was about to leave the room, the senior officer shouted my name—"Pflug!"—and I froze in my tracks. He then tried to be funny and said, "Hey guys, did you hear what our rookie did last night at the dead kid's call? He cried like a baby".

Back then, you did not confront an aggressor, let alone a senior officer, or complain to management about him, for fear of being fired. I thought to myself, "Who was I? I was just a useless rookie," and I believed him.

I promised myself that they would never again catch me in such a humiliating experience. I vowed I would allow no one to treat me like that, nor would I ever treat anyone else like that again.

Sadly, my internal response to such humiliation was to "be a man, don't cry, don't show emotion", and I did what all good cops do: I ignored that I was human, ignored my emotions, and I hardened internally.

Two things occurred that day: first, I vowed that I would never treat anyone like that and second, I'd never marginalize their feelings. But I shut down my feelings nonetheless. Sadly, we cannot just shut sadness down; my entire range of emotions fell victim, and I missed the joy in so many things after that.

It is genuinely unique how one man caused such a dramatic shift in who I was, who I am, and who I wanted to be. As you read this book, you see that this began my descent into darkness. This journey spanned 14–15 years until I eventually crashed under the self-imposed denials and weight of what I had allowed to occur in my life.

This story haunts me to this day.

*****

In the fall of 2010, I was the media officer for the Guelph Police. I was driving on Waterloo Avenue with Drew Halfpenny, a reporter from the *Guelph Mercury*, for a ride-along. As we approached a large pile of leaves placed by the homeowner in the gutter for the large elephant sucker truck to come by and pick them up, I saw a car in the oncoming traffic, stopped dead in front of the leaves, and froze for a second. The car passed me; I signalled and went into the oncoming traffic around the leaves, and the reporter asked, "What was that all about, Doug?"

I took a moment, cleared my memory of visions I had from that tragic day, and relayed the story to him. I told him how devastating it was for me personally and professionally to find the little boy dead in the leaves so long ago, and it prevents me to this day from driving in the leaves.

He asked how he could help, and I asked him to do a public safety story to encourage motorists to be incredibly careful when coming to piles of leaves on the roadway. I encouraged him to advise them not to drive through the leaves in the fall or, at the very least, to slow down and make sure they can see if there is anyone there.

He authored the following story[2]

Guelph Mercury **Headline: Guelph police warn kids not to play in leaves**
Wednesday, November 10, 2010

Guelph: It was sundown in late October 1994 when Guelph Police Sgt. Doug Pflug got the call. Some Halloween pranksters had left a bloody mannequin in a pile of leaves by the curb on Walnut Drive. Nothing to it, Pflug thought of a simple milk run, picked up the mannequin, threw it in the trunk, bring it back to the station as found property.

But when Pflug and his partner arrived at the scene, what they found was no prank. Concealed in a heap of leaves on Walnut Drive was a 12-year-old boy. He was dead.

"No training can prepare you for what we saw. It was devastating", Pflug said Tuesday. "I can still picture that vision in my head today as though it's right in front of my face".

This week, Pflug sent out a release asking local parents and teachers to remind kids not to play in yard waste piled on the street ahead of next week's loose-leaf collection.

But he did not tell the story of Terry Gatzke, the boy struck and killed in that senseless accident 16 years ago. It is not something he likes to think about.

Reports at the time said Gatzke "liked leaves". That day, he was horsing around in a heap left curbside for pickup by the city. Gatzke may have been invisible to a driver passing close to the curb. No witnesses came forward to shed light on the accident.

For Pflug, that day stands out as perhaps his most harrowing of 21 years of policing.

"It left a phenomenal impact on all of us", he said. "I was still 26 or 27 years of age, and we were just blown out of the water".

Pflug said that to this day, he refuses to drive through leaves piled at the side of the road and does whatever it takes to keep his wheels clear of the piles.

AUTHOR'S CHALLENGE

Years later, I spoke with my friend police Deputy Chief Bryan Larkin, who mentored me.

One day I was speaking to him and asking him for advice dealing with an oppressive boss I was working for, and the lesson he taught me was straightforward but clear through the following conversation. I genuinely hope that this simple conversation prevents you from traveling into the same dark place that I went to and allowed you to deal with.

NOTE: For this, we will change his name to "Bob".

ME: I just do not understand why "Bob" feels the need to pick on me; I work my ass off
     for him and one of the best producers on the shift.

BL: Doug, what do you think "Bob" is doing right now?

Me: I am not sure, sir.

BL: Doug, what do you think "Bob" is doing right now?

Me: Sir, I do not know.

BL: Doug, what do you think "Bob" is doing right now?

Me: Sir, I already answered you; why do you keep asking?

BL: Well, Doug, I will tell you one thing, he is not complaining about you like you are
     about him and right now wasting time and giving you headspace. Trust me, do
     not allow people headspace who have not earned it.

Point taken!

   Thank you, my friend. You supplied calm in chaos and light in the darkness.

AUTHOR'S CHALLENGE

Think of someone that you have let earn headspace and evict them.

NOTES

1. https://en.wikipedia.org/wiki/Guelph
2. www.guelphmercury.com/news-story/2677389-guelph-police-warn-kids-not-to-play-in-leaves/
[1] https://www.brainyquote.com/lists/authors/top-10-vince-lombardi-quotes

Foreword

WRITTEN BY LONG-TIME FRIEND MR. JOHN VELLINGA, FOUNDER AND CHIEF EXPERIENCE OFFICER ZIRKOVA VODKA

I first met Doug in Grade 9, early in our freshman year of high school at Waterloo Collegiate Institute (WCI).

Until I read his story, I did not know that he would have been the object of bullies. When I met him, Doug was already big and strong. What idiot would pick on him? He was also in what seemed like a permanent state of happiness and friendliness. He had a perpetual twinkle in his eye, possessed a shining smile, and was always ready with a kind word or hello to everyone. Who would want to pick on someone so nice?

But most notable was Doug's "anti-bully" approach. He would use his considerable heft and charm to dis-arm bullies: usually figuratively, but physically if necessary. He would stick up for kids who were weaker than their tormentors. He would befriend and support the unpopular, quirky, or cast out, even when he was an accomplished "jock", one of our school's most talented, diligent, and diverse athletes. He was great on the gridiron, in the gym, on the mats, and even on the track and in the field.

I was far from alone in thinking that Doug would make the perfect police officer—even when we were barely into our teens. He seemed to have been genetically engineered, both physically and mentally, for the job. He was strong and fit and not afraid to use his physicality to protect those who were not. He was friendly and slow to anger. He had a good relationship with everyone and could slip seamlessly between cliques. He would defuse a tense situation with a look or posture.

So, it was with no surprise—but a little relief—to hear that Doug had answered the call to serve and protect as a police officer. To do anything else would have been a profound waste. It was also without surprise—and considerable pride—to hear of his exemplary and award-winning career as it progressed. It delighted me when Doug started teaching at the Ontario Police College. He was the exact sort that should make a powerful impression on young officers just starting out.

What I knew little about were all the challenges Doug had faced, especially early in life, or even many of those that were unfolding when we were friends in school. To me, Doug seemed like he had already been fully formed the way that I perceived him. Strong. Fit. Friendly. Athletic. Decent. Principled.

Unknown to me and many, these character traits were the result of struggle, challenge, and even trauma. More ominous outcomes from the same backstory would have been possible. It would be far more predictable, even explainable, had Doug turned out to be an abuser or bully himself, rather than the opposite. Considering his physical challenges as a young boy, it would be easy to imagine him as a weakened or sickly teen and adult, but he remains strong and fit to this day. Given all the negative feedback and lack of encouragement, it would be perfectly justifiable had Doug believed his detractors and under-achieved or fallen into unhealthy habits like substance abuse or even criminal activity. With all the obstacles put in his way, it would be understandable if he had given up on his dreams. Most would.

But he did not.

That is what makes this an amazing story. It is not about a man's successful career as an athlete, police officer, and community leader. That should never have happened! It is a story about overcoming insurmountable illness, outrageous obstacles, and even trauma—then turning that into character.

With his knowledge of fitness, Doug would be able to tell you that a workout actually damages your muscles. It is in the constant healing that they become big and strong. It is in overcoming the aches and pains from the last session that makes the next one even more productive. Doug was not fully formed when I met him back when. He still is not. He is in a process of turning his hurt into healing, his pain into perseverance and his obstacles into opportunities. He is still finding and building his granite.

This is not a book about a celebrity CEO, entrepreneur, or a charismatic life coach who seems to have everything sewn up and put together. It is the raw and honest story of how someone who should never have made it, made it. I think for that reason, this is an important read. It is not airbrushed or idealized. For those of us who have led charmed and privileged lives, we can come to see our setbacks and failures in perspective and as learning and growing opportunities. For those beset by overwhelming odds, they can take inspiration from someone who turned similar circumstances into strengths and success.

Doug's is the story of a successful life that ought not to have happened.

But through extraordinary resilience, determination, and persistence, it did.

—John Vellinga

Who Was I?

"That Little Sucker Wouldn't Die"

1

I was born on September 23, 1966. I was just an "average baby" in an average family in Stratford, Ontario, a small town in southwestern Ontario. Paul and Joan Pflug are my parents. I was not born rich, exceptionally gifted athletically or intellectually, or with a predetermined destiny. Dad was 21 and Mom was 20; they were so young by today's standards.

Well, the "average" went right out the window several days later, when my parents learned that I had been diagnosed with pyloric stenosis[i]. The doctors scheduled me for immediate life-saving surgery and told my parents to say goodbye, knowing that there was a real possibility of losing me. The surgery went very well, and the doctors saved my life.

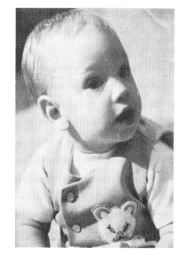

I am reminded daily of that day when I look in the mirror and see the 12-inch vertical scar that stretched from my sternum to my belly button . . . no six-pack for me.

Around three years of age, my parents noticed I was bruising a great deal, so they took me to the doctors. Initially it was thought I had childhood leukemia. Eventually, the doctors diagnosed me with immune thrombocytopenia (ITP). Upon diagnosis, the attending physicians placed me on a new aggressive medical treatment (1969), with my future uncertain. My parents were once again told the prognosis was not good, and the doctors suggested they once again say goodbye.

My Mom, Joan, recently recounted:

> Doug, you were three when you had idiopathic thrombocytopenia purpura (ITP) and were admitted to the hospital. You were under the care of Drs Bastedo, Whaley, and Friday. All the doctors thought you had leukemia. They admitted you to the hospital in the evening, and I could not stay with you.
>
> The next morning when I went to see you, you told me that the doctors were in your room last night and they thought you were sleeping, and you heard them say, "You may not make it", and I cried. After that, you said, "Mommy, don't cry because God told me I could stay with you for a while longer".

DOI: 10.1201/9781003187189-2

I remember sitting in the chapel thanking God when our family doctor, Dr Adelberg, walked by and saw me. He came in and sat with me. I was only 22 years old, scared, exhausted as this was your second brush with death. Today, you are a great father, husband, ex-elite athlete, retired decorated police officer, leadership instructor, and book writer. God certainly answered our prayers, and he had a plan for you.

In reflection, I can remember that around this time they brought a Christian Bible stories book into my room to look at and my mom would read me the stories.

There was one story that involved two young boys, one sick in the hospital and the other was his friend who visited him regularly in hospital. In the story the sick boy told his friend that he was extremely sick, was in a great deal of pain, and that he wanted to die and go to heaven. The friend told him that every night God visits the rooms of children and when you are ready, you just must have your hand raised, and he'll take you. So, the story moves on that the ill boy wants to go be with God and enlisted the help of his friend. The friend prompts the boy's arm with a pillow because he is not strong enough to do so. God came by the next evening and took the young, sick boy to heaven.

Well, because of that story, from that point forward to this date I refuse to have my arms outstretched in any fashion when I sleep for fear that if God pops by, sees my hand up or arm propped up, that it's game over. It is so funny how a minor story intended to supply comfort scared me for years.

*****

Several years ago, Dad and I sat by the cottage fire, and I asked him how he felt during this time. His eyes became glassy, and he told me how scared and devastated he was because of how sick I had been my first three years of life and how he could do nothing to help. Dad told me how he would hide his emotions from Mom because he did not want to further upset her. To do so, he would pray privately, asking God to save me. After telling me this, he paused for a moment, took a sip from his drink, took a puff on his cigarette, and then broke out into laughter. He told me that when the doctors told him I'd survive, he pumped his fist in the air and shouted, 'Man, this little sucker does not want to die'.

I wish I had the opportunity as an adult to sit down with these four doctors and thank them for investing so much time and ability into diagnosing my medical issues. I cannot imagine the associated stress they had using circa 1966–1969 medical treatments, saving my life, not once but twice.

Reflecting on my childhood, I had a bigger purpose or reason for being on this earth. I genuinely know I have something to do in life, a calling, a purpose, a goal, something. Time was the anchor holding me back, but I had to develop ready for that day in retrospect.

I am a Christian and believe in an afterlife, where one day I will be judged by a higher power on what I have done during my time on earth. I am confident that the doctors have watched as I have progressed in life and sure they each smile, knowing that their efforts were not in vain. These four are the angels surrounding me and continue to guide and protect me.

For most of my early life, I have always asked, "Why me?" trying to understand who I was, who I am, and who and what was I supposed to be. I wondered if I had a calling, or whether I was saved by God's graces for a higher reason or purpose in life.

I have always been very impatient, and though my life have refused to wait for life to happen. I have taken every step with urgency to live every second of every day. I genuinely believe that dreams are ideas I just haven't tried yet and that we should all shoot for the stars, and even if we don't reach them, we are better off for trying.

I had to go through this life-threatening adversity when I was so young to build my resilience for a bigger fight.

More on that later.

I have done some prior research on childhood trauma and associated resiliency and found an article entitled "Resilience in Children: Strategies to Strengthen Your Kids" that I genuinely feel supports where my resilient nature comes from. Those caring doctors saved my life for future service. I must also praise the "never say die" attitude and practices my loving parents, Paul and Joan Pflug, used. They saved my life at the time and placed systems and infrastructure in my life that would come to save me many times in the future.

Thanks, Mom and Dad.

The below article sums it up the best and may provide you with strategies for yourself or those you love.

"RESILIENCE IN CHILDREN: STRATEGIES TO STRENGTHEN YOUR KIDS"

Help your child build resilience in the face of obstacles including bullying, moving, divorce, and anxiety with these tips from an expert.

As I reflect and look at all the adversity and conflict that seemed to inject itself into my life, both physically and mentally, I sit in awe. After the incidents concluded, I would think to myself, WTF is going on, and why am I once again being challenged? Simply put, I could not believe that I had to face such weird experiences and wondered why I could not just live a simple life free of conflict.

These experiences provided me with the opportunities to nurture the skills I was born with that rose out of the early adversities fighting for my life. This has provided me with the credibility to help others that have been silenced by their real-life trauma and experiences.

Therein lies the debate on leadership: Is it nature or nurture? Based on "my story", it is seemingly a combination of both. Once the leadership seeds are planted, we must cultivate them to grow with time. We must eradicate harmful sources; they will take over and choke the good out if they succeed, just like weeds.

I will conclude that I was not born average. I was born with the opportunity to become a fighter, an advocate, a champion for the underdog. Lastly, I have become a tour guide for those whose "voice" is silenced and placed in the darkness of their adversities.

I can proudly say that I am a fighter, and I thank the casual and emergent battles that I have fought and will fight in the future. I have found "My Granite", and I hope to help provide you with a plan for the same discovery by the end of this book.

NOTE: People often ask me why I chose the analogy of granite in a presentation and future book.

I use granite because of its exceptional qualities.

Granite's characteristics include strength and durability. This unique and elegant natural stone is one of the oldest, hardest, and strongest stones available. A beautiful natural stone with hundreds of colours and patterns to choose from, Granite symbolizes strength and longevity—a sleek, rich feel (https://graniteforus.com/granite-characteristics).

The looks to be had from using this stone are versatile, from an unassuming elegance to a bold 'look at me' statement. There are hundreds of different granites available.

With this in mind, "Finding My Granite" has provided me with a solid foundation and place to plant my feet, move forward, and face life's challenges. It formed my core values of honor, integrity, passion, and accountability. It is the product of the love and support I have received my entire life during celebrations and tragedies. It is a place I'd like to share with you, hoping once your feet are firmly placed on the surface, you too will find your granite and begin to #RiseUpAndExcel.

AUTHOR'S CHALLENGE

Do not let past events in our lives hold us back from life's experiences in the future. #RiseUpAndExcel

NOTE

[i] https://10faq.com/health/what-is-pyloric-stenosis/?utm_source=6953445991&utm_campaign=11322987328&utm_medium=113734739889&utm_content=113734739889&utm_term=pyloric%20stenosis&gclid=CjwKCAjw-sqKBhBjEiwAVaQ9azEAnJnOEdEtv5I7TlA0rxVvvtBuTFliH7XBkdnQYVVZ5Ya2s9kazhoCv2cQAvD_BwE

The Early Years

Digging Deep and Building a Foundation for Potential Success

2

When the doctors said that I had miraculously responded to the new drug therapies, they continued to combat my sickness and eventually gave me a clean bill of health. I continued to grow stronger beyond my hospitalization. Over the next several years, my health improved dramatically, and I was a happy child. We lived close to a large forest where I had created many memories of playing Robin Hood in the summer and making cool snow forts in the winter.

I made some grand friends back then and remained excellent friends with some of them to this day.

Things changed though at my K–6 school, Sir Winston Churchill PS.

In grade 5, I became the target of two schoolyard bullies. Daily they would walk behind me and trip me or punch me in the arms or stomach. They would steal my lunches, hockey or baseball cards, hat, coat, whatever they could.

I remember one day during the winter months when they were following me home, taunting to provoke me to fight. At one point I ran, but as I arrived at our townhome parking lot, they caught up to me and jumped on me.

They both punched me at will, and I turtled, trying to cover my face and head. Luckily, I had a snowsuit on and toque that more than likely absorbed much of the force, but it was not the physical pain I remember to this day. It was the psychological toll that this beating took on me, and as I reflect, I remember an adult walked by and did nothing to stop this. I remember lying in the cold and wet snow crying, bleeding from my nose and mouth, fuelled by fear, humiliation and not valued. I remember thinking one day, when I grow up, I will be strong enough to stand up to bullies against me and others.

That spring I was in the schoolyard and the weather prompted us all to take our winter coats and corresponding padding off. The two walked up and began punching my upper shoulder and hurt me. I quickly retreated to the bathroom and cried. I felt alone, humiliated, and I withdrew socially from the playground. In class, I remember daydreaming about a better life.

When I went home, my dad asked me why my shoulder was heavily bruised, and I told him I fell playing football. I remember his pride when he said, "That's my boy". I did not have the heart to tell him I was bullied and beaten, or how I felt about myself.

DOI: 10.1201/9781003187189-3

Dad grew up with five brothers and would tell us stories about how they roughhoused, fought, and kicked butt when he was my age. He used to tell us how the Pflug boys would fight other groups of guys on the schoolyard, on the farm, or, in their teens, at the drive-in or pool hall. I remember thinking how cool they must have been; they were real men. I believed I was a wimp, a loser, a coward, and there was no way I wanted to let him down and let him know how I lived each day at school. Dad's little man pretended to be a man, even though he was not.

It is funny how we can vividly remember trauma and the corresponding damage it had on us mentally. Later, as spring moved to summer, I recall playing in the jungle gym at Winston Churchill PS. There were a bunch of tires bolted together in a web pattern and suspended from six posts like a makeshift trampoline. The two bullies knocked me off, and I fell to the ground extremely hard. As I got up, one kicked me in the groin and as I fell back to the ground, crying in pain. They stood over me laughing, yelling, calling me a baby, and called other kids to come over. As the other kids were gathering around and joining the laughter and I remember the pain, humiliation, and marginalization I felt. They treated me like garbage and felt I was garbage. It was near the end of the school year in May or June, and I remember the heat as I sat at the back of the class. I looked out the window and I remember the tears streaming down my face. I remember trying to hide them because only babies cry—right?

I remember having suicidal thoughts and wondering if it would truly matter if I even existed. I would think, "Would people even know I was not there? Would I even be missed?" That was a very tough time, and I remember I overcompensated and acted out in class trying to show "them" I was not a baby, and in the process of reflection I was a jerk to teachers in class and received well-deserved detentions.

My problem? I would not fight back nor had I the courage or confidence to do so. Dad enrolled me in judo to "toughen me up", but that was not for me. The problem I found was that after a few sessions, some other boys saw I was not one to fight and I met a new group of bullies. A brief time later, I feigned illness and quit judo.

In reflection, I won't call myself a coward, wimp, or nerd, but I just didn't like to fight and saw no value in getting a black eye to prove a point. The hard truth I did not want to face was that I did not see any value in myself and at the very least no value worth fighting for.

Luckily, for some unknown reason, I changed schools for grade 6 and went to Cederbrae Public School and met some fantastic friends that I remain in contact with today.

I really enjoyed my time that year and met a great bunch of kids who played with me as opposed to beating me, and as my confidence grew, I tried out for the school hockey team.

I could barely skate, but with the equipment on my chubby body, I could block part of the net and play hockey. It surprised me that I made it and was the goalie for our school grade 6 team. In reflection, I was the only guy who tried out for goalie, but that was success for me in any event.

As the year progressed, I continued to grow in confidence, and I had my first girlfriend.

For grades 7 and 8, all the small schools fed into MacGregor Senior Public School, a bus ride away from where we lived. Another new school meant another unique opportunity for me, and I was delighted and hoped this would supply another new positive start like I'd had going to Cedarbrae.

Sadly, this newfound confidence would not last long.

In grade 7, I remember sitting in gym class on the gym floor the first week of school, ready and excited to have a new beginning once again.

I was shy and an overweight kid who grew wide before growing tall. When it was my turn to introduce myself, I mumbled my name was "Doug Pflug". The teacher laughed and said, "Doug Plug", with a belly laugh as all the other guys laughed as well. He followed up when the laughing subsided and said, "No, from now on, we will know you as Fatty Pflug". He laughed and said, "Son, what kind of weird name is that?" I remembered my shoulders slumped; I devastated that a teacher of all people would be so harsh on me. He asked where I lived, so I told him, "Lakeshore", and he called me "a welfare piece of trash" and told me that I'd never amount to anything.

I believed him that day and went into my newfound shell and withdrew mentally.

A few weeks later, my friend and I were in the schoolyard, and a grade 8 bully approached us with a group of his friends. They formed a circle around us, called us names, and shoved us back and forth. We broke through the ring, and as we ran away, the guy took off his belt and started swinging it at us. We ran to the base of one of the massive maple trees that grew on the lot, and both tried to escape up the tree.

He whipped us violently with his belt on our buttocks as we desperately tried to escape by climbing a tree. I reflect and cannot believe the violence and humiliation we experienced.

A teacher ran over, stopped the beating, and took us to the office.

I remember the sheer humiliation coupled with searing pain from the belt and cried as we walked to the office, defeated once again.

Dad came to the school that day and spoke to the vice-principal. He was furious, and I had never seen him that mad before. At one point, Dad yelled at the vice-principal, banged his fist on his desk, and told him that if he didn't stop the beatings, he'd come back, take his belt off, and whip the principal so he could feel the pain like we did.

The violent attacks stopped.

Ironically, as I reflect, I had entered a random school draw a few days later for free tickets to the World Junior Curling Championships and won. Dad and I had a lovely night watching the event at KW Auditorium. In reflections, I wonder to this day if that was an overt way that the vice principal tried to apologize for his lack of action or make a kind gesture to help me heal.

Later that year, I spent time together with Dave Morrow and his Travel hockey buddies. They accepted me and we spent hours playing "boot hockey" on the school rink during winter months and touch football in the spring. That minor act of kindness unleashed some incredible human potential in me, and I thank him for this.

Dave and I have been best friends ever since, always helping each other out in tough times or sharing great times.

I am truly honoured that we have been grand friends for over 42 years now and continue to be there for each other when needed.

*****

In Grade 8, with my newfound confidence and sense of social acceptance and stability, I tried out for the school wrestling team and made it, and my love for that sport began. I shifted from a victim lifestyle to that of a survivor with this newfound passion.

I was 13 years old, and I genuinely saw that I did have value for the first time in many years.

It's incredible to look back at one's life and see those pivotal points in our lives or forks in our road that we take that led us to where we are today.

These were sad times for me as a young boy, but they also supplied me the ability to develop my resilience. This sword of resilience that I've developed assisted me later in life to fight away evil, trauma, or bad situations in life and further assisted me to advocate for those the very life experienced that did I for a time silenced those "voices" and give a voice to those who had their own voices silenced by their own trauma. It was a tough journey, but I'm glad I went down the path because if I hadn't, I would not be me and could have helped as many people as I have over the years.

*****

In 1980, I went to Waterloo Collegiate Institute (WCI) for high school, with about 1,500 students. I remember walking into this massive school as "a shiner niner," and I mentally reverted to "Fatty Pflug, welfare trash" belief and tried to hide in the large student population. I had another new beginning and set the goal to be the person I knew existed deep in me; I just wasn't confident enough to show anyone that "Doug".

My early life was a roller coaster with many lows followed by many highs.

In grade 9, I remember hearing a morning announcement and there was a call out for the try-outs for the junior football team, and it intrigued me. I loved football, played touch football with my friends, and was a huge Franco Harris fan of the Pittsburgh Steelers. I remember thinking back that I was just a "piece of trash," and no one would want me on the team, and so I did not try out.

I did not play any school sports that year.

Later, in the spring of grade 9, I remember we played touch football in the school football field end zone when I was approached by a gigantic man who introduced himself as Mr. John Carter, a Special Ed teacher at the school and football coach. He told me he liked what he saw and suggested that I work hard and try out for football that fall.

I was in awe; the guy stood 6'2" and had a muscular, intimidating presence; I was 5'6"-ish. I tried to find out who this guy was. I asked around and found out that he was a Wilfrid Laurier University grad[1] and drafted in the CFL. I remember thinking back that if he saw value in my abilities, I was not 'Fatty Pflug' and, in fact, someone of value and worth. In retrospect, John changed my life that day because he opened me up to possibilities and a different version of myself that I had never considered; one of value and #RiseUpAndExcel took root.

That summer I started running, doing pushups, and tried to work out in any way possible that I could find. I thought that if a man of such greatness saw value in me, I must realize he knew what he was talking about, and I did not want to let him down.

In the fall of grade 10, I tried out for the junior football team and made it.

John took the time to reach out with a minor act of kindness and changed my life direction. I made the football team, wrestling team, and track team that year and every year afterwards as I grew into the athlete and man I would later become.

*****

In 2006, when I turned 40 years of age, I made it a point to go back and thank everyone from my past that helped me along the way, and I called John. We had a great phone conversation that day reflecting, and what strikes me the most was John's humility and efforts to downplay his role in my life.

Sadly, on January 21, 2010, John died at 59 years old. I am so glad I took the time to reach out and thank him so that he knew what he had done for me.

John's simple belief and support over the years was an epic influence in my life. Upon graduation from high school, I celebrated being a captain of the football, wrestling, and track teams and was recruited by several universities.

Time passed under John's mentorship. "Fatty Pflug" died and became a distant memory.

Thanks, John. I am forever indebted for introducing me to the "me" you saw. When I became a coach, I modelled my athletes' behaviour and support as you had done for me. God Bless you and RIP Coach.

*****

High school provided incredible instances where it enjoyed some extraordinary experiences with friends and teammates. It saw me enter as a shy, chubby little boy and exit to a future of possibilities because of the relationships I had formed and athletic abilities I had developed during those years on some great teams, from some extraordinary leaders, and through a close, caring group of friends.

But as fate would prove, it also supplied a dark period in my life because of a devastating and life-changing event . . . and you will later learn about it.

******

I began to excel on the football field, the wrestling mat, and the track. Sadly, my English teacher and one of my physical education teachers took liberties with me and treated me like crap.

My class average was only 50 percent at the time because I was "voluntarily" missing tests on game days.

Sadly, I had bad luck in that I had the same English teacher in grades 9 through 13. She was academically minded, and we did not agree completely on athletes missing class for sports or giving them a chance to make up missed work. In the later years of our time together, in grades 12 and 13, they scheduled my English class for the last period of Friday.

That presented problems for me because football, wrestling, and track scheduled events on Fridays during the day or in the afternoon, so I would miss class.

In grade 12, I took the initiative because I wanted excellent marks to make more meaningful choices for University. I needed a 75 percent average to get into Wilfrid Laurier University, which was heavily recruiting me. In later years, the WLU coach was Tom Arnott, who would take over the head coaching duties in 2001 at the University of Guelph and bring me back on the team as an alumni Law Enforcement Mentor.

In speaking with Tom, he suggested I meet with the teacher, explain my future goals, and see if there was any way to work with her to make up missing work or write my tests before school on the days when they were scheduled during a sporting event. I made the appointment, politely pleaded my case, and asked if we could work together for me to earn a more significant mark, to write my tests accordingly, and get help with my future. She looked at me over her glasses in that condescending way and said,

> Douglas, I taught school in the States, and the athletes ran the school. That will not happen here. I will not reschedule tests for you; you must take them like everyone else. If you miss a class, you will get a zero, and you have to decide which is more important.

I was floored at how rude and close-minded she was, so I respectfully left the classroom.

It made me angry because I knew it was her biased opinion against "jocks" because she even admitted it that day. It was not like I spent all my time in the smoking pit, came to school drunk, beat people up, or engaged in any other destructive behavior.

What bothered me most was that one of my female friend's parents split up, and she allowed her to do well without having to work. Several times my friend even joked that I should pretend mine were and milk it the way she admitted to.

Grade 12 ended, and they assigned me an ultimate mark of 50 percent

That whole summer I worked my tail off by training in the gym, running hills, sleeping, and eating my mom out of house and home. It was all in attempts to follow the advice from Tom to make myself a much better football player.

I was told mid-summer that I'd be one of the senior football captains and looked forward to this year to implementing some of my leadership skills and athletic talent to help the team win games. I wanted to showcase the work I had done in the off-season by bringing my team a great season. I played middle linebacker, and running back and was also on every special team; I never left the field that year.

In the classroom, I found out on the first day of school that I would have the same English teacher, and I was angry. I tried to change but could not do so. The school offered one class of English A and another of English B. I quickly enrolled in English B to compare my marks from the oppressive teacher to the second teacher who liked me.

At the end of the year, I had an informal meeting with the vice principal, who was also one of my football coaches. We talked about my university athletic future, and when he learned my marks did not meet the grade to go to WLU, he was extremely disappointed in me.

As we went over my transcript, he saw the 50 percent in English A versus 80 percent in English B; I told him the story. He apologized and asked why I had not gone to him sooner.

Back in the day, you did not do that, because who would have believed me that a teacher would pick on me for such a trivial excuse?

As it was, my average limited my options, so they only accepted me at one school that was three hours away, and their team was terrible. Personally, it wasn't the right fit at the time, as my parents had divorced a year earlier, and I had a younger brother at home, so I didn't want to be that far from them. I needed to be home to support them, and I knew I had to stay in high school another year and upgrade my marks.

The concept of "adversity builds strength", came to full fruition that year when I enrolled in the neighbouring high school to upgrade my marks. This enabled me to take the next step in my future, and I was all set to go to the University of Guelph.

Truthfully, it wasn't a personal vendetta for me; WCI was a three-term per year school, while Bluevale CI was two semesters and would allow me a better opportunity to upgrade my marks. Had WCI been semester based, I would have never left.

I set off on both these journeys #StrongerFasterFitter using the "Magic Power" lyrics by a Canadian rock group named Triumph to fuel my way. Maybe if you click on the QR code below and take a listen, you too will find your "magic power". The entire lyrics of the song spoke to me, and I seemed to identify with them and in turn they helped motivate and inspire me to be better than I was. Throughout my entire life I would revisit the song and lyrics. "I am young, I am wild, and I am free, I got the magic power of the music in me" would be the simple boost I needed to #RiseUpAndExcel.

Source: Musixmatch

*****

Many years later, I was part of a team of writers and editors at the Guelph Police who researched, wrote, and published the *Fingerprints Through Time—A History of Guelph Police Service*.

We had many positive media and speaking engagements to promote the book. I was the master of ceremonies for the events and always opened up with, "Ladies and gentlemen, if my high school English teacher knew I wrote and published a book in anything but crayon, she would probably roll over in her grave". Usually, laughter and applause followed.

In 2010, I went back to Waterloo Collegiate Institute as part of the 50th Anniversary Celebrations and visited all of my favourite teachers. I went to the English B teachers' room and as I walked in, she laughed and said, "Oh, my! Doug Pflug", and hugged me. We chatted for a while about what I had done since she last saw me. She mentioned how she saw me on the news many times when as a police media officer. When I told her about the book, and how I prefaced every "meet the authors" sessions, she smiled and said, "Doug, she is still alive and has heard when you said." I was shocked when the teacher claimed she knew you had it in you; you just had to apply yourself.

We hugged and I walked out of my room. As I walked down the hallway towards the parking lot I heard, "Pflug, get back here". I turned around, and it was my senior football coach.

I flashed back and remembered when he was so overconfident, walked like he was a god amongst us, and treated us like garbage. I was the sure winner for Athlete of the Year because of my outstanding football, wrestling, and track seasons. Because of my poor academic performance in school, I had to change schools to upgrade my marks. When he found out I was going to play at our city rival, he took my name out of contention and they gave it to a grade 12 student. When that was announced at the athletic banquet, people were in awe, and it devastated me. I was never told why this happened until years later when I was coaching high school track and ran into one of my other coaches there, and he let me know they took my name off the ballot because he wanted 'get back at me' for transferring to the other high school to upgrade my marks.

To frame the context on this guy:

- When we were in grade 9 and 10 and still had the bodies of boys, he would grab us by the throat and throw us up against the lockers. We would smash our heads and get laughed at.
- He was the guy I thought, 'Just you wait until I grow to be in Grade 13; I will be as big as a man and will smack you silly'.
- He was the guy who would criticize us when we spoke to girls in the hallway, as though he was competing for their attention.
- He was the type of guy who bragged about playing football at Western and how great he was. When a fellow teacher and coach presented the game programs from those years, and his name was not even on them, he tried to make us believe that it was a mistake.
- Upon our graduation, he was the guy who was probably the most hated teacher we ever experienced, and he was standing in front of me, with that same cocky look and bellowing voice.

Now was my chance to settle this debt man to man. All those times that he had marginalized me physically and mentally, hurt me, and embarrassed me in front of my peers were running through my head.

As I walked closer, I was only thinking about how I was going to settle the score. To my surprise, he appeared smaller and smaller every step that I took. He was barely a threat, and my anger turned to empathy, finishing in raw pity for him.

I realized that aging was his punishment and there he stood before me, a withered-up older man. He tried to pull back his shoulders and stick out his chest as he once had, and he reached out his hand in a friendly gesture.

Pflug, you leave here a nobody and come back a star. Son, I am so proud of you; I have followed you through university football, your policing career, and heard about you as a football coach at the high school in Guelph. Well done, son, well done. I knew you were special.

We exchanged stories for about 30 minutes, and both relived some of the good times we shared. As I drove home, I reflected on all the teenage stress, uncertainty, fear, and obstacles that these two teachers had given me and how I almost let it destroy me, stop me, or prevent me from living out my dreams.

Success was my best revenge that day—not hitting him like I had wanted for so many years.

I learned some precious lessons that day reflecting on both those "teachers":

- I would never treat or target any young person the way I had been.
- I would always try to coach, counsel, and mentor youth and help them reach their potential; it is their new day, not mine
- I never wanted to be remembered the way I did him that day.
- I wanted to be a positive role model in the lives of youth.
- We only indeed rise in life when we help others rise.
- I would use my lessons learned to help others, knowing full well the pain they caused.
- Success is your best revenge when you use the negative to fuel to work towards your positive.

High school presented some fantastic opportunities through personal growth because of some outstanding teachers in my life and sadly from bad ones. I needed to experience both. As I look back, I enjoyed the successes and grew from them, but it was the hardships that I experienced where I saw the most significant opportunity and examples of my personal growth.

The adversity I faced, and corresponding resiliency learned, was a necessary growth period that I needed to experience. This growth would be dramatically challenged one fateful day near the end of high school—and the number 182 would change my life.

Side Note: With the list in mind, in 2006 I turned 40 and made a list of certain people I wanted to thank for investing their time and expertise in me. I also made a list of people I felt I had wronged and wanted to seek, and an "I'm sorry" list to right the wrongs and clear myself of the associated guilt I carried over the years.

In grades 11 and 12, I dated a wonderful girl. This relationship was so sweet and innocent. In grade 12, my parents split up, and I was going through a rough time, and I was confused about how this could affect my future dreams and goals. I had to tighten up and break up with her in my mind. For over 26 years, I felt guilt over that as she was a collateral victim of my parents' split. I owed her an apology because I believed that I had hurt her.

I asked around and found that she lived in Guelph and had done freelance writing for the University. I reached out and made contact, asking if we could meet for a coffee, and I had something I needed to tell her. When we met, she looked confused. I told her I needed to apologize to her for breaking up with her and that I was sorry for any pain that I would have caused.

She sat there for a moment with a puzzled look on her face and she smiled and said, "Thanks for the kind gesture, Doug, but you didn't break up with me. . . . I broke up with you back then".

I was dumbfounded, confused, and could feel the blood rushing to my cheeks out of embarrassment. We both laughed about the entire experience and the fact I carried unnecessary guilt for over 25 years. I felt like such a dumbass!

We still run into each other from time to time, smiling at the memory of that fateful coffee meeting when I turned 40.

*****

I worked from grade 9 until 13 (1980–1985) at a local grocery store in Waterloo. It was my first real job, packing groceries, and I loved it. I made $3.00 per hour and remembered my first paycheck of $90.00. I thought I was rich.

This was a fantastic opportunity for me to make money, learn responsibility, meet new friends, work with the public, and work on my time management skills juggling school, work, sports, friends, and family.

I belonged to a team of 25 grocery "packers" and an equal number of cashiers. The packers were all young guys my age, and the cashiers were all girls around my age. We got along wonderfully and had a lot of fun working together. I have remained friends with several people from that period to this date.

We had a store manager and assistant manager that I did not like or respect. One was around 45 years old, short, and pudgy in stature, permed curly hair, wore too much cheap cologne and his shirt collar was open to expose his ample chest hair. The other was young, leaner, but both used their positional power and managerial fear over all of us. Each shift it was a standard routine that they'd walk up behind the girls, most of whom were young enough to be their daughters, lean against them and ask for the cash drop bag. The girls would quickly give the bag, and they would go ahead to the next girl. They would usually run up against six to eight girls at one cash drop.

I hated seeing this because my parents always taught me to be a gentleman around ladies and never touch unless invited. These guys took positional liberties that today's standards would equate to sexual assault or, at a minimum, sexual harassment in the workplace.

One time I was on a lunch break speaking with one of my friends about this. This upset her about the way the older store manager would lean his "disgusting body" against her, and she could still smell his cheap cologne and cigarette smoke on her. I was 17 at the time and finally growing and seeing the results of working out and my confidence was building. They knew me to be outspoken, and I said, "The guy is just an old pervert, and he disgusts me", just as he walked into the lunchroom. He stopped, pointed at me, and yelled, "Pflug, my office".

I went up there, and for the next 30 minutes, he screamed at me, beat his fist against the desk, threatened me, and even challenged me to fight. This guy did not intimidate me; he was half my size and suffered from what we call "little man's syndrome". I kept self-control and did not act out and answered, "Yes, sir" and "No, sir" because my parents also taught me to respect my elders and bosses.

He ordered me to forget what I saw. I chirped, "Not likely. Maybe I'll call the police and let them know what I saw, or better yet, your wife", and I left his office. As I walked down the hallway towards the front of the store, I heard him yelling and screaming obscenities.

Word got around the store that I had chirped the manager and how he had treated me. Sadly, this scared a few of my friends, and it silenced some complaints about the store manager and assistant managers conduct. We were all inexperienced teens, and some of my friends were intimidated and feared repercussions. We needed the jobs.

After a brief time, they both began to micro-manage and pick on me.

I asked for a transfer from the front and was assigned to the deli meat counter.

This was yet another dysfunctional unit. The butcher changed prices on expensive meat to lower it for himself and friends, as did the girl who worked on the plastic wrap packaging machine.

One day when I was in the rear cleaning some equipment, I saw them changing prices again. The butcher saw me and came over to me with his giant knife and casually told me that "I saw nothing". That scared me, and I started working with my head down and eyes in the back of my head.

The two of them then attempted to discredit me as a "part-timer" and told the meat manager lies about me that I believe were to distract attention from what they were doing. The meat manager was an old school boss who believed that screaming at the top of your lungs and being a tyrant was how you led the unit. What once was an amicable relationship became one where he scorned my presence.

This all came to a head one Friday night when I was assigned the task to power wash the entire meat cutting room. This was a very labour-intensive job that easily required two to three people, but they assigned me it with no help. There was a massive high-pressure rubber hose with brass fittings attached to the tap. They seemed to bond, and it took me well over 30 minutes to finally loosen it and then put it away as part of my task. I did everything as described, booked out with the punch card machine, and left the store.

I came in the next morning at 7:00 a.m., and the manager, butcher, and meat packaging lady were looking at me funny. Around 10:00 a.m., they called me up into the store manager's office to see him, the assistant manager, and the meat manager. It was a small room and three against one.

I walked into the office and saw an opened package of Oreo cookies half-eaten. The store manager yelled and swore at me to sit down, and I did. He then picked up the box of cookies and threw them in my face screaming, "What the F is this?" I looked stunned, got furious, and tried to compose myself. I said I did not know. In my mind, I thought it was probably the butcher and meat packer whom I'd seen eat the cookies all the time, but they accused me of this. I wondered if I was being set up by them or by the managers for calling him a pervert the weekend before.

Over the next 30 minutes, all three took their turns yelling, swearing, and screaming at me, trying to coerce admissions of me. The bottom line to this date, I never opened nor ate them, nor would I do that. The three of them didn't know that my mom and dad also taught me not to steal, and as I say there, I remembered I was a millionaire based on dad's story, and I would not let anyone take that from me.

As I wrote today, with no fear or repercussions, I will honestly tell you I never did these things because I was raised so well by my parents.

I may not have had wealth in those days, but I was certainly not a thief, and I took significant exception to their allegations.

A TRUE SIGN OF CHARACTER IS ONE WHO STANDS UP FOR WHAT THEY BELLIEVE, EVEN IF IT MEANS STANIDNG ALONE

Standing up for those silenced by stupidity became a cause for me. I stood up for my friends who were assaulted by "grubby old men", and I am glad that I had that type of conviction at that age.

I worked that summer, and as school approached, I let the manager know I would not be available to work weeknights and that if scheduled Friday, I couldn't be there until after 6:00 p.m. The manager, an Irish guy, lost his mind and told me I had to choose between the store and football. I confided in him I was scouted and did not care.

I told my coach about this, and we worked around it to accommodate working and get my reps in. My boss refused to collaborate with me and to spite me and try to interfere with my dream, he scheduled me every Friday at for the 4:00 to 10:00 p.m. shift.

Our football season included seven regular season Friday after-school games. While I realize that whereas I now teach honour, integrity, passion, and accountability, I did not display those traits in the store. I had my mom call in every week and book me off sick to spite them. Wrong, yes—but in the big picture, it was the best thing I could have done.

Sometimes we face opposition when we seek our dreams. Life's lesson is to seek strategies to achieve balance in an issue. When both sides will not work together, we must take care of ourselves before others.

About five years ago, one of my friends sent me a Facebook friend request. We chatted about those days, and what I didn't realize was that all the girls had been grossed out at the time because of the actions of these grubby older men getting down on them, and that after I took the bullet for my comments, they stopped.

She then told me that the store manager lost his job a few years ago when several cashiers filed a sexual harassment complaint against him. It took over 25 years for this guy to receive the punishment he earned. I wish I had the courage back then to take a bigger stand, but I was only 18 and had not yet grown to be the person I am today.

Always remember the life lesson: Do the right thing because it's the right thing to do. Trust in knowing that one day you may find out how much you helped another person in a time of need.

Looking back, I remember these managers vividly, now through adult eyes and experience. It is so easy to see that they were jealous of most of the packers. We were all athletic guys, physically bigger than they, and we had youth and future possibilities on our side. We all represented everything they were not or could not have. These three "leaders" used their positional power to victimize our female friends through the cash run groping and shut us down through toxic masculinity, yelling, screaming, and intimidating.

AUTHOR'S CHALLENGE

With this, I want to challenge you all.

Please do not wait until you are 40 years of age; sit back now, make your list of those who made a difference in your life, and contact them and thank them. Their small acts of kindness helped you achieve your potential. John was retired and, just maybe, I made his day.

Sometimes the best compliments in life are never given. We all have an expiry date, so make sure you reach out before it is too late.

Years later, I would formalize this as a challenge that I give to everyone who will listen while I teach or on my social media feeds in John's memory. I now challenge you to make a stranger smile or mentor a young person because you do not know how those small acts of kindness can unleash some incredible human potential.

NOTE

1. www.psycom.net/build-resilience-children

Ram Tumkur and My Crash into the Abyss

Welcome to the Planet, Doug

3

The 1980s were a wonderful time in the world and my world. I had grand friends, an excellent job, loving parents, and a younger brother. The horrific memories and humiliation that "Fatty Pflug" had experienced became a distant memory where I used the lessons learned to fuel my future goals and desires.

This newfound internal drive fuelled my growth from a boy into a man with a 6'1", 220-pound athletic body. Many universities were scouting me to play football, wrestle, and run track at the next level.

Life was glorious, but, sadly, my academics were not great. I hadn't found the classroom's internal discipline yet like I had on the playing field and gym. In reflection, this is one area in which I should have worked harder and taken more initiative so I would have had better marks to include in my recruiting package. Frankly, I was lazy academically and that hurt me when I had to go back to high school an extra year to upgrade my marks; hindsight is always 20–20, my friends.

I look back often to grade 10 when I was walking home from school one day when I ran into a young man in my grade named Ram. We chatted the entire way, and it was incredibly insightful and rewarding. He did not talk about Doug the athlete but Doug the person. He thought it was cool that I had a brilliant future at the next level but dared me to challenge myself on who I was, who I am, and who I wanted to be.

Ram was not an athlete or popular, nor was he one of the "cool kids", but he was my friend and a staunch fan. He was a kind soul who saw deeper into a person than where they lived, the clothes they wore, or the group of people they called friends. His wisdom and empathy towards others were beyond his years; he became my confidant and never judged me. He realized I had a great deal of pressure that was coming from all directions—teachers, peers, teammates, coaches, university recruiters—plus the unrealistic expectations I placed on myself and future.

DOI: 10.1201/9781003187189-4

I often look back at the memorabilia I kept over those years and reflect on who I was before life began and, in the kind comments, to refocus on who I still want to be. We must always learn from our past to guide us towards the future, and this is a regular practice I constantly use.

I tried to hold it all together, and I do, now and then, speak with friends from that time, and they say I always seemed so in control of my life and even commend me for who they thought I was. They did not know that I had low self-esteem and confidence issues and that my parents divorced in Grade 11 and that I had all the associated stresses. I had economic difficulties and experienced bouts of depression. I started self-destructive physical training practices to failure and beyond. I look back and think that subconsciously I knew I could give up, but I suffered an injury that would end my career and the pressures associated with it.

I was scared and alone. It is funny now to reflect because those incredibly intense, devastating workouts did not strip me down or give me the negative desired result. They strengthened me, made me faster and fitter, and improved my game.

Once again, I faced incredible adversity through experience and trauma, and the groundwork for #RiseUpAndExcel formed. The trauma I faced, the resiliency built, and the lessons learned once again strengthened me. My resiliency and lessons learned would be tested in my senior year of high school when my world hit an incredible wall and stopped.

I have included my blog entry detailing this event on June 23, 1985, from www.riseupandexcel.ca.

One of the pivotal events that shaped who I wanted to be in my teen years involved my friend Ram Tumkur. Ram was bullied at school and often walked the halls stressed and scared of what might happen.

One day I saw three males roughing him up in the lower school stairwell and stepped in to defend this kind soul, who just wanted to fit in and belong. I pushed two of them away and smacked the primary aggressor. I threatened all three that if I ever caught them again, I would smack the hell out of them twice as bad as they did to Ram. Ram got mad at me for using my physicality against them and told me that they were just having a bad day, and we should never stoop to that level because it wouldn't solve anything.

Those were wise words for a man that was getting his rear end kicked, a lesson that I'd use over and over years later when I became a police officer dealing with people in both casual and emergent situations.

From there on, we arranged he would stay after school and watch my football, wrestling, or track practice and wait for me. I would then walk Ram to the bus stop beside the 7-Eleven on King St. and University Avenue in Waterloo every day after school.

During our routine, we would talk and dream about who we were, who we are, and who we wanted to be in our adult lives. We had it all planned out: University, jobs, family, life moving forward.

One day early in June 1985, as we walked to the bus stop, he told me how he and his sister would visit their grandmother at the beginning of summer break. He was so excited and shared his flight details, and we promised to get together upon his return so he could tell me all about his trip. We shook hands, said goodbye, and walked out to our respective busses.

On June 23, 1985, I listened to the song "Purple Rain" by Prince on the radio. The DJ interrupted, stopped the music, and announced, "Ladies and gentlemen, we interrupt regular programming; a bomb exploded on Air India Flight 182 flying from Toronto to London, England, killing all 329 people aboard, most of them Canadians".

I fell to the floor, feeling crushed, devastated, and alone.

A bomb planted by terrorists exploded onboard Air India Flight 182 off Ireland's coast. The plane crashed into the ocean with no survivors. Three hundred twenty-nine people lost their lives, including my friend Rammohan "Ram" Tumkur, and his older sister, Chitralekha Tumkur.

I remember crying at length because all my efforts to protect Ram were in vain. He was "bullied" by those terrorists who took his life.

The next day I looked at the *KW Record*. I saw the attached article, and I clipped it out and prominently placed it in my sports scrapbook as a memory of who I was, who I am, and who I wanted to be. A few weeks later, I came across this simple poem by Stephen Grellet, as a sign from Ram that he was OK, and I added it to that page.

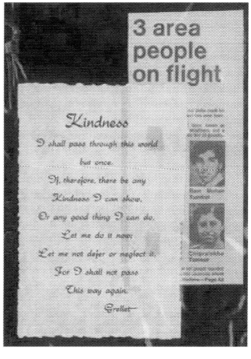

As time has passed, I often go back to that page, reminisce, and feel the poem's warmth. It continues to ground me, inspire me, and supply hope that tomorrow will be better. It also serves as a reminder that I still have much work to do to make the world a better place, one smile at a time.

KINDNESS

I Shall pass this way but once.
If therefore, there be any
    kindness I can show
or any good thing that I can do, let me do it now.
Let me not defer nor neglect it,
    for I shall not pass this way again.

—Grellet

I believe the groundwork for my life mission and "service heart" developed that day. I solidified the knowledge that I needed to earn each day I live through my goal to make at least one stranger smile per day, or, better yet, mentor a young person because we do not know how those small acts of kindness can unleash some incredible human potential.

It was that day that also solidified my dreams of one day being a police officer so I could "serve and protect". My goals were simple. I wanted to be a positive male role model and voice for those bullied, abused, exploited, or neglected.

God has a plan for me and spared my life so long ago to live that mission.

So, as I conclude, I ask you, who were you, who are you, and who do you want to be?

Always #RiseUpAndExcel my friends and lead with your best self, model the behaviour you seek from others, and always create an environment where others can succeed.

*****

The band Disturbed has a song called "Hold on to Memories" [i], and I believe they describe it best. I challenge everyone to follow this advice, and never let the memories of our loved ones slip away. Say their names and say them often.

It's been over 36 years since that fateful day, and I routinely reflect on my friendship with Ram. I am always cognizant that "the world's greatest tragedy, is Souls who are not remembered cannot survive".

Ram, you were my friend, you will never die, my friend; I will see you one day on the other side.

Until then, you will live with me forever. RIP Buddy.

—DP

Years later I would have the privilege of meeting the band Disturbed with my brother Don and I was able to replay to them what the song meant to me in times of sadness and they were honoured to know it made a difference.

HISTORY

For those of you who are unaware of what the Air India Flight 182 bombing was, I have included a section of the Public Safety Canada report to help you frame the context of my reference. In the early morning hours of June 23rd, 1985, Air India Flight 182 approached the west coast of Ireland. The flight began in Toronto, receiving passengers and luggage from connecting flights, and picking up more in Mirabel, Quebec. Their families joined children of all ages, looking forward to visiting their loved ones and friends in India. Most of the passengers were Canadians. Given the time of year—late June marks the beginning of summer holidays here in Canada—there were an especially large number of young adults, children and entire families traveling on the flight.

Unbeknownst to them, in the weeks prior to that flight, a group of Canadians had been planning to blow up the plane. The conspiracy was based in radical sections of the Sikh community in Vancouver and elsewhere who were pursuing the goal of an independent country, to be called Khalistan, in the northwestern province of Punjab in India.

Because of this conspiracy, a bomb was manufactured, placed in a suitcase, and taken to the Vancouver airport, where on June 22, 1985, it was checked through on a flight from Vancouver to Toronto. In Toronto, the lethal suitcase made its way onboard Air India Flight 181, which then stopped at Mirabel and became Air India Flight 182, en route to London and Delhi.

At approximately 12:14 a.m., on June 23, 1985, the timer on the bomb detonated a charge and blew open a hole in the left aft fuselage of the plane. The plane, which bore the name "Kanishka", was blown apart, falling 31,000 feet below into the Atlantic Ocean off the south-west coast of Ireland.

The children going to visit grandparents, young tourists looking forward to their first experience of India, women and men of all ages, flight attendants and pilots, in short, all 329 passengers and crew were killed.

It was, at that point, and up until 9/11, the worst act of terrorism against the traveling public in world history.

Meanwhile, at Narita Airport in Tokyo, a bomb exploded at approximately 11:15 p.m. on June 22, 1985, while luggage was being transferred from Canadian Pacific Flight 003 to Air India Flight 301 to Bangkok. Two baggage handlers, Hideo Asano and Hideharu Koda, were killed and four other baggage handlers were injured.

Numb with grief, families traveled to Cork in the west of Ireland where they were met by an Irish population who rallied to receive them. The hospital in Cork became a temporary morgue as the grim process of collecting and identifying bodies began.

Canadian authorities were not prepared for such a disaster. Family members were overwhelmed with grief, angry that this had been allowed to happen, furious that not enough was being done to answer their questions. That grief and anger has not gone away with the passage of time.

The Canadian government joined with the government of India and the local and national governments of Ireland to build a compelling memorial site on the south-western shore of Ireland in 1985–1986. It is here that the families come to remember their loved ones. Prime Minister Paul Martin led a delegation of Canadian political leaders to join the families on the twentieth anniversary of the bombing. It was the first such visit by a Canadian Prime Minister.

While statements were made in the House of Commons in the immediate aftermath of the disaster, many families continue to express their profound sense that the Air India bombing was never truly understood as a Canadian tragedy.

Let it be said clearly: the bombing of the Air India flight was the result of a conspiracy conceived, planned, and executed in Canada. Most of its victims were Canadians. This is a Canadian catastrophe, whose dimension and meaning must be understood by all Canadians.

For reasons set out below, I am recommending that a focused, policy-based inquiry be held to deal with questions from this mass murder that remain unresolved. We know the location of the conspiracy that planned the bombings, and the identity of some of the conspirators; we know how the bombs got on two planes; we know the details of the bombs' detonation. We do not need to revisit these questions. They are clearly proven. What 'we need to know more about is how Canada assessed the threat, how its intelligence and police forces managed the investigation and how its airport safety regulations did or did not work. Twenty years later, these questions are still worth asking.

The Air India bombings were the worst encounter with terrorism Canada has experienced. We cannot leave any issues unresolved.

Note: The University of Waterloo has a memorial graduate Scholarship entitled Ram and Lekha Tumker memorial Graduate Scholarship in their honour and memory.

AUTHOR'S CHALLENGE

We all have the defining, pivotal time in our lives when we reflect on our "who we were" phase in life. That time shaped "who we are" and "who we want to be" moving forward.

Take some time to reflect on your pivotal moment and write it down to capture it as I have done mine. Focus on the positive you have learned from it because it shaped you.

In this process find three to four people who helped you navigate the time and to move forward to #StrongerFasterFitter.

Call them and tell them the lasting impact they continue to have in your life and celebrate your successes with them.

Over the years., I have found that some of the nicest compliments people have for one another remained in their thoughts and never said.

Always remember that we cannot guarantee tomorrow, so let us share them today.

NOTE

[i] https://www.musixmatch.com/lyrics/Disturbed/Hold-On-to-Memories

The University of Guelph "Gryphon" Football and Wrestling

4

Grade 13 was a special time in my life, where I saw a future and goals to work towards.

That fall, we had a great football season, making it deep in the Waterloo County Secondary School Athletic Association (WCSSAA) football finals. I perfected my game on both sides of the ball; I was an outside strong side linebacker on the defensive side of the ball and running back on the offence. I had a great season on both sides of the ball, being named part of the WCSSAA (Kitchener/Waterloo/Cambridge) City All-Star Team that garnered attention from many universities.

One of my favorite memories from that season was the quarter-final game we played against the Cameron Heights Gaels. John Cater was transferred to that school that year and was coaching their football team. I wanted to have my best game and impress my old friend, coach, and mentor. I remember rushing the ball for over 100 yards that game and totally shutting down Cameron's left side

running game, playing my linebacker position. At the end of the game when we shook hands, John winked and said, "Good game, Doug", and hugged me. Little did I know that this would be the last time I ever saw John.

DOI: 10.1201/9781003187189-5

The next day I read the *KW Record* sports section "Friday Night Football Game" recap and saw that they had quoted Bob Serviss, my head coach: "Serviss had a lot of praise for Pflug, stating it was the best game of his life".

I remember receiving my first recruiting document for Wilfrid Laurier University from Assistant Coach Tom Arnott after that game. It was a form letter, and he personalized it with, "Doug, I saw your game against Eastwood and was extremely impressed. Let us get together and chat". We had played Eastwood the week before, securing our chance for the quarter-final game Against Cameron Heights. I still remember the joy of opening that letter, and the tears ran down my face. I reflected on all the years of bullying by students and several teachers, the name calling, the self-doubt, the suicidal ideologies and corresponding mental health side effects. This letter was validation for me that all the sacrifice, the punishment, the hard work was worth it and, once and for all, that "Fatty Pflug" died and Douglas Pflug was born.

*****

As I reflect back to my time of rebirth in grade 10, I remember the school had an assembly one day for all the students and played a movie of a motivational speaker who talked to high school students about how great their experiences are—followed by a short ad for Josten class rings and yearbooks.

The video was an eight-minute edited version of the Silver Screen and Golden Apple award winning *Greatest Days* film, featuring Mark Scharenbroich encouraging students to make the most of their high school years, followed by a series of short clips on the best of high school. Seen by millions of students in the 1980s, it was written, performed, and directed by Mark Scharenbroich with an original song by Billy Barber. It was produced by Jostens Class Rings and Yearbooks. Strong connections are vital in our lives, yet in today's "virtual world" it is often difficult to make meaningful connections.

Audience members continually note that his Nice Bike messages take them on a roller coaster ride experience with stories that touch the heart, brilliant comedic timing, and actionable strategies. Plus, it is motivating, fun, and engaging. When team members are truly connected, retention improves, sales increase, customer loyalty soars, and your business grows.

Emmy award winner, Hall of Fame keynote speaker, and entertainer Mark developed the Nice Bike metaphor to drive home the power of connecting in a more genuine way. Part motivational keynote speaker, part thought-provoker and pure entertainer—Mark delivers every time.

I truly encourage you to watch it, reflect, and plan your greatest days.

Mark Scharenbroich
"Greatest days of your life . . . so far"

To watch more from Mark Scharenbroich, check out his YouTube Channel by clicking the following QR Code:

*****

It is funny how when we were young, we would find a movie or character in a movie. That year, in football I personally identified with the main character Stefan Djordjevic in the movie *All the Right Moves*. The parallels between his young career and problems with his coach mirrored mine. I can honestly say I watched this movie well over 50 times.

The plot:[1]

Stefen "Stef" Djordjevic (Tom Cruise) is a Serbian American high school defensive back who is gifted in both sports and academics. He is seeking a college football scholarship to escape the economically depressed small western Pennsylvania town of Ampipe and a dead-end job and life working at the mill like his father and brother Greg (Gary Graham).

He dreams of becoming an engineer right after he graduates from college. Ampipe is a company town whose economy is dominated by the town's main employer, American Pipe & Steel, a steel mill struggling through the downturn of the early 1980s recession. Stef gets through his days with the love of his girlfriend, Lisa Lietzke (Lea Thompson), and his strong bond with his teammates.

Most of the film takes place after the big football game against undefeated Walnut Heights High School. Ampipe appears headed to win the game when a fumbled handoff in the closing seconds—as well as Stefen's pass interference penalty earlier in the game—leads to a Walnut Heights victory. Following the game, Coach Burt Nickerson (Craig T. Nelson) lambastes the fumbler in the locker room, telling him he 'quit' the game. When Stefen retorts that the coach himself quit, the coach kicks him off the team.

In the aftermath, disgruntled Ampipe fans vandalize Coach Nickerson's house and yard. Stefen is present and is a reluctant participant but is nonetheless seen by Nickerson as the vandals flee. From there, Stefen deals with personal battles, including the coach blackballing him among colleges because of his attitude and participation in the vandalization of Nickerson's yard and house. Stefen gets in an argument with Lisa, and his best friend Brian (Penn) declines a scholarship offer to the University of Southern California and plans to marry his pregnant girlfriend.

Frustrated by what Nickerson did, Stefan angrily confronts his former coach, which ends in a shouting match out in the street. But Lisa decides to talk to Nickerson's wife to try and help. In the end, Nickerson realizes he was wrong for blackballing Stefan. He has accepted a coaching position on the West Coast at Cal Poly San Luis Obispo and offers Stefan a full scholarship to play football there, which he accepts.

*****

I was always a big Vince Lombardi fan and read everything I could to get my firsthand information about him. I thought that if I could find some small piece of him, I could identify with him. I too would achieve something great. I came across this quote that I still reflect on today.

"IT'S NOT WHETHER YOU GET KNOCKED DOWN, IT'S WHETHER YOU GET UP"

To me this is the ultimate Vince Lombardi quote, so simple yet so profound. His quote directed his football team, the Green Bay Packers, but we can all contemplate it for so many things in life both inside and outside of sport. I have fallen and failed often. My journey in life was to find out what or why I got back up and it would take me years to figure this puzzle out.

The greatest periods of my personal growth came because of such failures and falls. It is in those places of failure or darkness that we truly find the light. My light included my four core values and the love and support from my family. Getting knocked down was not my learning lesson in life; it was my response to adversity, my perseverance, and dedication to #RiseUpAndExcel that sings to me.

*****

When football was over, the football recruiting letters began showing up in my mailbox, and I genuinely believe I had a chance to "be somebody" one day, and my confidence continued to grow.

I would recite the Vince Lombardi quote when I woke up, throughout the day, during training or practice, and right before I went to sleep that night. I knew I was not a gifted athlete, but one that was built by blood, sweat, and tears.

With the upcoming wrestling season, I had to dig deep and quickly drop ten pounds and wrestle varsity at the 198-pound category.

That year I had a new wrestling coach, Mr. Ed Goddard. We bonded instantly and can say that he was not just my coach, but my guidance counsellor, teacher, friend, mentor, supporter, and lifelong friend. Ed was an extraordinary man in that he wanted us to develop as not only athletes, but as young adults, and he prepared us for the next adventure in life at university.

Under his coaching and leadership, I won Gold at the WCSSAA City Championship and Gold at the Central Western Ontario Secondary School Athletic (CWOSSA) Championships that year, earning the opportunity to wrestle at an invitational tournament in Lowell, Michigan, USA. This was an exceedingly rare occurrence in the mid-1980s as no one travelled that far, let alone in high school sports.

I remember how intense it was to be exposed to a small-town iconic wrestling program. In my experience we would all just show up, warm up, and prepare ourselves to wrestle. In the US, specifically Lowell, Michigan, we were at an iconic wrestling powerhouse school where they had a storied history of success.

On Friday night they took us to a room as a staging area, the lights went dim in the room, we could hear loud, thunderous music in the main gym, and suddenly the doors popped open and the bright lights blinded us. They then asked us to stand as they marched the other school into the auditorium as the bands played, fans cheered, and the place went nuts.

There must have been a thousand people there, which blew us away because we would have 10–15 people at our meets. As the nerves built, the music stopped, and we heard the Canadian National anthem begin and the announcer yelled, "Ladies and Gentlemen, Team Canada!" and again the crowd went nuts. As we walked from the dankness to light, my adrenaline pumped through my body and I thought, "Holy shit, this is the big time".

I fell in love with the pomp and circumstance of American High school sports that night and prepared myself for battle. I remember my billet and fellow wrestler "Big Jim" Johnston came over to me. He dwarfed me with his 6'5" and was about 270 pounds, standing beside my 6'1", 198 pounds. I remember thinking I was lucky to not have to face him. He looked at me, told me, "you have this, Pflugger", and slapped me on the back as they called my name.

I went onto the mat and faced a wrestler from Sparta, and the match began. I remember shooting for the guy's legs, and he sprawled to avoid my attack. I fell to the mat, and he backed up. I quickly jumped to my feet, and I refocussed my attack. I had always been an extremely aggressive wrestler and thought I was representing Canada in my own way. I wanted my new friend from Lowell to respect me, and truthfully I loved the crowd. I went in on the guy, locked his upper body up, and as he pulled back, set him up and I used my trademark "pancake move" and threw him onto his back, and I was on top. The contact was so flat that I was awarded an instant pin, and the match was over and my 'new' Lowell teammates and team from WCSSAA cheered. That was one amazing experience I will never forget, I felt like a king that day.

The next day we battled several wrestlers from there, and I ended up in the gold medal match with the Lowell wrestler. As we met in the middle at the match, we both shook hands and said no hard feeling towards each other. We battled for the full two-to-three-minute match and in the end, I lost a close battle 4–3 to the host Lowell HS wrestler.

It was funny. He later told me that night that he saw my pancake and promised himself that there was no way that I was going to catch him in that lethal move . . . and I didn't.

*****

I had amassed a substantial record that year of 27–3 and prepared for the Ontario high school championship meet known as the Ontario Federation of School Athletic Associations (OFSAA) Championships hosted by Brock University.

The two weeks leading up to the OFSAA championships were extremely hard, and we trained to exhaustive levels. We trained extremely hard, just not very smart by today's standards. Back then, we wrestled two-to-three minute halves in a meet which could be exhausting given the sport's nature. With a week remaining, I took a break, blew off some steam, and went out with two friends. My friend drove up to Toronto to go to a dance, and the three of us jumped into his parents' brand-new VW Jetta. We left Waterloo and hit the 401 eastbound towards Toronto.

In retrospect, we should have never gone that night, but hey, we were invincible, right?

It was a cold February night; the roads were snow-covered and icy, and as we neared Guelph, my friend tried to pass a car on the inside of the fast lane. The front tire caught a rut, and suddenly we shot into the median, corkscrewed two to three times, and flipped end over end. I was sitting in the rear passenger seat, and as we rolled in the ditch, I grabbed onto the front seat, fighting to stabilize myself and fight for my life as glass, debris, and snow flew everywhere. When the vehicle came to rest, I was pinned in and lost my mind and went blank. I remember then standing outside the car, and we could not find our friend who had been in the seat in front of me.

The traffic was heavy; it was a Friday night, and we screamed in sheer terror for our friend. As we looked back in the direction we came from, we saw our friend lying on the road half on the lane; we saw traffic coming from the distance towards him, and we sprinted to his location and pulled him into the snow-covered median, where he lay unconscious. It seemed like hours, but we could finally summon help.

I remember getting into the ambulance because we were frozen as we only had dress pants, a dress shirt, and a light coat on. We were taken to the Guelph General Hospital and treated for our injuries. They kept our friend that night for observations because he suffered a brain injury when he was thrown from the vehicle and knocked unconscious.

The officer came and spoke to the two of us and accused my friend, the driver, of being impaired. He did not want to hear what happened, only to prove what he thought occurred. Only after roadside screening tests on both of us confirmed the officer wrong did he warm up to us.

That night I vowed that when I became an officer, I would not make being a young person a crime or pass judgement on anyone regardless of the situation I met them in.

They charged my friend with careless driving—rightfully so.

We went to see the vehicle at the auto wrecking yard and were shocked to see the extensive damage to the car and that we even survived.

I heavily bruised my lower back that night and had lots of facial cuts from the glass. The driver was unhurt, and after a week, they released our other friend from the hospital. Our family doctor suggested that I take a few weeks off, but who was he? I also thought I had a goal to achieve.

The following week of practice was very tough given my injuries, but I had a dream, and let nothing distract me from it. I deeply challenged myself not to let this stupidity ruin my experience; my teammates and my coach were going to OFSAA. I went into the Provincial Championships with a 27–3 record and wanted to defend that.

I am proud to say that even though I had faced such physical, mental, and spiritual pain the week prior, I finished fourth that year at OFSAA. I had hoped for not that result, but I could finish what I started. It was not a medal around my neck but the satisfaction of facing trauma, enacting my resiliency tools, and finishing what I had started. This point will be referenced again later in the book when I supply my tools for you to succeed.

*****

It was funny, though, in reflection, the "pancake" move that I had learned and perfected was not from a coach, a fellow wrestler, or an instructional video; I learned it from the movies.

In 1985, they released the movie *Vision Quest* in theaters.

The plot was a simple one[2]

Louden Swain is a wrestler at Thompson High School who has just turned 18 and decided that he needs to do something truly meaningful in his life.

He embarks on a mission or, in a Native American term, a vision quest, to drop two weight classes to challenge the area's toughest opponent, Brian Shute, a menacing three-time state champion from nearby rival Hoover High School, who has never been defeated in his high school career. In his zeal to drop from 190 pounds to 168 pounds, against the wishes of his coach and teammates, he disrupts the team around him and creates health problems of his own.

Meanwhile, his father has taken on a boarder named Carla from Trenton, New Jersey, passing through on her way to San Francisco.

Louden falls in love with her and begins to lose sight of his goals as a wrestler. Worse, his drastic weight loss culminates in an unhealthy situation where he gets frequent nose-bleeds which, Louden assumes, are due to a lack of iron in his diet (which costs him a match that he should have won). The two finally admit their love for each other, but Carla realizes she is distracting him from his goals. She decides to move out and continue to San Francisco, but not before seeing Louden's big match in which he pins Shute in the final seconds with a hip throw after suffering a nosebleed.

As Louden celebrates his victory, he monologues to the audience, "I guess that's why we gotta love those people who deserve it like there's no Tomorrow. 'Cause when you get right down to it—there isn't".

I rented the movie and played the final movie sequence about 100 times to learn, practise, and perfect the move.

That season, I used my "pancake" many times as it fueled my amazing last season in high school wrestling. I have supplied the QR link to the final sequence of the movie so you can see the "pancake" as well, as I did over 35 years ago.

*****

That spring, I continued to train and ran track and threw the javelin. I had a gratifying season making it to OFSAA for both the 4 by 100 and javelin throws. I was the first runner for the 4 by 100 as I worked the blocks very well. That track season further helped me improve my strength, fitness, and speed as I had committed to the University of Guelph for the fall.

That summer I hooked up with a large group of guys from all over the city who were moving on to University football. We trained like freaks in the gym, field, and track. We would spend hours together training, dreaming, and becoming friends, all in our respective pursuits of excellence at the next level.

I was not the best or most gifted athlete around over the years. I am immensely proud of my work ethic I put into my training and preparation physically, mentally, and spiritually and would put that up against most.

*****

As high school ended and I prepared to take my next step in life towards the University of Guelph and the two-week, three-practices-a-day training camp in late August I'd reflect that my high school could be summed up by three movies: *All the Right Moves*, *Vision Quest*, and *Breakfast Club*.

I encourage you to watch all of them and see if you too can identify with any of the characters and better understand "who you were, who you are, and who you want to be" moving forward.

I have been going through my scrapbooks while researching this book and came across the graduation present from my dad that came in the form of two amazing 8 x 10 photos commemorating my high school football days and a letter of advice.

June 1986

Doug,

I had these pictures redone for you so that someday you can look back at the "glory days" of high school and the feelings you had at the time.

This was achieved by demanding work, cuts-bruises-pain, and tears to prove you had the will-ability and stubbornness to do it and make your mark in life.

Remember the recognition and the glory others gave you will soon fade, and you will be replaced by a younger "hero".

Currently stay strong and work hard at putting this energy into what you want in life.

But remember, take the will—and apply the ability—to achieve, change stubbornness to compromise.

Doug, with this advice I hope you find friendships—lasting love and success in the future.

With Love, Dad

*****

As I write and reflect on these words from 34 year ago, I am floored, amazed, and honoured what was bestowed upon me by dad. I had always thought that *iron will* was my idea, but I am wrong. Dad foreshadowed the concept to me so long ago, and the fuel needed to achieve life successes: hard work, cuts, bruises, pain, ability, energy, and stubbornness; and at times compromise.

Wow. Thanks Dad

P.S. Dad, can you now foreshadow six numbers 1 through 49 and we can have a real proper time.

*****

Later in August, my buddy who had been lying on the 401 drove his parents' car to my place, I packed up, and we left for a football training camp, where I met another influential leader, head Coach John Musselman.

Back then, the team had just come off winning a National Championship, the Vanier Cup in 1984, and the work ethic and culture of that team were terrific. The veterans worked so hard to recapture the glory from '84 and win another Vanier. They showed excellence in their practice and play and demanded the same from the newcomers.

We opened the two-week training camp of three-a-day practices, and I began running the ball as a tailback against some powerful men. After three days of running the first team offense in the morning, I remember that meat squad to get RB reps against the first team defence in the afternoon, and I had made all the special teams for full special team practice at night.

I remember standing in front of the mirror after a shower in the change room after the third day of camp, and my entire body looked like one massive bruise.

Some of those guys hit harder than a freight train, and I was utterly in awe of the power transfer they delivered on me. I remember quietly thinking to myself, "I am so glad they are on my team and felt bad for opposing players who felt their full force".

I hurt and ached in several layers of bruises. My body was battered, beaten, sore, overwhelmed, homesick, and defeated. I even questioned my right to be on the field with these fantastic elite athletes.

A day or so later, as I walked out of the change room past the coach's office, Coach John Musselman saw me and called me into this office. He shut the door and asked if I was okay. That morning during offensive practices, I had uncharacteristically fumbled the ball twice, and when the practice had finished, I had walked off the field with my head hanging low.

We talked for about an hour, and he shared that all young players who come to the next level face some form of doubt; it's a bigger game, with more prominent players, and we were no longer the big fish like we had been in our high school ponds. I shared with him that I was tired, beaten, and mentally flat and that self-doubt had crept in, and it was affecting my confidence.

John encouraged me to give it a few more days until camp broke and classes began, and I agreed. Shortly after, we had our rookie initiation, and upon completion, they invited us back into the change room; the vets and captain invited us all to join them and sing our team song, and we became valued members of the team. We fought many battles that year and got great successes because of that, on and off the field.

I went back to my dorm room and took out Dad's note and reminded myself that that "the fuel needed to achieve life successes[included] hard work, cuts, bruises, pain, ability, energy and stubbornness; and at times compromise".

They assigned me a veteran mentor and had the privilege of meeting my now lifelong friend and brother Paul Wright. Over the years have helped each other fight some of life's battles, and I genuinely love him as a "brother from another mother".

Paul and I are remarkably close, even today. It is amazing to look back when we met. He commuted from Kitchener to Guelph every day. I was living in Waterloo. We had an arrangement that he would drive me daily, and I would help with gas money. I was poor during those years because I did not save properly to cover the expense of university. Paul did not let this interfere with helping me; many times I paid him in "cash" through the new cassette tapes I'd receive weekly from the BMG club or whatever I could barter with.

Paul is an amazing man, and I am so glad he is reaping the rewards of a glorious life because he was so charitable back in the day.

It is truly insightful chatting with Paul from time to time as we reflect on who we were, who we are, and who we want to be moving forward. I genuinely enjoy our conversations because he has been there the whole way and knows me and I know myself.

I had many talks with John that year, each as supportive, caring, and directive as the last. I enjoyed a great rookie season, earning my way up to dressing from the second game on as a second-string tailback and starting on all special teams.

We played one helluva game against Western in the Yates Cup that year that we eventually lost, but I kindly reflect on the friendships I made that year. Although we lost that game, we won in how we came together as strangers and left the season as friends and teammates.

I have had the privilege last year of speaking at length with John about our talks and how he helped direct my attention and energies forward from that of a teenage boy filled with "piss and vinegar" into the man who I later became. Under John's leadership and the lessons learned through my Gryphon Football brothers' team, I am grateful.

The following year, I would befriend another teammate, Jefferson Frisbee, who was one of our linemen. Years later, we connected when he was a West Virginia University professor and the hockey team general manager. It is incredible to see how later in life, we would again work together as Gryphon brothers but in a new family, the WVU Mountaineer Hockey family.

These incredible experiences of personal growth as a player and person are why I returned years later to the program in a mentorship role to assume a similar position that John had in my life and to mentor other young players the same way I was.

Gryphon Football pride runs deep; it runs proud and forms the bond that joins us all as family.

In my second year, I returned to the football off-season mat to keep my fitness level. It was another fantastic experience in my life where I would team up and sparred with Doug Cox, a two-time Olympian (1988 Seoul, South Korea | 1996 Atlanta, USA). He routinely beat the crap out of me physically and mentally on the mat, but after a time he further taught me how to be a man, face adversity and loss, learn from it, and #RiseUpAndExcel. I learned a great deal of humility during those years wrestling with Doug and am a better person because of the experience.

You will rarely hear of someone thanking another for delivering such punishment to them. Still, I appreciate the lessons Doug taught me on the mat because they quickly translated to the street, where I would have to put those talents to work in many emergent situations.

Doug and I have remained good friends over the years, and he quietly laughs when I remind him of the stories where he routinely rag-dolled me around the practice.

*****

In 2009, I would return to the University of Guelph and Guelph Wrestling Club teams serving as the Wrestle Canada National Strength and Conditioning Coach—Guelph Training Center until 2011.

In 2019, I had the pleasure of meeting and speaking with John at an event at Alumni Stadium. I told him what he meant to me that day and praised him for his insight and caring for a rookie player. I further said that I took a lot of what I had learned from him and used those same skills to coach my own athletes. With tears in his eyes, he said, "Thanks Pflugger, you made my day". We are still friends to this day.

In 2001, I rejoined the Gryphon Football team, where I currently serve as the team's Law Enforcement Mentor and Community Liaison Coach spearheading and highlighted by:

2015–present. I formed a partnership with the Avalon Group Homes for at-risk youth. This partnership enables players who wish to work with youth the chance to earn a part-time job with the agency. To date, Johnny Augustine, Orion Edwards, Dean Yaromich, Akeem Knowles, and Elijah Woods have worked for the group home and gained valuable experience to put towards future employment opportunities.

2015–present. Stu Lang and I created the Gryphon Football 'Community Heroes'. This program recognizes community heroes in Guelph for their outstanding contribution in making Guelph a nicer place for all to live, work, and play. We invite the recipients to a home game, give them a block of free tickets for family and guests, and we bring them on the field at the end of the first quarter to be recognized. A brief bio is read, and each person receives a Community Heroes jacket. To date, there have been 10 School safety patrols of the year, 40 YMCA Women of Distinction Award winners, 3 Special Olympics Coaches, 12 Big Brother/Sisters with little brothers/sisters and several other local business owners.

2015–present: The University of Guelph Gryphon Football Pflug Family Community Service Award is given annually to the graduating payer who has performed the most community service during his four years on the team.

2018–present: The Annual "Salute to Service" game honours our first responders in police, fire, EMS, corrections, and military

2016–present: The Annual Gryphon Football Special Olympics Powerlifting meet

*****

"Barrie Boys"

During my first year, I enjoyed meeting and hanging out with one of my teammates, Dave Lloyd, from Barrie. We were two guys who came to camp not knowing anyone and quickly formed a lasting friendship when we discovered we had the same family and core values.

As the school year ended, "Lloydy", as I know him, invited me to go to his place in the summer in Barrie and meet the buddies he grew up with from high school. We arranged a time, and I drove up to Barrie and met Randy Swears, Pat Langdon, Terry Le Clair, and Barry Hughes. I was accepted and, with pride, carried the "Barrie Boys" label.

We spent time together those three summers 24/7. We worked hard at our summer jobs, trained like freaks in the gym, field, and court for our upcoming seasons, and played hard on the beach and in the bars. We fuelled every moment with continuous chirping, laughter, and growing respect and love for each other. We did not know it, but the "Barrie Boys" were growing into the "Barrie Brothers".

We were competing against each other all the time, jockeying for positioning within the group. Continuous chirping and insulting each other always fuelled this. We worked out hard, played hard, and partied hard. To improve ourselves for our upcoming seasons, by hanging out at the beach and bar, we would play touch football and continuously chirp each other. If you came at one of us in anger, that meant you came at all of us. Our friendship grew over those three summers that saw us grow from dumbass teenagers into successful men.

Looking back, I am so proud of my guys. We all achieved elite athletic successes; Lloydy, Barry, and I played University football. Randy and Pat played University basketball, and Terry played Junior Hockey. The best part about this is that we have the memories, scars, and aches from a life lived and not watched from the sidelines.

We all have the same core values and love of family and each other. We get together from time to time and chirp each other the same way we did many years ago. We have helped each other through marriage breakups, sickness, our parents' deaths and have sup-ported each other as our families grew.

It is so nice to know that we have shared over 35 years of friendship.

If "life" were to come to one of us, it would come to all of us. We "Barrie boys" always rally to help a brother up.

AUTHOR'S CHALLENGE

Try to give back to someone or something.

Robert Ingersoll says it best, "We rise by lifting others". [3]

I honestly believe that regardless of who or what you call 'God' or the energy, you believe in karma. Kindness begets kindness.

When you see someone with a smile on their face, always look deep into their eyes; they are the gateway to their soul. Some people try to hide how bad they feel, disguising it with a weak smile. That is where you will learn how a person really feels and can step up and help them.

Want to change your life to the positive? Change someone else's life to the positive first.

NOTES

[i] https://www.goodreads.com/quotes/8119455-we-rise-by-lifting-others
[1] https://en.wikipedia.org/wiki/All_the_Right_Moves_(film)
[2] https://en.wikipedia.org/wiki/Vision_Quest

Answering the Call to Serve and Protect

5

I will never forget the day I received my employment letter from the Guelph Police Force. I was so proud to be given the opportunity to serve and protect.

However, it forced me to make a life-altering decision. I was going into my fourth year of University with high expectations of having incredible seasons in football and wrestling. In the end, my decision was based on two facts for not finishing my degree. I was offered my dream job, and in doing so I was going to receive $729.00 every two weeks. No more Kraft dinners10–15 times per week . . . I was rich.

*****

I can't remember who gave it to me, but I received a card of congratulations back then that had a poem on it, that once read became my goal or mantra as a police officer. They call it "Little Eyes Upon You" and I would like to share it hoping it inspires you.

There are little eyes upon you
and they are watching night and day.
There are little ears that quickly
take in every word you say.

There are little hands all eager
to do anything you do.
And a little boy who is dreaming
of the day he will be like you.

You are the little fellow's idol,
you are the wisest of the wise.
In his little mind about you
no suspicions ever rise.

He believes in you devoutly,
holds all you say and do.
He will say and do, in your way
when he is grown up just like you.

DOI: 10.1201/9781003187189-6

There is a wide-eyed little fellow
who believes you're always right
and his eyes are always opened,
and he watches day and night.

You are setting an example
every day in all you do.
For the little boy who is waiting
to grow up to be just like you.

Author Unknown

So, I accepted the position and left the safety of being a University student-athlete where the sense of Team and covering your brothers' backs echoed through everything we did. I felt sadness and regret, but it excited me at the challenge that would span the rest of my life and supply one day for my family.

*****

When the Guelph Police Force hired me, Richard Stewart was the Chief of Police; a position he held from 1988 to 1994.

As I reflect on my first day of work and attending his office, I have very fond memories. Chief Stewart was a stately gentleman and exemplified what I thought someone in his position should be. He shared his love for the City of Guelph and the citizens that we swore to "serve and protect" at all costs. Chief Stewart reminded me that we police with our communities which I believe was ahead of his time in his thinking, and many of the points he shared mirror  the current police and community shared goals we teach. He shared his love for sports and told me he was a season ticket holder for the University of Guelph varsity basketball team. He even said that he had seen me play football at the school.

There is an old saying that "it's hard to teach an old dog a new trick".

Here it was an old dog teaching a pup a new trick or two on how we should police with our communities.

In reviewing this project, Chief Stewart offered the following comment,

Very kind words Doug. Thank you. I always made it a point of seeing new recruits and new hires as soon after they started as possible, thinking it was important, early on, for me to get to know them, and important for them to get to know me, and hear a bit of my philosophy. Each interview was of course different but covered the points you touched on. I did like to think I may be a bit ahead of the curve, one phrase I used often, when speaking with the "white shirts" (Senior Officers) when looking at policy and procedure was—the status quo isn't necessarily correct. It was my hope that by pointing this out we would move ahead rather than stay stationary.

I'll once again confirm through my years of experience that Chief Stewart was way ahead of his time, and I hope future leaders learn from this simple lesson knowing the lasting impression our meeting has had over 35 years.

Chief Stewart retired in 1994 and moved to the corporate sector. Over the years, we would run into each other often at charity events, police-community events, and sports games at the University, and our friendship grew from chief to constable to mutually respectful friends.

In 2005 I approached him as asked if he would join the Guelph Police history book committee, and he readily accepted. We would release the book detailing the Guelph Police history spanning from 1840 to 2010, 18 months later, a feat many thought impossible.

In 2016 I was nearing my "policing expiry date", and I shared I had applied to the Ontario Police College. And it elated him. He challenged me that one day if I secured the job, he would like to attend one of my lectures.

In 2020, that challenge became a reality when I hosted Chief Stewart at the college, and he sat in my basic recruit constable community policing lecture, where over 250 were in attendance.

As I reflect, I felt like a child performing for his parents who was hoping to win that proud smile of pride. The lecture that day went off marvellously with full engagement by the recruits. As the class neared its end, I introduced the special guest to the audience. I relayed that Chief Stewart was the man who gave me a chance to live out my dream very much as they had just received their police services. I relayed the support he had given me as a Chief, mentor, friend, and confidant; in response, the entire class gave him a round of applause.

I then took the Chief out for lunch in the instructor's lounge, introduced him to many of my colleagues, and shared some marvellous stories and memories. He expressed his pride and respect for me: I was so happy to show the man who gave me a chance to earn it and now pay it forward by providing other recruits with the same support.

A few weeks later, I ran into the OPC Sergeant Major, and we spoke about his meeting with my Chief. He responded, "Now that's what a Chief of Police should look like and act. He's an impressive man, Doug".

I totally agree.

On December 21, 2020, I received a kind note from Chief Stewart detailing that day.

Hey Doug, I was going over the last year in my mind, and one highlight was your invitation to sit in on your class at the OPC. I thoroughly enjoyed the day and was so happy for you. The enthusiasm you showed was sincere, and those young minds will remember your sage advice for their careers. So, thanks for being so thoughtful. Merry Christmas, and I hope Santa brings you that bigger boat.

Chief Stewart, thank you for believing in me and my potential by giving me the chance to " 'Serve and Protect".

*****

As you know from the prologue entry, this turned out to be a complete disaster in the early years because of my assigned shift. The police leader did not promote the team, covering a brother's or sister's back, and lacked understanding of leadership's fundamental concepts.

We had such talented people on that shift, and we just lacked an excellent police leader.

This was such a disappointment to me. I always had thought policing would extend the elite teams I had contributed towards, but in those days, you did not complain about your boss, you did not question them, and in most cases, you were told to "shut up until I speak with you".

I looked back to the first weeks in August 1989, and they detailed me to attend a post-mortem because "everyone had to do it". I was very naïve and had no experience with death, let alone had seen a dead body. I was dropped off at the Guelph general hospital and given direction to where the morgue was and sent off on my way.

I do not blame my shift supervisors or my coach officer because, simply, they did not know any better at the time. That said, I had the benefit of meeting with someone from my organization and was briefed on my role, what I would see, feel, or think to better prepare myself for this experience. That was not the case, and as I have detailed this task in the lineup, the stories of other fellow officers' experiences at their autopsy filled the discussion and with attempts to tease me or freak me out.

I never have nor will ever like the blood, guts, filth, and gore that come with policing. I am not a prude, but it makes me uncomfortable, no more, no less.

They dropped me off at the hospital and I found my way down to the morgue. I introduced myself to the doctor and said that I had never seen a dead body and had never been to an autopsy. He kindly gave me a brief intro to the case and pulled back the sheet covering the body. I remember my knees buckling under my weight when I saw the body; it was a lady who had died by suicide of carbon monoxide, and she looked like my mom, having the same hairstyle, body style, size, and weight.

He was truly kind to me that day and walked me through the entire process . . . I am sure out of necessity. He did not want me to pass out and risk continuing the autopsy by stepping over and around me.

When the autopsy was over, I thanked him and left. I called the station to get a ride back and went outside to get some fresh air and wait for my coach officer to arrive.

I remember it was a sultry August afternoon; I was sweating and not feeling well when he picked me up. When I got into the cruiser, my coach officer asked how I was; I was honest with him how the whole thing troubled me, and he took no time to laugh and scold me.

I told him I was remarkably close with my mom and how this bothered me because she looked so like mom. He turned and looked at me, started laughing at me, and said, "Great I'm riding with a momma's boy".

When we got into the station, we all went to the report room, which was our custom at the end of shift to meet everyone, and our supervisors would sign our daily notebooks.

This provided my coach officer with a greater audience, and he took full advantage of berating me and poking in jest.

This was not the first nor the last time he took runs at me. But again, in those days, who was I? I was just a newcomer trying to make a positive name for myself and could not speak up. He would negatively document me on things like:

- not being a team player because I protested going to garage sales every Saturday and Sunday
- making fun of me and laughing at drivers I had pulled over and gave tickets to because he would not have and that I was trying to impress the boss
- I was too gung-ho and wanted to learn the job
- I worked out and ran during my off time

The worst thing he did, which haunts me to this day, was not allowing me to wear hearing protection at the outdoor range because "you need to hear a gunshot so you can investigate one".

Ok, but 2,000 times?

As I have gotten older and had my hearing assessed, the audiologist draws direct parallels to my hearing loss.

He would always chime in with some insult or "chirp", as we all called it, to bring negative attention my way throughout my entire career. I never knew why he enjoyed being so rude and stayed away from him as much as possible.

I used my athletic resiliency tools to deal with stupidity and trauma, and I became stronger because of his relentless persecution. Timing plays a massive role in our lives, and the timing of his placement in my life and corresponding personal growth served me very well over the years. I am warped; looking back, I'm almost thankful he acted the way he did because it made me focus on what I was doing and work hard to achieve my professional successes.

*****

About six years ago, Michelle and I walked through Riverside Park in Guelph during the Ribfest weekend when we ran into this guy. He retired several years ago. He was wearing one of the powder blue police shirts we used to wear but had removed the Guelph Police shoulder crests; he wore jeans and his old police boots. Yes, he was that guy.

I introduced him to Michelle and reminded her, "This is the coach officer I told you about" and smiled. I explained she was a Police Sergeant with Peel. He stepped back, looked her up and down in a perverted sort of way, and said, "Well, little darling, I can see why they promoted you"'. And he asked her, "Who did you sleep with?"

Michelle is not one to respond to·such rude behaviour; she is very professional and reserved, but on this occasion quipped, "You are a jerk" and walked away. I gladly joined her.

******

I graduated from the Ontario Police College on February 2, 1990, and returned to the police service. I had several great coach officers, including "Johnny" and "Don". They were incredible guys and even better officers, who taught all the things I needed to be successful and set me up for many significant experiences down the road. They were truly ahead of their time and follow tenets that I now teach in leadership:

> **Lead with your best self,**
> **Model the behaviour you look for from others and,**
> **Always create an environment for yourself.**

On February 7, 1990, Don and I were parked in some lot going over the details of the last call we attended when we saw a car come into the parking lot at a high rate of speed. The car pulled up beside us and the frantic parents who told us they were lost but needed medical help for their 11-year-old son, choking and in medical distress. I quickly grabbed him and jumped in the back seat of our cruiser so that we could speed off St Joseph's hospital's emergency department.

I performed the Heimlich maneuver on him, dislodged a big candy that he had been sucking on that got stuck in his throat, and told the parents. We then drove the young man to the hospital to get checked out while his parents followed. We arrived at the hospital and helped check the young man into emergency. We said goodbye and continued on our way.

At the end of that work block, I went to Florida to visit my friend who lived there.

When I returned to work a week later and attended lineup, a lot of my shift mates joyfully teased, "The rookie is now famous". I did not know what they were talking about, and "Johnny" pulled me aside and gave me two newspaper articles outlining the day I helped the boy.

Headline: Policeman saves boy

February 1990—**Guelph Mercury** *Newspaper: Letter to the editor*

My husband and I would like to take this opportunity to thank God and the two police officers who were so providentially in our path on February 7, 1990.

Our family was en route to a hockey game when I turned to notice that Mark, our 11-year-old son, was choking. He had accidentally swallowed a candy with it later lodged in his throat.

I tried repeatedly to remove the candy, but with no success. By now, Mark had been choking for a considerable length of time, and we decided we must get him to the hospital. In a state of panic and confusion, my husband made a wrong turn. Fortunately for us, his error allowed us to notice two parked police cars. We quickly pulled up beside them and called the officers to help. What a sense of relief it was for us when the young officer who came to Mark's aid said the candy was out.

He had used the Heimlich technique to dislodge it. We are eternally grateful to this wonderful young officer. His calmness, decisiveness, and ability saved us from what could have ended with tragic results. We have no doubt in our minds that he saved Mark's life. We also appreciate the kindness and dedication of the other police officers involved in this situation. May God bless you both.

Jack and Monica Glazier/Rr2 Guelph

As I read the article, I thought it was such a gracious gesture by the family and frankly thought that Don and I were doing our job that day. I asked him, "This is what we do, right? Save lives and are calm in the chaos?"

With that, he gave me the second article dated February 27, 1990, that Tony Saxon of the *Guelph Mercury* did in follow-up to this letter to the editor.

Headline: Officer saves choking boy: Parents took wrong turn on the way to hospital.
February 27, 1990— *Guelph Mercury* Newspaper
By Tony Saxon—*Mercury* Reporter

THANKFUL FAMILY—Members of the Glazier family, clockwise from top, Jack, Mark, and Monica, had a scary experience earlier this month when Mark began choking on a candy. Luckily, the family came across Guelph police constable Doug Pflug, who they feel saved Mark's life by performing the Heimlich Maneuver.

A Guelph area family is calling Guelph police constable Doug Pflug a hero after he saved the life of their son Mark earlier this month.

Jack and Monica Glazier were on their way to son Mark's hockey game when the parents heard him choking in the back of the van.

The Glaziers panicked and took a wrong turn on the way to hospital and ran into a cool, calm officer who performed the Heimlich maneuver.

Mark had been sucking on a hard candy and started to panic when choked.

"Try as I might—and I tried lots, I couldn't get the candy dislodged", said Monica. "I even tried the Heimlich maneuver, but I'd only heard about it and it didn't work. I didn't know the person had to be standing".

The Heimlich maneuver is a simple, yet effective technique used to dislodge items a person is choking on. It involves applying a quick, intense pressure with a clenched fist at the point directly below the center of a person's rib cage. It is a learned technique and can be dangerous if applied by someone not trained in its application.

When it became clear Mark was in serious trouble, Jack decided to head for the hospital, but became confused and took a wrong turn off Speedvale Avenue. "We were actually heading in the wrong direction, out of town, but just as I turned, I noticed two police cars parked in a lot," said Jack. "I pulled in and waved the officers over". Jack adds that his thought was that the officers could get their son to the hospital faster. One of those was Const. Pflug, who had only been on the force for six months.

The officer quickly took control, grabbed Mark, and took him in the cruiser, quickly applying the maneuver and instantly dislodging the candy that was slowly choking their son to death. "He acted quickly and made the right decision", Jack said. "If he had waited, I don't think Mark would be around".

Monica, who called the experience "the most terrifying experience of our lives," said she doubts they could have gotten to hospital in time to save their choking son.

The irony of the situation is that Const. Pflug told the couple he had only learned the life-saving technique two weeks before the incident, but to Monica, he still seemed so self-assured.

The couple feel God also played a part in putting the officers in their path that day, but still put most of the credit on the shoulder of young Pflug. "That guy saved

Mark's life", said Jack. "They save a number of lives in the course of a year and they just look at it as their job. For what they do in our city, they don't get enough pats on the back". Echoed Monica, 'If we could give him a medal, we would'.

*****

I had the privilege of meeting Mark socially around 2007, and it was so lovely to chat with him and kindly reflect and learn about his life from the day we first met.

As I reflect, that event's timing was crucial in my policing history and career. I had a terrible coaching session before going to police college and, upon my return, was questioning if I made the right choice in coming to the Guelph Police. I am so honoured to be part of the Glazier family story, but that event gave me hope, and I stuck it out with the Guelph Police.

*****

COMMUNITY POLICING CAN SAVE YOUR LIFE; IT DID MINE

That fall I was asked by my team Sports Psychology Professor Dan Yarmey if I wanted to join him and help coach an up-and-coming senior football team at Our Lady of Lourdes Catholic School. I jumped at the chance because it allowed me to continue to work with Dan. He was a significant part of my athletic and psychological development in university, and I felt he could help me bridge the gap between them and law enforcement.

I wanted to coach as it was something I felt I'd be good at, giving my experiences and being in a spot where I thought I could make a real difference in the lives of these young men. Last, it provided me with a positive bridge between policing and the community.

That season was extraordinary in that we came together under the incredible direction and mentoring of Doug Cummings, a teacher and football coach at the school.

That season we faced great adversity, tight games, injuries to crucial players, differences in coaching philosophies and game strategies, and eventually won the District 10 Championship.

We celebrated with the players, and I got home late that Friday night after our pizza party. I caught a few hours of sleep and went in for the 11:30 p.m. to 7:30 a.m. shift. That night was uneventful, and I completed it with ease, still riding the adrenaline from the glory of victory.

The next night they assigned me to walk the beat. Back in those days, we could not walk in pairs; we had to stay on our side of the street. If there was a fight on the other side of the road, our sergeant made us ask for permission to go.

It was around 1:00 p.m.; I was walking the beat in downtown Guelph when I approached a large crowd waiting to go into a club. Everyone seemed happy, and admittedly, I was complacent thinking about the win for a second night when out of nowhere, bam! I was sucker-punched in the face. I dropped my head into my hand as I looked up, saw a lot of blood; they broke my nose. As I realized what was going on, my legs were pulled from underneath me, and I was slammed on my back. I could grab my mic chord and say, "I need . . ." and the mic was ripped out of my hand and detached from the radio.

The fight was on, and I felt the weight of my attacker on my front, so I tried to slip out. I remember hearing,

"Zone nine responded . . .

"Zone nine respond . . .

"Zone nine . . .

"Station to the units, we have lost contact with Zone 9, last known location was on Carden Street".

I remember automatically shifting my weight as I had a thousand times on the wrestling mat to get onto my front to prevent being pinned. Here being pinned was not a lost match; instead, it could have been my life given the random attack.

As I got to my front, I could hear several units yell, "Zone 6 going, Zone 15 going", and the sound of distant sirens filled my ears, and my adrenaline surged. I felt a moment where the attacker grabbed for my .38 in the crappy Boss holders we had, and fear and anger raged in me.

I began to experience extreme fear and rage as I knew that I was fighting to preserve possession of my gun. I remember feeling his hand pull at my gun, my gun belt shifted because of the force, and I knew that I was fighting for my life.

The hours of gun retention training kicked in and I thought that there was no way I was letting this guy get my gun to turn on my shift mates or me, and I fought even harder. We wrestled for control for what seemed like 30 minutes, but I would not give up, knowing my shift was coming; the sirens filled the air, and the dispatchers were encouraging me to fight harder, that help was on the way.

I remember getting to my feet and striking at the upper body between my feet with everything I had in attempts to create time, distance, and space from the person who hit me and was fighting me and going for my gun. As I tried to gain control of him, I noticed a circle was forming around us, and negative comments filled the air, attaching to me.

The blood was rushing out my nose when I looked slightly up and saw a pair of cowboy boots point in my direction. The unknown person pulled back his right leg in a kicking motion, and I grimaced and put my head into my shoulder, turned my left shoulder towards the future kick to my head as the attacker continued to struggle between my feet. I remember falling slightly onto the attacker and securing the handcuffs on him to his rear.

As I stood him up, the stress-induced tunnel vision lessened and the auditory exclusion lessened and I was able to see that there were 15–20 pairs of athletic shoes, toes pointing to the aggressive crowd and formed in a protective circle around me. I continued to battle to gain control of my attacker and realized that there were guys from my high school football team, and they formed a protective circle around me that night. They took a stand to protect me that night, to risk personal injury from being hit, and throw punches back at the crowd, because as I've later been told, "No one was going to hurt Coach Pflug".

In reflection, I am so fortunate to have the chance to collaborate with these young men and the fact they believed in me. Two days prior, we became a District 10 Championship football team, and on that night, we became a family.

I took a good beating that night and would have certainly lost had it not been for those guys. Looking back, the beating I took was temporary, but the pride and family we created will last our lifetime.

The next week we met to order championship football jackets and to make sweatshirts that said, "Pain is temporary, but pride is permanent".

When the meeting was over, I addressed the crowd, my face still showing the effects of the attack, and said, "Hey guys, thank you again for coming to my aid last weekend. I know that if you had not stepped up and some of you even took shots, I would not be here today. Thank you. Now if I ever find you downtown underage again . . .". And the room filled with an enormous round of laughter.

To this date, I see the guys regularly, and they share many on field and off field stories with my family on what I mean to them and how I helped them in their process of growing from teenage boys into men.

It is incredible when I run into them in the mall, on a field, a pub or just around town and they introduce me to their children. When introduced, they always say, "This is Coach Pflug, the man I told you about".

That was very fitting on multiple levels, don't you think?

*****

When I became a Coach Officer myself, I knew I had the chance to differ from the coach I had. This is such an important role in the life of a young officer because the Coach Officer provides a personal supervised learning environment where the officer takes the knowledge gained in a safe academic setting and uses it in a real-world call for service. This coaching time supplies an incredibly solid base that the young officer can expand on as he or she continues to learn and develop.

Trust in knowing that in the Coach Officer role, I did the opposite of everything he did, made for easy success training some incredible recruits.

When I was promoted to the Sergeant's rank, I further used this knowledge to ensure that the officers that we asked to coach recruits were a good fit and made them aware of our recruits' personal and professional importance and changing corporate culture. Coach Officers in policing are so critical.

This continued for a year or two after I found the boy in the leaves and blew up one day when I came into work and found that someone had painted a Gryphon and the words "chosen ones" on my locker with Liquid Paper. This was the same tattoo that all the football rookies had placed on various parts of our body out of a sense of pride, acceptance, and belonging by our older teammates. The tattoo is on my right hip, and someone must have seen this in the work shower.

I was so pissed off with by this stupid act, and I immediately tried to clean it off with solvent, and as I did, I once again felt hands on my shoulders, and they spun me around and threw me back into my locker.

It was the same officer who took joy in publicly insulting me. Again, this guy was no version of being in shape but loved to bully others. I was told to "watch my back, I'm no better than the shit-heads on the street, and I'd better be careful when asking for backup because the boys don't like me".

I vowed I would treat no one anywhere like this, and regardless of the side of the line I found them, I would treat them as a person first. One day, my desire for promotion in my organization was born out of a need to not be like the tyrannical Staff Sergeant or senior officers in the platoon.

To manage this newfound stress, I went back to my safe place, the gym and track, where I could control effort and receive rewards. It was funny, when I was at work some older officers would even come up to me and laugh and try to marginalize me to the others. "Look at the young buck—thinks that if he can pump iron, he can be a cop. Weights don't help a street fight, son", and once again I was the subject of bullying.

I could have easily sat back and become part of the problem or #RiseUpAndExcel and be part of the solution and be a change leader. Remember, you cannot lead unless you have followers.

*****

It was around this time that I received an invitation to hang out from another younger officer named Tom Gill. Tom was a big guy with a gregarious smile and well liked by everyone, and I wondered "Why me?" To add to my curiosity, Tom lived with four guys, one of whom was happy to pick on me, and I was naturally suspicious as I thought he was friends with all those guys.

I cannot remember what we did or where we went, but remember we got along marvellously. In the evening he told me he had heard all the stuff people were saying and doing to me. He then told me that regardless of what was said or done, he was the type of guy who bases his own opinions on his own personal experience with people.

He said he really enjoyed hanging out that night and that I could consider him a friend and brother.

Tom and I have celebrated over 33 years of friendship. He is a guy who I consider a brother and would do anything for. He recently retired as a Staff Sergeant and an incredible career of service to our community. His leadership was exemplary, and empathy, understanding and incredible police skills, knowledge, and abilities always fuelled it.

As time went by, I had enough and applied to two other police forces because I was disheartened by my experiences because of poor coaching and supervision.

Little did Tom know, but that was the first time I considered staying and proved to be a huge turning point in my decision to stay at the Guelph Police Service because I was applying to other places to start over.

Thanks, Tommy, had it not been for your small act of kindness, I would have left the Guelph Police Service and not enjoyed the successes my career provided. I hope that you enjoy your well-deserved retirement, you truly "Served and Protected" in the best way you could, just by being you.

*****

I loved policing because it allowed me the opportunity to enter people's lives when in conflict or chaos and use my critical thinking skills and problem solve to help them move forward. When I graduated from police college in February 1990, Mom challenged me, "Doug, don't become an asshole. Make sure you make everyone's life better because you are in it than worse". This was such a cool challenge, but in an unhealthy mind, as I moved too, it became so heavy a burden and a noose around my neck.

A few months after I began this process, there was a supervisory shift, and it saved my career at the Guelph Police Service when Staff Sergeant Pat Martin took over our platoon. Pat was a great police leader and indeed created an environment where I could develop and succeed.

Our platoon included some amazing officers and civilians. We worked hard and had some wonderfully positive experiences that we all shared under his direction. It was a considerable experience, and I would try later in my career to mirror some of his leadership practices, knowing how positive they were for us.

I am grateful to have worked alongside these people and received the positive influences they provided.

AUTHOR'S CHALLENGE

I challenge you to give what you can in mentoring youth; they need us to help plan, find, and seek their paths. When you mentor a young person, never lose sight that you will help in the release of some exceptional human potential.

Just maybe, that potential will turn into reality, and they may even save your life like they did mine.

At the year-end awards banquet, the guys presented me with Our Lady of Lourdes Unsung Hero before the school to thunderous applause.

Thank you, guys, you made this friend smile.

When Darkness Creeps In, Try to Focus on Any Light You Can Find

6

Over the next few years, the darkness appeared more often between the momentous events I experienced. As I reached out to my work friends during times of stress, we would go for wings and beer or have a few "shots to take the edge off". On off days I'd hit the gym track or University of Guelph football stadium stairs and train for hours alone, trying to understand and expel the energy generated from the rage growing within me and free me from the growing darkness.

That was how we were "culturally" trained: no one would acknowledge or accept weakness in any form. Work hard, play hard, train hard.

> **Stress—Ignore it**
> **Have too much stress, eat chicken wings and beer**
> **That does not work, have a few shots to take the edge off**

I do not blame the past for the lack of mental health knowledge, recognition, or lack of education, awareness, and help. This was not an issue people focused on, and they did not teach us coping skills or tell us to use or at least know where they were if we were having a hard time.

In the mid-1990s we were all young officers with about five years of experience, working out tails off trying to get to the "infamous" Detective Office. Talking about pain and stress or admitting you were having a mental health problem or letting anyone know you did would instantly disqualify you. The policing culture was in denial that police officers could be simple people, hurt and have issues with the horror the job presents, so you suffered in confusion and silence.

So, I did what most did and hid it. If they don't see it, they don't know about it, and can't judge you for it.

As I think back, remember that between 1990 and 1996, I started a very unhealthy practice when I came off the seven-day night shift block where we worked 11:30 p.m. to

DOI: 10.1201/9781003187189-7

7:30 a.m., seven days in a row, followed by six days off. We finished on Thursday and I would not sleep that day, so that I could force a fatigue-induced crash that night to flip my body from the night mode to day mode. It usually worked, but about four or five times each year I would struggle and, as for "my blowing off steam time," I would go to the basement alone, crank up the heavy metal, drink rye, and in most cases, cry to "take the edge off".

Eventually, I'd fall asleep, and wake up the next day and shrug off the previous night's events, trivializing them as stupid and justified them by believing it was due to lack of sleep and extreme fatigue. I would then start a new and brighter day.

Hey, that made sense, right? Wouldn't you simply justify the previous evening and laugh it off as tired after seven hard night shifts and lack of sleep.

This flawed strategy would follow me through my life and one day take the feet from beneath me and force me to crash—hard.

*****

I am a man of faith, and I truly owe my life in service to Jesus Christ. I believe that his caring hands gently guide me in making life-altering decisions or move me towards certain paths. There is always a lesson to be learned that I can one day draw upon to help others. To expand on this, we are at a time in history where false facts are thrown at us daily, the media bombards us with their profit-driven narratives, and some people have lost their faith regardless of whom they call god.

I believe in a higher power, yes, one that I cannot see but know its presence surrounds us.

I also believe that since this higher presence does not have a human form, I am given the responsibility to be 'godlike' in everything I do. With that in mind, I trust in him. If I am placed in a time of turmoil, confusion, or darkness, then this is not punitive. It is a personal time of significant growth where I crash, reflect, and I am reborn with the knowledge, ability, and skills to help someone down the road when they crash. Life is linear and A + B = C. My life of service allows a physical presence for God's teaching to fuel my actions.

I believe that my staying at the Guelph Police Service and experiencing adversity happened for a reason. I learned from it and gained personal and professional growth.

On April 24, 1995, my decision to stay was once again put to the test when I backed up Constables (CST) Attila Korga and John Martinello. They were attempting to rescue a male who was experiencing a mental health episode and drove his car onto a pond, broke through spring ice, and sank in the five to six feet of deep water.

When I arrived minutes later, John and Attila were already in the water trying to steady the bobbing car and keep the man's head above water. They shouted for my help, and as I ran down the bank, I took off my police gun belt and bullet-proof vest and jumped into the frigid water to help. John kept the male's head above water while I steadied the car and Attila dove under the water through the back door where he could reach around the man and cut off his seat belt. I could then use my height and leverage to pull the male out of the car and carried him to the shore.

Headline: Guelph's police heroes "just doing our jobs"
May 1, 1995—*Guelph Mercury* Newspaper: article
By Marg Petrushevsky

Three Guelph police officers have been recommended for recognition of their bravery after they rescued a city resident from drowning on April 24.

Constables Attila Korga, John Martinello and Douglas Pflug may be heroes to the community, but to them, they were just doing their jobs.

In an interview Sunday, Martinello said he and Korga were driving down Victoria Road just north of College Avenue at 2:54 p.m. when they were flagged down by citizens concerned about a car that had just gone into a drainage pond at the intersection. The car was about ninety meters back from the road but clearly visible from College Avenue.

"I could see the car and the guy in it", Martinello said. "The incredible thing was it was sinking, and he wasn't doing anything to get out".

The men shucked some of their equipment, then while Korga radioed for emergency response teams, Martinello waded in. He called to the man to try to get him to undo his seatbelt, but the man seemed disoriented or in shock and was not responding. When Martinello reached him, the driver was already underwater but only for a matter of seconds. Martinello was able to reach through the open car window and get the driver's face above the water but told Korga they would need something to cut the seat belt.

"I couldn't get him up any further, and his ears were still underwater", Martinello said.

A citizen was able to provide Korga with some sort of pruning scissors so he could cut the shoulder belt when he waded out to the car.

By this time, Pflug arrived at the scene and helped Martinello support the driver's head while Korga went in through the rear door, ducked under the water and undid the lap belt catch.

They aided the man ashore and Korga returned to the car to ensure no one else was in it.

"I have to give Attila credit for thinking that", Martinello said, "because I did not. And there could have been someone else in there. We were so busy with the driver we'd never have noticed if he had a passenger".

The citizen had also given Korga a blanket so they could get some of the man's clothes off and wrap him a bit before walking him to the edge of the road. By that time Guelph firefighters were on scene and supplied blankets to counteract the cold before Royal City Ambulance staff took the man to the Guelph General Hospital.

Then the firefighters began treating the officers for hypothermia, Pflug says. "I was cold", he admitted with a grin. "I'm 6'1' and the water was up to here", he explained, showing almost the top of his shoulder with his hand. "We're lucky it wasn't any deeper. But even so, I was having trouble breathing. I was gasping and couldn't get a good breath".

Martinello, too, had problems with the cold, although mostly with his hands. He had not been able to get them out of water while he was supporting the driver's head. The firefighters helped them strip off wet clothes and provided them with warm, dry blankets.

"I can't thank those guys enough", he said. "They were really caring and concerned". They also drove the officers back to the station in their cruisers.

Pflug admits being a bit curious to see a video of some bystander shot during the rescue. "My training just took over", he said. "I don't know what I did, so it will be interesting to see what's on tape. There was a stronger hand guiding us because we did not think. We just reacted".

Martinello also found their experience to be positive. "It was most gratifying to see the man in hospital later with his wife and kids around him. It was great to see the citizens in the community getting involved and concerned—bringing the scissors and blanket. We deal with a lot of negative things, so it gives you a real boost to be able to do something positive".

The entire rescue took about half an hour.

A few days later, Chief of Police Lena Bradburn called to us in her office and we each received a Chief of Police Life Saving Award.

A few weeks later, the adrenaline high of doing a good deed continued. I received incredible recognition at our awards banquet and was recognized as the Guelph Police "Member of the Year" for my efforts to Guelph through my community involvement and emergent situations.

After that day, I never saw the gentleman again. I received annual notes or phone calls of thanks from him on the anniversary of that day for ten years afterwards.

*****

That summer, I continued my "normal" schedule where I worked full-time as a police officer and from May to August each year full-time as a strength and conditioning coach, training OHL and NHL players. The specialty that separated me from other trainers was that I was alongside the guys. I hoped that seeing a guy ten years older than them would further motivate them through my physical efforts to lead them to excellence independently.

*****

On March 10, 1996, on the eve of Reighan's birth, my mom sent me this letter with simple but very insightful advice for a new dad.

> Dear Doug,
>
> As I have told you before, I can write down my thoughts and feelings better than I can say them.
>
> Almost 3 years ago when I told you I was letting you go as my little boy to become a husband. How time flies. I remember being so proud when you told me you wanted to walk me down the aisle. My heart was bursting with "pride, Love and Joy". That day I felt as if I could conquer the world on my own. I was blessed with two wonderful sons.
>
> Since then, Doug I have sat on the sidelines and watched with pride at your success. Even though Doug I wasn't there beside you, don't ever think I was not interested or didn't care. I guess I felt that you deserved all the glory, you are the one who went after what you believed in.
>
> Having you and Don in my life I felt complete and when you told me about the baby, again a new piece of my heart opened. I was so happy and proud to tell everyone.
>
> I know Doug you will make a wonderful father. Be there for your child always. Don't criticize, don't try, and live your life through them, live it with them. Most

important, let him or her be what they want to be, not what you want them to be. Let them learn from their mistakes, not yours.

Doing this is the last advice I give you unless you ask me.

Remember Doug, when you son or daughter is born, put them first and everyone else second. Let yourself become one with the baby. Give them the greatest gift of all, "love" because without love there in nothing.

When you hold your baby for the first time; I can never explain to you how it feels, soon you will find out for yourself. Remember your baby is your future, grandparents are the past.

If you ever need anything, you know I will always be there for you,

Please don't do this. I'm an old fool for writing this. Just think of me as a proud Mother, Mother in law and grandmother. Without you, I would be any of the above.

I love you more today, than you will ever know.

Love Mom

On March 11, 1996, my beautiful daughter Reighan Lottie Pflug was born, and I was so thrilled. I was a dad to this amazing little girl. I promised myself and her that I would be the "best dad ever" and try to give her the best life I could.

I felt myself hardening and feeling numb as I suppressed my emotions from what I was regularly experiencing daily. I was used to dealing with the worst in humanity and what one person could do to another. I took risks at work, drove a little faster to each call for service, volunteered for the higher risk calls, and took on extra details in attempts to reclaim myself and feel as I once did.

Little did I realize that I was not only running hills and the track with my clients, but I was also running from myself. There were genuine pain, memories, and fears that I was profoundly suppressing. This became the norm for me to train hard in my heart, body, and soul as I marketed "Strengthen your game".

Success and training like a pro became my drug and addiction, and I pushed the limits harder and harder to see what my breaking point was.

Reighan was the only light or source of joy in my life, and I do not know how I would have survived had she not come into my life. She was my only sense of joy and positivity. The tighter I held on to keep myself "right" and healthy for her, the greater I would display untimely or inappropriate displays of sadness, grief, or weeping when I was alone.

*****

One-night shift around 1998, I remember breaking up a fight on Wyndham Street North, Guelph, where I put one of the two intoxicated combatants in the rear of my cruiser. I made a mistake that night and did not handcuff him because I knew him.

As we left the scene towards the station, the guy told me that he knew where I lived on College Avenue. He described where our unit was, the car I drove, where my wife worked, and what she looked like. He got very dark and told me, "Doug, I know you work tomorrow night and know where you live; I'm going to break into your house, rape your wife, and sodomize your baby girl," and laughed. As we continued to drive to the police station, the rage filled within me as I could feel years of past abuses against me coming to the surface. I wanted to flat out kill him with both my hands.

When we arrived in the sally port, I looked in the back of my cruiser at the suspect and I still tried to be a nice guy to not escalate the situation by handcuffing him as policy had suggested. He was violently kicking and punching the inside of the cruiser and we needed to get him out of there and control him. As I opened the cruise door, he sprung out at me and tried to attack me. For a split moment, I thought this was perfect as I wanted to retaliate for his threat towards my wife and baby girl . . . he just gave me the opportunity.

I did not succumb to my emotions that night or become the evil I summoned from the darkness to seek retribution. I remember feeling an instant sense of calm as I regained my professionalism. I calmly turned him around, put the cuffs on, and walked him to the holding cells. In reflection, whether it be God or my loving deceased grandparents, Gordon and Lottie Kerr, some angelic presence entered my body and prevented me from being worse than the man I had arrested.

Grannie and Grandpa had always taught me to look for good where I can only see darkness, and that night I did. I was immensely proud of myself and my self-control because I had the ability to physically hurt the guy, just not the desire at that point.

*****

I have worn a silver St. Michael's pendant on a chain since I started in 1989, as it was one of the first "police" gifts I bought myself with my first paycheck. I genuinely believe he has been on my shoulder my entire career protecting me. However, on this evening he just had to work a little harder.

ST. MICHAEL THE ARCHANGEL: PATRON SAINT OF POLICE OFFICERS[1]

Angels have long played a role in the Catholic faith—from creation to Jesus' death and resurrection. Often depicted in art as chubby cherubs or serene figures with wings wearing white, angels are described by the Catechism of the Catholic Church as "spiritual, non-corporeal beings that glorify God without ceasing and who serve his saving plans for other creatures". St. Augustine describes them as "servants and messengers of God".

Angels are mentioned many times throughout the Old and New Testaments—from when God revealed the Ten Commandments to Moses and said, "Behold, I send an angel before you to guard you on the way and to bring you to the place that I have prepared," (Exodus 23:20–21) to when the angel Gabriel delivered the message to the Virgin Mary that she would carry the Son of God, and beyond.

Angels bring us a sense of peace and security. How impressive is it to know that as the Catechism of the Catholic Church states: "from its beginning until death, human life is surrounded by their watchful care and intercession. Beside each believer stands an angel as protector and shepherd leading him to life".

While there are countless angels, Gabriel, Raphael, and Michael are the only angels referred to by name in the Bible. These angels were each entrusted with extraordinary missions and played a specific role in how our salvation would play out. St. Michael, also known as an archangel (an elevated angel), called "Prince of the Heavenly Host", is considered the leader of the angels.

As a police officer's role is to protect the public from the activities incited by the devil it is natural that St. Michael is the Patron Saint.

I remember wearing the medal for a few months when a friend told me I needed to get it blessed by a priest to make it more protective. Great advice, I thought. The next day when I was working, I drove to the Basilica of Our Lady in downtown Guelph and walked into the church. After a few minutes I met Father Dennis Noon, who inquired about my presence in the church. We spoke at length and realized we had met several times at various events in the community. I explained my request to have my medal blessed, so he asked me a few questions and found out that I was not Catholic. We talked about that for a few more minutes, joyfully teasing back and forth about why I thought he should bless it and why he thought he should not. The defining point in our conversation came when I asked him, "Father, what if a Catholic suspect is pointing the gun at me?" He paused, reached out his hand, and blessed the medal.

I proudly wore that medal from 1990 until 2010. When my relationship with Michelle heightened, I gave it to her to protect her while she was on duty in Peel Region, where I thought the crime was more severe and she'd need the help.

A week later, Michelle bought me a St. Michael's medal and asked me to see Father Noon and have it blessed. A few days later, I met with him and he asked if I wished to convert to Catholicism. We laughed and reflected on the conversation so many years ago, then he blessed the medal and me. We have remained grand friends over the years, and I am glad he could think out of the box and help this Protestant out.

*****

I had two incredible supervisors during this time on a platoon in Sgt Maurice "Obie" Obergan and Sgt Greg "Zing" Zinger. I not only respected their rank, but with these two I also appreciated them as men. They both possessed excellent police knowledge, the IQ (intelligence quotient) as we say, but they equally excelled with leading people or with the EQ (emotional quotient) as we say in leadership. They knew how to establish balance, and at work, we quickly called them "Sergeant" because we respected them so much and worked our tails off to make them look useful to their supervisors. When we were off work, building someone's deck, playing ball together, or merely having a beer, we fondly and respectfully called them by their nicknames.

Recently, I was chatting to "Obie" while researching this book project. I told him how I thought that he and Zing were way ahead of their curve in the way they led us in the early 1990s, and it humbled him. I asked what their secret was, and he said, "Dougie, it was simple; it was about two things. We wanted people to work for us, but we also wanted people to collaborate with us. We tried to make you want to come to work each day and treat you like family. Our job was to be there to assist you develop and not get in the way".

Remarkably, the more I study leadership, the more I realize that the old-fashioned virtues are still constant today.

Looking both at "Obie" and "Zing", they were great followers and that made them influential leaders. Their leadership provided us with a safe place to learn and be great followers, increasing our ability to be leaders ourselves one day.

Simply put, we loved working for and with these two guys.

They say that imitation is the best form of flattery. Well done, guys. It is in this spirit that one day I would discover my four core values and what I wanted my leadership dash to be: Gone, but not forgotten.

Sadly, in 2019, "Zing" died of cancer. I will always remember him as the fantastic leader, boss, and friend he worked so hard at being for me.

RIP, Zing.

*****

Around 1995, they dispatched several of us to a fight at one of the many bars in downtown Guelph. It was a gong show down there during those years. There was a guy who would even come down and video the fights and post on YouTube. It was crazy. As a result, people used to come down after midnight, grab a slice of pizza, and sit and watch fights like an actual UFC night.

We all went to the bar around the same time. As I got out of my cruiser and ran to the location where my team was trying to arrest the combatants, one of them saw me and shot at my legs like a wrestler. Wrong person to try this on because I quickly got him in a "Gaboury" head and arm headlock. The move involved grabbing the person in a front headlock, but instead of just grabbing someone by the neck, we would also bring an arm in the restraint. The support of the upper shoulder assembly supports the neck in the event you had to go to ground with a person. This is far safer than a front headlock where, if you fall, you could guillotine chop a person and break their neck. They did not teach this at the Ontario Police College but was far safer and less likely to really hurt someone.

As fate would have it, the guy pleaded not guilty to the assault police charge that I had charged him with.

We went to trial, and the defence questioned me why I used this move and why did I do so if admittedly it was not an approved move? In the cross-examination I tried to relay that the front headlock was very unsafe for the person being held, because that if we fell, I could most likely break their neck.

The defense counsel went at me for about half an hour until the judge finally stepped in. He asked me to explain the Gaboury move again, and I once again highlighted the safety part of this control move. He asked where I had learned it, and I let him know that Guelph Olympian Doug Cox had used it many times on me as I sparred him preparing him for the Olympics.

I explained that the embedded safety of adding the shoulder girdle to a conventional head lock was essential to reduce the possibility of serious injury, and my use of it was not to punish the suspect, but rather to add protection and maintain safe control of them. I then explained how I felt when I was in a Gaboury hold far too many times than I wished to remember at the hands of Doug Cox. I then explained how I had used it hundreds of times with proficiency in people while wrestling.

The defence counsel again attacked me for using this and asked to have Doug Cox come and supply expert testimony on the move and challenge the court to rule on this.

The judge sat back, reviewed his notes, and asked me to further qualify my wrestling experience and how long and to what level I had wrestled. I let him know a general over-view, and he paused, looked to the ceiling, and came back with his decision, something to the effect of.

Ladies and gentlemen, I have reviewed the evidence of Constable Pflug regarding his use of the Gaboury Wrestling move to secure the accused in the fight. I have heard that he used it to add safety in a combative situation and that he has used these many times in his freestyle wrestling career in high school and university. I appreciate his honesty and humility when explaining that it was used on him multiple times by our Olympian Doug Cox, and Constable Pflug says "rag dolling" him on the mat on regular occasions. It is the opinion of this court that Constable Pflug knew what he was doing and clearly articulated his safety concerns so I, therefore, declared him an expert witness on the "Gaboury" wrestling hold.

The defense counsel asked for a recess, and when court resumed, the accused changed his plea to guilty and we concluded the case.

When court broke, I ran into the judge as he was leaving, and he smiled and winked and we both parted ways.

I bet that was the first such ruling to date.

*****

In 1995 I entered a competition for a newly vacated spot in the Young Offender Office. I jumped at the chance and prepared my résumé for the competition and interview. I won the competition and was assigned to the detective office as a Young Offender Officer. At the time, I worked alongside two other detectives and our Sergeant, Reg McKean.

Reg was a fantastic officer and supervisor, and I credit his firm but fair investigative and supervisory style as a framework for what I'd try to do later in my career. He genuinely cared about the victims that we aided and the officers in his charge. He was just a well-re-spected, all-around good guy who I am still friends with today.

One night they sent us up to the University of Guelph on a suspicious medical emergency call. When we arrived, we found that a student in his early 20s had been walking in the residence hallway, collapsed, and been transported to the hospital. We investigated the scene where the male had passed away, and Reg called in for additional resources.

As the evening progressed, Reg suggested we attend the young man's room but cau-tioned that he heard there might be an outbreak of spinal meningitis at the University. I did not know what that was but thought, "Heck, I'm healthy . . . let's go". We gained access to the young man's room and found nothing suspicious. Reg and I learned the male had spent some time in his room before with his girlfriend, and we found out that she was working at a fast-food restaurant. We drove to the restaurant and sadly had to let her know of the death and our investigation concerns. She was understandably crushed, and we comforted her as we tried to get more information for our investigation.

We left work that night around 1:00 a.m., and Reg advised that we'd come back to work early the next day and go to the autopsy to find out the cause of death.

I arrived home and went to bed.

At around 4:00 a.m., I woke up with sweats. My stomach and bowels were rumbling. I ran to the washroom and used a nearby wastebasket to aid as my body dumped everything. As I lay back in bed, I thought, "spinal meningitis", and I freaked out, bearing in mind that we were in pre-cellphone or pre-Google days. I lay there freaked out, thinking I was going to die. I made desperate calls to find Reg, and I left him messages.

I booked off sick and asked the night Sergeant to make sure Reg knew I was extremely ill.

At about 11:00 a.m. Reg called back and advised that the young man did not have spinal meningitis. He died from an enlarged heart because of a viral infection.

I remembered the relief of his words and continued to ride out the seasonal flu.

When I got back to work a few days later, my partners and Reg took good-natured shots at me and we all laughed.

*****

I really enjoyed those four years because they gave me a daily opportunity to work with at-risk youth and try to be a positive role model in their lives. That was especially important to me; I had a great dad, some amazing coaches and I knew the value that those relationships can provide. A lot of the young men I dealt with during this time did not have a positive male role model. I truly felt that maybe, just maybe, I could help them through the troubled years.

Last year when I turned 54, I saw a message appear on my LinkedIn profile from one of those young men I had worked with.

His message read,

"Happy Birthday Doug, you don't know it but growing up you had set me straight a few times. I have never forgotten and am thankful for your empathy. Please genuinely enjoy your birthday and continue to show compassion and empathy because it changes lives.

"Hats off to you, sir!!!"

His profile picture showed his two daughters with him, all smiles. I felt like I won the lottery after reading that message. It is a stark reminder to everyone that small acts of kindness in any form are pivotal in a person's life and affect the rest of their lives and unleash some incredible human potential.

*****

At work over the next few years, I would experience successes working as the Young Offender Officer for three years and then returned to the Uniform Division as a Coach Officer and later Acting Sergeant. During this time, I continued to perform community service, like medicine for a tortured soul. In these roles, I would put myself in a position of need to the people or charities and work to fill that need. This worked two-fold in that it provided the people and charities with what I needed and kept me real. Knowing that I was of value, it required of me that I had a purpose in life professionally.

*****

In 2000, I became a single dad, sharing 50–50 custody of Reighan and attacked that role with the same tenacious efforts I had in policing and in training elite athletes and myself. To me this new venture was one where success was the only option and that I would not fail my sweet little girl.

My primary goal was to focus on her development and try to shield her from having the divorced parents' "negative" emotional reality. My family, police family, and Guelph Storm family really stepped up and rallied around me to help me navigate these tumultuous waters ahead of me.

I am eternally indebted to those folks. We were a team and "family" on and off the field. I hope that over the years I have let them know I would not have been able to move forward in my personal and professional lives if it had not been for them. They listened as I spoke, helped problem solve, lent me a shoulder to cry on, joined me in a run and talk, and provided me with laughter or light in the darkness. They even helped babysit Reighan if I needed a few hours to blow off some steam in the gym or reflect and plan-assess and act on my desire to move forward. Thank you again, guys.

However, I find that my most significant period of personal and professional growth resulted from a massive debrief and the dissection of the many failures or traumatic events that I have experienced.

I tried my best over the years, but sometimes it was not enough. I wish I had a healthy sense of what "winning" or having a successful call outcome was that would have helped me cut myself some slack when I was unnecessarily hard on myself. I always joked that "no one could punish me as I can punish myself".

At this point in my life, I was not debriefing situations the way I do now, where I try to find the positive and learn from it. Instead, I was falling under the surface because of the bad. This book is about the journey, personal and professional human tragedy, and associated lessons learned I wish to impart to you and help you #RiseUpAndExcel.

I took Reighan with me everywhere, and we became a regular fixture at East Side Mario every Friday night for our Daddy-Daughter Date Nights. She would have her airplane chicken nuggets every single time. This is where I believe that her exposure to my community service work helped develop her own service heart. In later years when she graduated high school, she received a Disciples Award for her 340 hours of Community Service work over her four years when the requirement was 40 hours.

Two events that I created and am enormously proud of were:

1. **The Annual Guelph Police vs Guelph Storm hockey game**

   This was a ten-year annual event that helped raise over $40,000 for Guelph Wellington Special Olympics. This allowed me to join three loves, the Guelph Police, the Guelph Storm, and the Guelph Wellington Special Olympics.

2. **The Guelph Police Bike Helmet Positive Ticketing Youth Engagement Program**

   When I retired in 2016, we had given out over 18,000 tickets to area youth found wearing their bike helmets, entitling them to a free Dairy Queen treat. We also drew from the collected tickets and gave out 36 free bikes to children each year as grand prizes. The program continues to this day.

In later years, when I began teaching at the Ontario Police College, I would share that Community service was my medicine for the Post Traumatic Stress Injuries I had experienced.

I challenged everyone who would listen to follow this lead because it genuinely supplied me perspective when I slipped into the darkness.

*****

PERSONAL REFLECTION

As I reflect on the late '90s, I remember receiving medical help as I found I had two unexplained bald spots on my chin. They were the size of a quarter; one on the bottom left of my chin where no whiskers grew, and the other back right upper portion of my head. I treated the area with medication by the doctor for three years, and it eventually went away.

I wonder if this was another symptom of the stress I was holding.

That said, the calls for service, the memories, the sheer horror, devastation, and human tragedy and casualties that I was dealing with regularly all increased. These experiences weighed on me and led to my night terrors.

As I continued to function each day, I felt so empty and dead inside from 1990 to 1997. I embarked on what I now believe was a journey to self-destruction through the constant pursuit of excellence and success under the excessive weight that I had placed on myself. The harder the task or goal, the more inspired I became to "win it". In the end, there were many hollow successes because of the efforts I put into them. However, I descended to a place where I became devoid of any emotion; I was empty and felt I was running on fumes.

What was my response? I set my sights extremely high and chased more demanding tasks and goals to challenge me. I became an adrenaline junkie and placed myself in some potentially harmful situations chasing that high.

I am a proud and confident person with what I believe are fantastic core values to guide everything I do.

I ignored and removed the conscious possibility that I could fail and continued this hectic pace piling up on myself. This was a cry for help, but I was too proud to ask. I hoped that it would crush me under the self-imposed weight because I was too proud, or my ego refused to ask for help. In reflection, I know I was hoping to crash through a physical injury to have an "excuse" to ask for help to admit that I was hurting so badly and, in fact, human. Sadly, it would be a long time before this crash, and as designed, it wasn't a physical injury, but a psychological one that came from the past and wiped me out.

I became addicted to the infused adrenaline of chasing success in many forms the same way a cocaine addict chases the high. When the high subsides, you need your next fix. Whether it be cocaine high chase or adrenaline high chase, they are both destructive addictions, nonetheless.

The ironic thing I marvel at was that I was also an incredible actor. No one in my sphere of influence—not friends, family, those I coached, or even those I arrested—knew of my internal burden, pain, and emptiness.

The learning point for me was that some common self-medications like alcohol, drugs, sex, and a host of other things were not what I needed. The quest for excellence became my drug. Over the years, I still seek excellence in what I do. As you will later learn, we may place realizing goals and measures of what we define as success before we begin. We may get lost again in the pursuit and process.

Adversity and the corresponding pursuit of success became my drug, and I became an addict.

I have always believed that I "must live every second of every day and I'll rest when I'm dead". There is no doubt if I continue this pace, I would have killed myself through this addiction and the quest to feel and regain what I denied for so many years. To frame this, I have listed some extra weight and responsibility I took on, remembering this was also while I served full-time as a police officer:

- I trained and did cardio once a day, sometimes five to six times per day, every week and month without fail. Christmas day supplied a better opportunity because the gym was empty, and I could have it all to myself.
- I competed provincially, nationally, and internationally at many Law Enforcement Track and Field meets, winning 32 medals highlighted by a silver medal in the javelin and a bronze medal in the hammer throw 1998 World Law Enforcement Olympics held in Birmingham, Alabama.
- As a rookie rider, I trained myself and won a Silver Medal–Canadian Police Law Enforcement Mountain Bike Championships in 1997.
- In 1991–1995, I coached senior and junior football at Our Lady of Lourdes high school, donating hundreds of hours and achieving many successes.
- In 1991, I started Ironwill Strength and Conditioning, training many up-and-coming OHL and NHL hockey players from May to August, sometimes two to three times per day while working full-time as a police officer.
- 1991–2011, I joined the Guelph Storm Hockey Club's coaching staff as their office conditioning coach. I remain with the team as their Law Enforcement Liaison officer. Since 2011, I have continued to serve as their law enforcement mentor.
- In 2009–2011, I took on the role of a National Strength and Conditioning Coach—Wrestle Canada
- In 2009–2011, I added the role of strength and conditioning coach for the University of Guelph Men & Female Varsity Soccer

It is important to note that from 2000 on, I also began coaching both my daughters in track, soccer, and whatever else they took part in. I was in a position where I was on a rocket of destruction going full speed from the time I woke up in the morning until I crashed my head on the pillow for bed, exhausted.

Looking back, I do not know when I slept, recharged, or even took a few moments to take a breath for myself.

I unconsciously kept piling the weight on my shoulders and was on a rocket to destruction. I didn't see it, and when it crashed, I finally saw what I had done to myself.

Time would become my enemy, and it was running out.

*****

In 2000, I received a very prestigious Committee of Youth Officers for the Province of Ontario Award for Community Award for Youth Service.

> The Committee of Youth Officers for the Province of Ontario awards a community member for outstanding interaction with youth in their community. This individual proactively builds a lasting, meaningful, and productive relationship with youth. The ideal nominee will make a positive difference in their community through the development and delivery of programs and leadership. The award is presented to an individual who mentors and engages youth to help them become stronger citizens. The award is presented annually at the COYO Conference in Niagara Falls.
> The Community Award for Youth Service is an award that is dedicated to recognizing the work and contributions of a community member who has shown outstanding commitment to youth in the community.

*****

In 2003, I received the Guelph Police Service Community Service Award for Excellence in Community Service. The award recognized remarkable volunteerism by a member of the Guelph Police Service.

*****

In 2004, my youngest daughter, Alexis, was born. The birth of another little girl blessed me, and I met Alexis for the first time and instantly fell in love.

Alexis, my blondie, joined Reighan as my two only sources of joy in my life and the reason I woke up a day and continued my path. I was a proud dad of two incredible young ladies. If I did not have this purpose, I do not believe that I would have become the man I am today.

That being said, I continued to find that I had misplaced emotions and cried at inappropriate times.

My response was to deny, ignore the root causes, and suppress the feelings. This created incredible conscious and subconscious stresses upon me, and I noticed I was developing a nervous tick in my right eyelid. The greater the pressure, the more it flickered.

*****

In 2005, I was in the Cancun Airport when I received a call from the Deputy Chief of the Guelph Police. After some small talk, he advised I was being promoted to the rank of Sergeant and assigned to the leadership team on B Platoon under the guidance of my lifelong friend and mentor, Staff Sergeant Neil Young. It thrilled me to be in a leadership position where I could make a real and lasting impact on my platoon.

AUTHOR'S CHALLENGE

I wish media were not being so ridiculously hard on the police as of late.

Yes, there are corrupt officers, but we do not judge based on our skin colour, so please do not just judge me on my uniform colour. All I ask is for everyone to understand; Police, Fire, EMS, Corrections, and our military have answered a call to service.

Some of us have experienced or suffered from a Post Traumatic Stress Injury (PTSI) or Post Traumatic Stress Disorder (PTSD) in some form or another. Some may not even know this yet, as it has not come to the surface.

Please understand that this is not an excuse for abusive actions towards others; understand that we are just like you, human beings once we take off the uniform.

Do not focus on the negative stories you see or hear. Trust in knowing that most people genuinely believe in the job we do to make our communities safer.

Your challenge is twofold:

1. Thank a frontline worker for their service.
2. Create an email folder and store all the positive comments you receive. Then, on a difficult day, re-read those comments and appreciate, respect, and need them.

NOTE

1. www.catholicfaithstore.com/daily-bread/st-michael-the-archangel-patron-saint-of-police-of-ficers/

The Crash into the Pit of Despair

7

The year 2006 was an exceptional year that ended with the OHL News doing a feature story on me for their December 2006 edition entitled.

Strength and Conditioning Key to Success, by David Burstyn
"Your on-ice performance is certainly going to show if you make a committed effort to improve yourself off the ice". -D Pflug

Strength and conditioning have evolved throughout the years. The days of a player reporting to camp and getting into game shape, as training is a year-long process with no off-season, are long gone. Times change and today all 20 OHL teams employ a trainer as part of their staff.

"Teams realized about 10 years ago that they needed to parallel the stuff that NHL clubs utilized", says Doug Pflug, the strength and conditioning trainer for the Guelph Storm the past 12 years. "In that, they needed to cover the same roles/experience to develop their young players so that one day it could assist the OHL team in winning more games, but also prepare their players for life in the OHL. I also believe that because of the competitive market for players south of the border with US colleges, the OHL teams had to provide such expertise to keep kids here".

Based in Guelph, Ironwill Strength and Conditioning is run by Pflug, a Police Sergeant who has over 25 years of experience working with amateur and professional athletes. His facility is well tailored for the development of hockey players. It has 22 Monarch bikes, three squatting cases, leg press/squat hack machines, treadmills and dumbbells varying in weight, all in a relaxing environment to stimulate and motivate the athlete.

"We really have more weight available than we can use", jokes Pflug.

OHL players now have more than never recognized the importance of conditioning and emphasized as much attention to their stick handling as they do their plyometric. While skill level is there, players still needed added strength to help them in corner battles, in front of the net and in open ice situations. Bobby Ryan of the Owen Sound Attack is a perfect example of what increased strength and conditioning can do for an athlete. When he broke into the league, they criticized him for carrying too much weight. However, as a player with an abundance of skill, his dedication to strength and conditioning always came into question and at one point affected the way NHL scouts looked at him as a pro.

Ryan used that as motivation and trained rigorously in the off-season before his NHL draft eligibility. He changed his diet, which resulted in a 6% reduction in body

DOI: 10.1201/9781003187189-8

fat. Coupled with extensive cardio workouts helped him shed fifteen pounds of excess body fat.

"They brought it to my attention that it is essential in today's game", admits Ryan. "It was not something that I paid close attention to early in my hockey career, but I have learned over the past few summers what dividends it could pay.

"Your on-ice performance will certainly show if you make a committed effort to improve yourself on the ice. If you are doing the right exercises, getting the proper training, and concentrating on your nutrition, you will notice a tremendous improvement in your game".

The sacrifices made in the season certainly paid off for Ryan, increasing his point production by 50 points, and what was even more impressive was that he went from a -18 in his rookie season to a +30. The weight he successfully took off allowed him to be more involved and keep up with the game's pace, thus improving a desirable prospect. At the '05 NHL Draft, the Anaheim Ducks second overall selected him right behind Sidney Crosby.

Ironwill takes immense pride in setting up personalized programs to target a player's strengths and weaknesses. They recognize that no two players are the same and set up customized programs for their clients. They supply functional and strength training programs. Functional strength training (FST) is more sport-specific and concentrates on using body core muscles—abdominal and back to enhance coordination and endurance. FST mimics the movements of the sport while working against resistance.

"When I train a person, our first sessions are a client questionnaire, health history, ParQ fitness form and lifestyle questionnaire. It is prudent that you must get their information down first so you can fully understand your client and their needs", adds Pflug. "With most clients under twenty-one, I encourage parental participation. I would suggest that if a trainer is not taking the time, they are not doing their job completely. As a trainer, you must also look at your client's goals and counsel them to make sure that they are realistic and attainable".

Pflug has worked with many great NHL athletes, including Jeff O'Neill, Manny Malhotra, and Dan Paille, just to name a few. Pflug has a simple philosophy in his approach to fitness training. "I always try not to only train them, but function as a life mentor and teach them important things about life and themselves", adds Pflug. "My job is to improve a player, not set them up to fail".

*****

I genuinely believed that my world would open to incredible possibilities of having such an inspired purpose in life. That purpose was to be the best dad a girl could have. I had always wanted to be a "dad" and not just a "father". I remember doing extensive research into what a dad needed to be to successfully raise a daughter. An article that I read was pretty straightforward when it mentioned that this would be my daughter's first relationship with a man. I would set the tone through our relationship for her acceptable norm on how she allowed a man to treat her the rest of her life.

I took this challenge seriously as I am the type of person who is all in at 110 percent or not in at all. There is no point in dipping your toe in the lake of experience . . . you must jump right in.

After Reighan was born she melted my heart, and it filled me with amazing love, joy, and purpose. But I had anxiety bouts, unexplained nervousness where none should exist, which manifested itself in what I deemed at the time was inappropriate expressions of sadness, grief, and tears. I spoke to friends and they just dismissed this as my heart being softened by my sweet little girl. In the past I tried to ignore these feelings and lock them down just like I had done in 1991–1993 because of the tyrannical Staff Sergeant.

As Reighan grew and her needs increased, I retired from playing on an elite slow-pitch travel money team. Retirement from this was a simple choice because I had my day already.

I divorced in 1999 and then began life as a single dad just trying to transition as easy as possible for Reighan. I was a teenager when my parents divorced and knowing how I felt at that age made me try with everything I had to minimize the breakup. I held a great deal of stress, anxiety, and guilt knowing that my part in the divorce would also inflict pain in her life like my parents had mine.

As my policing career advanced, I was constantly reminded of this to always #RiseUpAndExcel, and I tried to be with her as much as possible. After Reighan was born, I looked everywhere to gain better knowledge and spoke to many people to gain insight and understanding into how I should conduct myself and be a better dad.

In 2004, my second daughter, Alexis, was born, and again my heart melted when I first saw her sweet little face. I once again experienced misplaced tears and emotionally displayed and dismissed this, believing that my two wonderful daughters were making me "soft".

I cried during TV shows, at football games, times of joy, sadness, and other inappropriate times and always dismissed and joked I was tired, or my allergies were acting up. Deep down, I knew I was struggling; I didn't fully enjoy the positives in life to the extent I thought I could. I felt guilty for even feeling joy. I was scared, and I realized I was a broken man.

*****

One of the recurring themes in this book is the knowledge, skills, and lessons learned through adversity born out of conflict. Reflecting, I am glad the events described in this book happened. Had I not experienced the trauma, fought it with resiliency, and grown from the experience, I would not be the man I am today. I challenge you to use the same simple formula and view the situation through the eyes of possibility versus eyes of darkness. The simple shift in mindset or lens we look at things can dramatically change the outcome. View adversity with a positive lens versus a negative one, and I know you will come out the other side as a better person as well.

*****

As I think back to the time months before they promoted me, I was an acting Sergeant much of the time. Sgt Neal Young, my friend "Woody", was my Sergeant, and we had a new Staff Sergeant that came to run the shift. I did not know this man very well but knew that he was not on his "team" or part of his "silo". Before they promoted him to Staff Sergeant, he was a Sergeant on our platoon, and I had thought we were okay and remembered giving him free tickets to the Guelph Storm hockey games that I couldn't use so he could take his son. He was a short, stout little man and rubbed me the wrong way with how he conducted himself. I thought we were good, but I found out that I was wrong.

There is a philosophy I currently teach, and that is "to praise in public and punish in private" when dealing with employees. When you praise in public, you promote outstanding work, and the employee feels better about themselves, and the shift can celebrate. Punishing or bringing someone up to standard in private is a respectful way to inform a person what they did not meet a standard and collectively work together to remedy the situation.

This is what I thought to be such a simple concept regardless of the date. When you praise someone in public or in front of their peers, you uplift them, empower them, and make them feel good about the effort they put into a situation. Over time, they will continue to trust you, work for you, and become great followers and even better leaders themselves one day. To punish in public works the complete opposite. Not only do you shut the person down, but you shut the group down because they lose trust in your leadership. When times get tough, you will most likely throw them under the bus as well.

This Staff Sergeant had no clue about this, or at least with me, and I endured his lack of common sense and supervisory conflict management problem-solving abilities.

Prior to his coming to our shift, I had earned my supervisors' respect and had been an Acting Sergeant on and off for about two years. One night I was working 2:00 p.m. until midnight shift, and Woody had called me in after lineup to show me my annual performance evaluation. I was happy with it as it would be my last one as a constable and used towards my impending promotion to the rank of Sergeant. I had earned 10 "exceeds standard" out of the 12 categories and was thrilled that my demanding work and efforts were recognized.

I left the office and went out on patrol. Around 3:00 p.m. they dispatched me to the bus station because there was a passed-out intoxicated female. I arrived, and an officer backed me. The lady passed out cold due to her extremely intoxicated state. We could not wake her and certainly not leave her there as she could not care for herself. We put her in the rear of my cruiser, and I drove her to the station to lodge her in the cells in a safe place to sober up as we routinely did for others in the same state. When we arrived at the station sally port, we tried to hoist her and move her into the station. Her deadweight and overall body weight made this a challenging task. As we tried to pull, carry, and move her, we had to stop several times to readjust.

When we got her into the cell block, I left so that the officer could search her. When my partner came out, she had advised the lady had fresh red marks that she believed were from us trying to carry her. Her bra and shirt caused the redness to her upper body and we documented them.

The Sergeant came back to review her and asked us to take the lady to the hospital as she was far too intoxicated for our cells, and we transported her there.

Later that night around 11:30 p.m., we received a call to the hospital that our intoxicated lady complained she thought "she had been sexually assaulted" when she was passed out. She believed that the unexplained redness and marks she found when sober on her upper body under her shirt resulted from being sexually assaulted. I read the call on the computer and realized that I may have a good explanation for the marks and in 30 minutes our detectives finished work.

I placed a call to the Staff Sergeant and advised what had happened before he came into work and how we documented the redness. He was working a 5:00 p.m. to 3:00 a.m. shift and was unaware of the arrest. I thought I was doing the right thing to give him a "heads up" and thought the detectives would be happy knowing they didn't have to stay on overtime that shift.

We went back to the hospital and my partners checked the lady and found that the marks were, in fact, the ones my partner had documented earlier. I called the Staff Sergeant, and we left the hospital.

The shift was over, so I drove into the station and booked off service for the night.

The next day I went into work early as I had always done to get the lineup information ready.

At 1:50 p.m., I walked up to the lineup room and began briefing my shift on the memos left for us.

The Staff Sergeant suddenly walked in, which I thought was odd as worked at 5:00 p.m. and abruptly stopped me and the lineup. He then walked over to me at the lineup podium, told me to take off my Sergeant's chevrons, put out his hand, and told me to give them to him.

Extremely puzzled, I took them off and handed them to him, and he said, "Go sit with the other constables, constable", and he took over and continued the lineup.

It bewildered me, and I was embarrassed, angry, and confused. I had no understanding of what had just occurred. He scolded and punished me like a child in front of the entire shift . . . I was furious. When the lineup was over, I collected my things and went out on the road to start my shift.

Woody came in that day at 5:00 p.m. and sent me a message to meet him in the back-parking lot. I was relieved my friend was calling me, hoping to let me know what happened. I had no clue what was going on, nor did my shift.

When I arrived, he let me know that the Staff Sergeant was severely pissed off at me and claimed that I disobeyed the policing and procedures of our organization for the intoxicated lady, reporting that she had been sexually assaulted the night before at the hospital. He said that the Staff Sergeant went into my evaluation and changed every category to simple "meets" and even failed me on two. I went from ten "exceeds" and two "meets" to ten "meets" and two "does not meet" standards in 12 hours.

He then told me that the Staff Sergeant had met with the Deputy Chief and tried to remove me from the promotional list. I was second on the list for promotion and slated for promotion later that year.

A brief time later, I was called into the station and told to meet the Staff Sergeant in the second-floor Sergeant's office. I reluctantly went up there and met the man who was actively trying to sabotage my career. When I arrived, he told me to close the door and began to yell and berate me for over 15 minutes. In the process his face reddened the entire time, and I honestly thought he was going to have a heart attack.

In the end, he asked me why I breached the policies; I was shocked.

He finally stopped yelling, and I tried to explain that all I was trying to do was save the organization some overtime and give him the heads up so she probably wouldn't have to hold the three detectives and forensic officer on overtime.

He refused to accept my reasoning and told me I could leave. Before I left, he asked me if I had anything to say and I said, "Well, Staff, that's the last time I ever give you a 'heads- up' on anything".

He was a short, stout little man in extremely poor shape, and I was genuinely concerned for his health. I hated him that day and truly wished him no harm and hoped he didn't come to any because I was not helping the mood with the way he was scolding me like a child.

For friends or people that I respect, I would "run or risk my safety to help", but for him "I'd walk".

Woody took a stand based on his core values and influence up and changed all the ratings back to where there were before the incident. He would later share with me that he was challenged several times to justify why he supported me because the Staff Sergeant complained to the Inspector that he did not support him. Woody explained to the Inspector that he would not help pick on and intentionally sabotage anyone's career as the Staff Sergeant tried with me.

He joked, "I was guilty as charged not supporting him".

For the next several months I hated working for that Staff Sergeant because he continued to micromanage me, and I could do nothing correctly. He actively tried to discredit me and have me removed from the promotional bank list.

In the end, I was promoted to the rank of Sergeant.

This adversity, resiliency, and lessons learned prompted me to promise myself that I would never lead like this or treat anyone like this, especially those who worked for me. A supervisor's job was to create followers, support their career development so that one day they can take over when we retire. That Staff Sergeant made our work environment toxic and, by today's standards, heavily sanctioned under the many processes we now must prevent such tyrannical behaviour.

*****

Conflict breeds credibility and knowledge from lessons learned and professional growth. It certainly did after this subsided. Sadly, this would not be the last time he took a run at me; the next time they had promoted him to Inspector.

I told him it was probably the same marks on the woman we had documented and would go there and get back to him as soon as possible so he wouldn't have to hold the detective office on overtime.

There was a real dichotomy of leadership when they did, and an influential leader would help me through the conflict with a poor leader. I genuinely am richer for the experience and glad that I was the positive leader that helped others.

In 2005, they promoted me to Sergeant's rank, and I transferred to B Platoon, led by Staff Sergeant Neal Young, my dear friend. "Woody" was a big, tough, strong, and caring man who was so far ahead of his time in the progressive way he led people.

Woody and I had been lifelong friends, and I was so happy to learn from a man who I respected as a brother, father, friend, and boss. I knew he would fully commit to my leadership development and was the type of guy who would do everything he could for you when he believed in you.

I have a funny recollection of the one-week spot since being promoted. I came to the shift, and with my usual crazy energy I was running around trying to learn everything as fast as possible. One morning he asked to speak to me in his office. We walked in, he closed the door, turned around, placed both hands on my shoulders, and said, "Dougie, I love you like a son but please do me a favour . . . slow the hell down, you are driving me crazy".

We both laughed and went back to work.

I truly loved working for Woody because he always took the time to explain things as we went along, regardless of the stress that may have been a template on the issue. He encouraged me to make sure I kept a bible of all the new things I was learning for quick reference down the road. Well, I went a bit overboard and quickly had created a manual that other "New Sergeants" would later use.

I remember another time when I released a prisoner that the drug unit had brought in.

My role as an officer in charge of the station on that day was to review all prisoners who came into the station and assume custody and corresponding safety while they stayed in our cells. The arresting officers wanted me to hold the accused for bail. I did not feel we had enough grounds to keep them and released them on a Promise to Appear and an Officer in charge Undertaking with conditions like what they would have received in bail court.

The next day the drug Sergeant came down and rudely questioned my actions, so we got into an argument. I told him my station, my responsibility, and that I stood by my decision. A day or so later two Inspectors came down to see Staff Sergeant Young, who oversaw the Drug unit and the other the Detective division. They were also both personal friends with the Drug Sergeant. They both protested my actions days before the accused's release and demanded that I be reprimanded for not doing as they demanded.

Woody knew that these two Inspectors took liberties regularly, taking shots at me and discrediting me. On this occasion, he asked me to cover the desk, and he asked them to go with him to the prisoner reception room to discuss the matter. He knew they had both targeted me several times in the past for frivolous and vexatious reasons.

They left the Sergeant's office off the general office and went to the garage.

There was a great deal of yelling and screaming as they both ganged up on Woody. Woody has a powerful personality and was not swayed easily. He fully supported what I had done and stood up for me, eventually telling them both to back down, and he would "take this up higher".

He came back to the office and assured me that I followed the correct process that day. If I had any further issues with the three of them, then I was to let him know.

Leadership is easy when times are good, and it is challenging when the times are critical. And in this case, two officers with a higher rank than Woody called them to the task. He did not buckle under the weight of their targeted demands; instead, he rose and stood his ground on knowing what I did was right, supported by his core values and leadership practices.

This was such a great lesson learned that day, one that I also used several times when others came at my people through me.

Woody truly helped me create my leadership mantra would I used to this day:

Lead with your best self.
Model the behaviour you look for in others.
Always create an environment where others can succeed.

Thanks, brother Woody, a man I love like a boss but as a lifelong mentor and friend.

I owe a great deal to Staff Sergeant Neal Young, aka "Woody", and attribute many of my successes as a Sergeant because of the time and effort he invested in me as a friend, son, and colleague.

*****

We had such a significant shift back then, and we indeed were more of a work "family" because we were all so invested in working together with and for another

These officers were so impressive that we did not need to supervise them traditionally. Instead, we supported them and created an environment where they could succeed. It was indeed one of the best leadership development opportunities I have ever had. I was not perfect, but they appreciated that I was a new Sergeant and cut me some slack knowing that I was trying my best. It indeed was fun to go into work alongside those officers, and we continued to develop a team atmosphere and mutual respect, understanding, and corresponding friendship in and out of work. We could always count on this group to volunteer for any work assignment, and for when we needed work done at one of our homes during off time. We had an abundance of help.

*****

In 2007, I went to a call for service with my shift that would dramatically and forever change our lives.

This is where my final descent into the darkness of hitting rock bottom began. This is a devastating story that was the most challenging experience for me, both personally and professionally—one that required extensive post-incident counselling to deal with the crash and destructive mental health space I was in.

It would be incredibly irresponsible for me not to provide you with this caution so that I do not traumatize you. This story is traumatic and fuelled with intense emotions for all those involved, and I want to prepare and protect you for this respectfully. We all experienced this call for service in our own way. Some have healed, some have not. This call forever bonded us, and I truly hope everyone involved finds peace one day in dealing with it.

I wish to inspire you, teach you, and help you reflect on "your story" so that you too could use the lessons learned to find your light in the darkness.

In December 2007, I was on routine patrol as the Road Sergeant for my platoon. They dispatched us to a location on a medical call that involved an infant child, and every available officer on our shift jumped on the call. We all raced to get there and arrived randomly, running up the apartment and taking part in attempts to save a drowned little girl.

She did not survive that day.

*****

Everyone involved that day in their various abilities, from those who took the call, dispatched us, or attended as police, fire, or ambulance was severely traumatized. I tried to be strong and an excellent leader for those involved that day, while also covering off my supervisor on scene duties that day.

I went back to the station to fill out my paperwork and remembered several colleagues asking if I was okay. I told them I was, but in full denial. I left work that day, went to the gym, blew off what I thought was the stress of the day, ate supper, hung out with the girls, then went to bed. As I lay there, I remember thinking to myself, wow that was a bad one, but I have survived stuff like this before.

The answer was simple. I will hide from my emotions like I always did and move on like I still had in the past. I will be okay . . . Right? Right!

In reflection, I hope I made a bit of a positive difference in their lives that day, but later learned I failed to take care of myself with the same empathy and compassion for those I worked for and with that fateful day.

I was proud of our organization because our peer support team arranged a critical incident debriefing and respectfully suggested Employee Assistance Program (EAP) counselling to each of us.

My mind started playing horrific tricks on me and the trauma-induced stress combined this sweet little girl and Alexis, my two-and-a-half-year-old daughter at home. I was good at suppressing my emotions, or so I thought, and continued to do so in this case. I struggled in silence for quite some time, trying to separate the two, but did not do so. For several weeks I would wake up and see anonymous infant eyes on my ceiling, and with the massive loss of sleep my mind continued to spiral downwards.

I ached in my heart, body, and mind and spiralled downwards to levels that I had never been. I just wanted to sleep, feel numb, and break. I began to self-medicate with rye whiskey. This was not to get drunk, but an attempt to feel numb and hopefully fall asleep.

*****

A brief time later, I crashed and could no longer move forward and felt that I was "stuck in darkness". In my mind I had failed my daughters, my family, my city, and myself. I realized I needed help but did not know how to get it.

In this state, I could finally put the past practices of denial and suppression to the side, remove my pride and ego that I used to protect myself, and ultimately be vulnerable. Initially, I viewed this through the years of hurt as though this vulnerability was an example of personal weakness, but later learned it was a position of strength where I was now open and ready to ask and receive help.

I made an appointment with our EAP (employee assistance program) and met Mary Margaret.

The three best parts of our sessions were:

1. I learned that we all hurt, we all need help, and realized that I was not going "crazy". The tighter I tried to hang on to my sanity was resulting in more significant loss and the physical, emotional, and spiritual control which were all typical symptoms that can occur after someone goes through a Post Traumatic Stress Injury.
2. We dealt with the years of insecurities that resulted from the "Fatty Pflug" days that were cultivated and brought forward in my life and how to minimize those and move on with those.

3. Strategies that I could use moving forward to deal with or combat PTSIs in Life. Everyone's trauma, treatment, and strategies are as personal as the first impact on them.

   a. I was journaling my thoughts during or shortly after the crisis to take time to reflect and act. This was not a "call for service" that required immediate resolution.

   b. Viewing who I was, who I am, and who I wanted to be in the future and set a practical plan for that growth

   c. Promoting that I use the systems and infrastructure I did as an elite athlete. When under stress, train my heart, body, and mind as I did then. I knew the template and just had to shift focus from using it as an athlete to a police officer or whatever role I found myself in.

As part of my counselling process, I realized I was stuck and had a difficult time dealing with the fact that I wanted her family to know the valiant efforts that were taken by all the police, fire, and EMS workers that attended that day.

I also needed to express my condolences to start my grieving closure because that is simply for the type of person I am. They then encouraged me to call the family and see if we could chat and provide each other with our respective perspectives.

I remember calling and speaking to her grandmother, and as I spoke with her, I cried deeply. We then both chatted for 15 minutes and shared an incredible moment in time.

I could share that everyone involved that day had tried their best to save her grand-daughter's life. We were all dramatically affected by the loss and seeking help to deal with the loss. I could express my personal condolences that day and she was very thankful. In the end, she thanked me for putting a personal reference to all those that had attended that worst experience in her life.

Several weeks later I was sitting on the living room floor while leaning up against the couch with my daughters. I remember my body locked up and went rigid and I thought I was having a heart attack. All of sudden I felt an incredible energy like a spinning basketball in my chest. As the energy increased in intensity, I looked up to the ceiling to my right and I saw a bright light that also appeared to be spinning. I felt the energy inside me peak and I felt like it almost shot out of my head, arms, and legs. As I looked up to the light, I heard, "I'm okay" and the energy inside my body and light on the ceiling disappeared in a flash.

As I have stated before, I am a Christian and I honestly believe her angel came to me that day to release me of the pain, stress, and internal devastation I was feeling. As time passed from that day, I feel better about the entire incident and my faith in Jesus Christ is reaffirmed.

Side note: for the research of this book, I have gone back and looked at my scrap-books, my collection of newspaper clippings, cards, and other documents to refresh my memory. I came across the newspaper clipping obituary for the little girl the other day and was amazed to see she looked nothing like my Alexis.

In reflection, it is incredible how when the mind is sick it pays terrible tricks on you. Until I recently saw that clipping, they looked identical. A lesson for all of us I would suggest: When we look at things through one set of eyes or a negative stress induced lens, the reality we see then is not the truest picture like I have come to discover.

*****

I still use a combination of these tools as they continually assist me out of the darkness that I may descend into and remind me that there is a light, and that light was found within me. As we move forward in this book, I genuinely hope you use one or a combination of these tools to help you move forward. They helped me, and I hope they help you in your journey.

It was not long until I let go of the past negatives holding me back from moving forward and saw the lessons learned from this adversity. I felt good about myself and my future and "who I wanted to be". I practised a positive mindset every day and looked toward the future with excitement, positivity, and hope. The early thoughts of Ironwill 360° Leadership began and I realized that my policing career had an expiry date, so I went back to school.

They always say you must "hit rock bottom before you can rebound". Well that definitely happened to me in 2007.

Looking back, I am grateful for the crashing and hitting rock bottom. The process was a very difficult one, but it helped me put my pride and ego aside, ask for help, receive the specialized help I needed, release me from the memories and horror of the past, and assist me in moving forward in my life. The process also helped with the associated denial and allowed me to open my Pandora's box[1] of emotions and no longer lock them away but free them, allowing them to develop, grow, and mature.

It was truly a unique experience in incredible darkness at rock bottom, and this is where I found my light. That light was not an external source; I found it within myself. I based my light on my four core values taught to me by my loving parents, Paul and Joan Pflug.

Once found, it illuminated my life, calmly set in, and replaced chaos, and I personally and professionally grew at an incredible rate with a new set of rules. My efforts were not to destroy me under the weight of the pursuit; they were there to build me up to be the man I am today. All I had to do was believe and embrace who I was, who I am, and who I wanted to be.

Recently I came across the "Train to Win" article by Brian Willis. "The article identifies the parallels between competitive athletes and police officers' performance requirements and always recognizes the importance of/tactics for staying mentally focused and in control of their emotions.

Practising physical/technical/mental skills with a "Train to Win" focus will better enable officers to access executive function thinking under stress and increase the chance officers accurately assess the situation, plan and act appropriately when an officer or public safety is being threatened in emergent situations.

Research has found that an officer's performance, like those of professional athletes, is causally related to their physical, technical, and mental readiness.

Therefore, to maximize officer and the public's safety, training must educate new officers on the qualities of a winning mindset, on the importance of maintaining emotional control in high-stress situations, and on providing opportunities for skills integration by training physical, technical, and mental skills together".

As I look back now, I am very thankful to have been an elite athlete in high school and university. This was where I learned of physical, technical, and mental readiness through practice, pregame prep with our sports psychologist, gameplay, and post-game reflection. I was not aware that these skills would one day save my life and get me back on the rails and allow me to move forward #StrongerFasterFitter in my #HeartBodyAndMind. I would assess continually these strategies in my future but am confident I have great systems and infrastructure in place to deal with anything life can throw at me.

AUTHOR'S NOTE

This is my story about experiencing a Post Traumatic Stress Injury, from my perspective and corresponding descent to a dark place and recovery. While this is the process I used, all the people who went through that day have their associated stress symptoms and healing processes and ways to deal and reflect on that day. We all had our personalized trauma, ways of dealing with it, and hopefully the means of treatment and strategies to move forward.

I am honoured that we all rose in our way that day to better others. Sharing this terrible day with such an incredible group of frontline emergency personnel means a great deal to me, knowing that we did not face this alone.

I genuinely respect you all and hope that you sought help, have recovered from it, and moved forward to everyone there that day. I genuinely wish you all peace and resolution in the future.

*****

Five years ago, I had the privilege to meet up with Mary Margret for coffee as she was in town visiting family. It was so lovely to sit and talk with her. I thanked her for what she did for me by freeing me from the darkness and teaching me how to move forward.

Looking back on the trauma that I experienced, I can see that my resiliency developed, and I learned lessons that proved to be precious in my life. Life works alongside a more significant schedule or fate, and that timing is of the essence. By this, if we don't grow to be the person who is required at a time, then maybe we won't experience what we should have until we are ready to be "that person we need to be".

I now believe that everything from my past has prepared and will continue to prepare me to enable me to deal with and learn from every positive and negative situation that presents itself.

I have adopted a more positive perspective in life and now embrace the opportunities and fight through them rather than running or freezing in them.

******

As I reflect upon the years, there are three areas where I still struggle to put "rational thought" towards an irrational act: suicide, death, and the level of violence one person can have for another.

I have learned to rationalize suicide because that was the most rational thought the person had at the exact moment in time. Nothing I say, do, or think can put me in that place, but that was the only way out for some people.

I have been to drug overdoses, hangings, carbon monoxide, wrist slashing, people who have jumped in front of trains or off bridges and many other forms of suicide and still can't wrap my head around it.

In our police service, it was the policy that the road Sergeant was to attend to every death, inspect the scene, summon additional resources if required, and sometimes attend the loved one's home and advise them that their loved one had died. Sadly and morbidly, I became very good at these because of the sheer volume of them and the goal I always set for myself to "always be the type of officer that I'd want to come to my door in the event of a tragedy".

Over the 12 years of performing this role, I experienced every emotion known to man. Some would laugh, cry, be violent, faint, locked in shock, and the list goes on. I always came to expect the unexpected to be ready for whatever was going to happen.

What I truly hated was that last face they saw when they answered the door and said, "Officer, what's wrong?" I carry this guilt with me to this day and can still see their faces wrought with wrenching body pain. For me, it is a dichotomy of emotions, extreme sadness versus the extreme honour of being there to help someone in their worst hour.

I remember one specific case where I knew the gentleman whose wife had died because of unlucky circumstances. As I drove to his home and tried to prepare myself mentally and plan a kind, direct, and compassionate script, my anxiety rose tremendously. My goal in death notifications was simple: "Be the type of officer that I'd want to attend my home for this horrible notification".

As I pulled up to the house, I noticed his lights were on, and the front door was open. As I walked up, he appeared in the doorway, smiled, and said, "Hey Doug, what's up?" through the screen door.

I solemnly asked to come inside, and he opened the door, and we went to the living room.

Once inside, he turned around and teared up and asked, "Doug, what's wrong?"

He looked into my eyes, which was when I ruined his life with my news.

He initially was in shock, went white, then collapsed, and I caught him as we fell to the floor. I helped him up, and over the next half hour, he went from one extreme emotion to the next. One minute he was beating on my chest in anger, the next sobbing in my arms in intense grief, to stand back in shock and disbelief. Time seemed to stand still, and what felt like 3 hours was 30 minutes.

I know my kindness, compassion, and empathy helped him that day, and I was glad a friend gave him the news. After a few days, my anxiety subsided, and I went back to "normal".

About a year later, I walked through Canadian Tire when we met up again. When he saw my face, it instantly transported him back to that life-crushing night and he became very emotional. Sadly, we embraced and worked through the immediacy of his grief and later parted ways.

We have run into each other several times over the years since, and although he didn't break down, I can always see his pain in his eyes and memory of the pain I caused that night with the death notification. I have seen him from a distance occasionally, and he quickly turned and walked the other way in recent years. I know my face reminds him of one of the worst days in his life, and I do not want to re-traumatize him.

I have spoken to a counsellor on this several times and must resign myself because one of my greatest strengths of empathy and compassion for others is also my greatest weakness.

As time passed, I moved towards that "dark place" under the accumulated stress weight and was fighting to keep things tight. I remember working a seven-night block in 2005-ish that would end with a vacation for my daughter Reighan, seven or eight years old. The plan was for me to work the seven nights, then we'd fly a few hours after the night shift was over to the happiest place on earth, Disney in Florida, for six days.

Simple plans, I thought, right? Nothing is ever simple in law enforcement.

During that seven-day block, it seemed like fate was working against me, and by the end of the week, I had attended eight to ten sudden tragic deaths, and on the last night, we had a double fire fatality where we found the couple deceased at the bottom of the staircase that led to the upstairs by the front door. My entire shift pulled together that week and helped each other professionally and emotionally. They were a fantastic bunch who faced such horrible things one cannot even imagine.

That last night bothered our whole platoon working that night. I held them all in such high esteem and was immensely proud to lead them.

A few hours later, we went to the airport and we flew off to Disney. During the flight I once again suppressed my feelings from the week so that I would not ruin our vacation.

I recall meeting with my Divisional Inspector some time after this and saying I needed a change or a fresh start in another area as I was burnt out.

*****

Recently I had a bad dream and was transported back about 15 years ago, when I attended a medical emergency call. As I walked up to the front door, I saw the ambulance carrying a dad of about 45 out of the house on a stretcher and his son was holding his hand talking with him. As they spoke, the dad assured his son that everything would be "okay". He took a deep, laboured breath and died right there in mid-sentence.

The son was devastated and became hysterical. I had to aid and hold the young man back as the EMS workers tried to revive him and transport him to the hospital. I drove them both to the hospital and sat with them in the quiet room for what seemed like an eternity. I remember thinking, "What in the hell could I say or do to make this better? How could I make their lives better when I came into them than worse?" It defeated me when the doctor came in and respectfully said that they could not bring him back to life. I sat there with them for about an hour and felt their pain, the pain of knowing a wife would become a widow and a teenage boy would be raised without a dad that day.

It was that time in deep grief for a man I never knew, a family I had never met, that the seeds of "live every second of every day" were planted. I realized that life was not guaranteed.

I have never been comfortable with death, and most are not. What profoundly affected me that day was that one minute you could talk with a loved one, and one second later, you are gone.

It always blows me away when such dreams come back to haunt me when I believe issues from the past are closed. Maybe, just maybe, they are a subconscious reminder that death should be life and promote that I live "every second of every day" and share that thought with anyone who will listen.

*****

Over the years, I have seen so many dead bodies that I cannot even try to inventory them in my mind. Truthfully, I believe my mind has shut those memories down out of a subconscious type of self-preservation. I do have flashbacks of when I find people deceased or see someone in distress at the time. I especially have them when I walk by buildings or even rivers where I had found someone. During these "flashbacks", sadly, I relive the experience of my stress, anxiety, and even the emotion.

I remember several where we found deceased persons crawling on the floor, and when you looked at the sightline, you learned they died while trying to crawl to the telephone for a summons to help. Dying alone and in distress like this is a genuine fear that I have for myself and my loved ones, and it bothers me as a human to know that they died that way. I genuinely want to be the guy who died peacefully in my sleep. But these people did not have that.

I cannot remember who suggested that as a coping mechanism, but I genuinely appreciate that gift. It better enables me to clear the bad thoughts, celebrate the life lost, and remove the negative sights, smells, and situations of where the death occurred. The strategy I have harvested for myself from a caring soul was to find a picture of the person living. Then, as I leave the place and the "scene", I look at the picture of the person living. Forget the biological mass; I must view, celebrate the life mentally once lived, say a small prayer, set the picture down, and leave the place.

This advice and practice have helped me through some tough calls and memories.

As a Coach Officer and Sergeant, I always tried to share that same strategy to supply the surrounding officers some comfort as it has done for me.

We all manage death as individuals as the person involved. Let us all try to be empathetic and better help our friends, colleagues, and strangers move forward when they experience this. This small gift of compassion and strategy could save a life one day.

*****

Since retiring from active service, we have bought our retirement home and have some incredible neighbours. In February 2018, we woke up, and a frantic neighbour texted me and came to our house. He asked us if we had seen or heard from Bill. Bill was an 80-year-old dear friend called the "Mayor of Boblo Island". Bill was one of the most interesting people I had ever met. He was a retired school music teacher, learned to rollerblade in his 70s, often spoke of his daughter and grandkids, was a social butterfly, and shared many dinners at his place or ours.

Everyone loved Bill. As we walked down to his unit, memories of the earlier holiday season filled my head; between December 26 and New Year's Eve, we had four straight dinners with Bill. He was like a grandfather to us.

I remember questioning the neighbour when he last saw Bill, and he advised a few days prior when he "checked" the apartment and my stomach sunk, knowing that we would probably find Bill deceased. As we walked down the hallway, Michelle, my wife, and also a retired Police Sergeant, and I stood outside for a moment, and the neighbour looked at us in confusion; we stood there to see if we could detect "that odour" that we both had smelled so many times over the years of our respective service.

No odour present—whew.

We opened the door and looked around his condominium while the neighbour stayed in the doorway to the unit. I went directly to the bedroom, Michelle to the bathroom, as experience has shown, there are usually the two places people die. As I entered the bedroom, nothing. I walked deep into the room to "clear it" as many times before, and there I found Bill, slumped over, deceased.

He was getting ready for bed and simply slumped to the floor. In my mind, he died instantly and not in distress, as I have described before. He looked at peace and almost angelic. I called out that I had found him, and Michelle ran into the room, and we knew there was nothing we could do. We both hugged in apology, and she said, "He's almost smiling", and we both recounted how at dinner a few weeks prior he made us jambalaya based on his wife's recipe. Michelle reminded me of our conversation with Bill asking why he never remarried, and he quickly quipped, "Why would I remarry? I'm still madly in love with my wife and miss her so much". We looked into each other's eyes and knew they are now together in heaven.

His death was very peaceful. We called 911, and although we were both retired, we immediately assumed the Sgt Pflug roles we once held and covered off: I needed all that for the "call".

Bill had been there for a few days. The neighbour that summoned us said he had checked the bedroom, not to the same level we did. I did not tell him this as I tried to protect him from the guilt he would have had.

We grieved extensively over the following weeks. Bill was our friend, a mentor, a member of our family, and we would miss him.

RIP Bill.

*****

It is incredible to think that some will say that people are police officers 24/7. I do not subscribe to that thought process. We must have time off, or the weight of the position will crush you.

Looking back, I have been retired for over three years now, and although I no longer have the power behind a badge, I still have the knowledge gained from it.

On that day, Michelle and I were extraordinarily strong for the people, and after grieving, we also reminded ourselves to be strong for our grieving.

*****

Once you have smelled death, you will *never* forget it. There were many times I would bring my uniform home, wash it, the scent stayed in, and I had to throw out the clothes. It truly is distinct as a punch full-on in the face; you never forget it.

I think back to two years ago in 2018 when Michelle and I drove to Boblo. It was a sizzling summer August/September evening. The drive involves getting off 401 Highway and driving through country roads for about 20 minutes to Amherstburg. As we neared the edge of the city, windows open, warm air in our faces, we suddenly both turned, looked at each other and said "dead body" to each other at the same time. We both shook it off, thinking our minds played tricks on us and went ahead to Boblo. When we left two days later, as we neared the location, the police blocked the road off. We later learned they found a body in the field.

Once you smell death, you will never forget.

AUTHOR'S CHALLENGE

Hopefully, you are not near your end as you read this book. My challenge is to seek the resources you may need one day. Know how to access them and get the help you may need.

Please, need help, ask for help, get help.

NOTE

[i]   https://en.wikipedia.org/wiki/Pandora%27s_box#:~:text=Pandora's%20box%20is%20an%20
    artifact,and%20emotional%20curses%20upon%20mankind

Lessons Learned as an Elite Strength and Conditioning Coach

8

GUELPH STORM HOCKEY CLUB STRENGTH AND CONDITIONING COACH

I looked back on the amazing police leaders I had worked for and those with the Guelph Storm Hockey Cub in the Ontario Hockey league that I joined as their strength and off-ice conditioning coach in 1995.

For those of you that do not know this league, the OHL is part of a greater league known as the Canadian Hockey League. Hockey fans will know that this is the development league where young talent play who wish to be drafted into the National Hockey League (NHL). My goal was to compare the elite leadership I saw from both areas and take the best I saw, "take it, tweak it, make it my own", hoping I too would succeed.

When I joined the team as their strength and off-ice conditioning coach in 1995, I quickly learned that I was around four giants in the game and leadership: E. J. McGuire, Mike Kelly, Jim Rooney, and Dr Neil Widmeyer. I carry each man in extreme esteem for their leadership styles and what they did for the young men, staff, and organization but also how they positively influenced me in my life.

A bit about E. J. McGuire:[1]

DOI: 10.1201/9781003187189-9

E. J. McGuire was born in the Old First Ward in Buffalo, attended Canisius High School and then played hockey for the Brockport State Golden Eagles, where he was named captain his senior year. He started his hockey at Caz Rink and played travel hockey for the Regals.

He became head coach of the Brockport hockey team in 1977 and led the Golden Eagles for five seasons. In 2009, E. J. was the first ice hockey player/coach to be inducted into the Golden Eagles Hall of Fame.

While at Brockport, he met Mike Keenan and formed a lifelong friendship. After concluding his Brockport hockey stint, E. J. aided Keenan in winning the Calder Cup for the Rochester Americans (AHL). The coaching tandem worked together for 11 years in the NHL with Philadelphia, Chicago, and Ottawa winning five divisional titles and twice going to the Stanley Cup finals. An innovator during his coaching tenure, he was instrumental in using video for education and motivational techniques and developing extensive statistics for analyzing line matchups in its earliest form of coaching strategy.

E. J. also coached at the University of Waterloo, where he obtained his doctorate in Kinesiology/Sport Psychology. Coaching stops also included stints at Guelph (Major Junior OHL) and in the AHL for three seasons with Hartford and Maine.

In 2005, E. J. was hired to work in NHL Central Scouting and over the next six years he became Vice President of Hockey Operations, where he revolutionized NHL scouting. He created the NHL scouting combine borrowing the format from the NFL and was one of the executives that developed the "war room" in Toronto, that reviews plays in real time.

E. J.[2] was the Head of Central Scouting in North America and an architect of many of the innovations of hockey scouting; his efforts provided NHL clubs with the most comprehensive list of NHL draft-eligible prospects.

At his passing at the age of 58, NHL executives honored his memory by creating the E. J. McGuire Award of Excellence. "Excellence is what E.J. person-ified", Central Scouting's David Gregory said. "It was imperative that the winner of this award be named after E.J. had the strength of character and competitiveness because these traits exemplify what E.J. brought to the hockey community every day".

E.J. died from cancer in 2011 and is survived by his wife, Terry, and two daughters, Jacqueline and Erin. When you asked him what E. J. stood for, in his Irish wit, he would always say, "Edward John, but my parents saved me the trouble of trying to spell that".

E. J. was a man I learned so much from in the three years I directly worked for him and in the later years we were here we'd see each other at the rink when he was scouting. What I loved about him was that he combined his academic training and excellence to coaching and leading. This hybrid set him apart from most at the time, and I truly learned so much from him.

We both joined the team for the 1995–1996 season. We played 66 games that year, winning 45 and only losing 16. As we entered the playoffs, they rated us in the Top 10 of the CHL, and expectations were extremely high. To prepare for the playoff run, our GM Mike Kelly made key trades to strengthen our lineup for future draft picks because the organization felt we had a real chance and took a legitimate chance at winning the OHL Championship and earning a spot for the Memorial Cup.

One of the best lessons I learned from him came in the first period intermission of our first playoff game. With expectations extremely high, we came out flat during the first period, and it shocked all the players. One of our captains threw his gloves in his stall. He was obviously angry and disappointed that we came out so flat. He took a breath and walked around the room in attempts to motivate the guys. At one point his positive speech became negative, and he started pointing his finger at different players in the room that he did not feel were pulling their weight.

E. J. came into the room and shouted for him to stop. Once he had the room's attention, he spoke in a calm and directed voice. He was the player to hold his hand back up in the same fashion he was pointing at others. The players responded, and then E. J. told him to keep his finger pointed but shift so his palm faced the ceiling and asked him, "What do you see?" The player looked bewildered and said, "My hand". E. J.'s lesson was simple. "When you point your one finger at the players, look at your hand because three fingers are pointing back at you. Before you demand others to step up, fix three things about yourself or your play before you point a finger at others".

He then challenged everyone. "Guys, calm down. I love your passion because it means that you care about the outcome of this game. We have practised for this, let us go out and not think so much. When you think, your feet slow down. Go out there and play and work three things of your own game, and when we all do that, that's seventy-five things we are working out and will win this".

At the end of the second period, we tied the game. Leading into the third period the guys were flying, and our fitness took over, and when the final buzzer sounded, we won 6–3.

That season we:

- won the Hamilton Spectator Trophy as OHL Regular Season Champions
- won quarterfinals series vs Niagara Falls (4–0)

- won semi-final series vs Belleville (4–1)
- lost in OHL Championship in final game seven vs Peterborough (4–3)
- competed in Memorial Cup (4th Place) in Peterborough

One experience I savour to this day was during the Memorial Cup Tournament that year. E. J. asked if I would like to be on the bench with the team during the game.

The first period was full of action, and I was a cheerleader for the guys, trying to help verbally as they went on/off the ice like the way I helped them push out another rep in the gym. During the first period intermission E. J. pulled me aside. He thanked me for my efforts and asked me to not say a word and watch him during the second period.

I stood on the bench the entire period and analyzed everything he said, did, his facial expression, body language, and simple presence on the bench.

In the second period intermission, he asked what I saw and learned. As I recounted everything I saw, he praised my efforts. He said,

> Pflugger, sometimes it's not what we say on the bench that leads, it is the confidence the players see in how we conduct ourselves. They always look to me to be strong and consistent. Coaching is not always about the plays or what we say, it is also about the atmosphere we create.

"Create an environment where others can succeed" is a philosophy I would one day incorporate in all my leadership and followership opportunities

In the third period, I mirrored everything he did while he continued to coach both the players while watching his protégé. At one point, one player came off the ice and I gently and quietly tapped him on the shoulder and E. J. he looked at me smiled and nodded in approval When I looked up, E. J. smiled and nodded at me. So much was said in that exchange where no words were said.

E. J. was a firm believer in practising what we teach as well. He and I mirrored this type of coaching style. I would train, do plyometrics, quick feet, and sprint work with these guys to earn their trust. E. J. would during training camp walk to the front of the group each year and place four hundred-dollar bills on the table. He was 41 years of age at the time and would challenge any player in camp to beat him in the mile and a half run. If they did, they could claim one bill for themselves.

Over three years, the guys would all get so excited to see the prize and think they could "beat the old guy". No one could ever claim they beat E. J., and his training camp record stood during the two years he coached with us.

E. J. left the team two years later to coach in the American Hockey League. We kept an incredibly special close friendship until his sudden death in 2011, when cancer took him away from us at the early age of 58.

Over the years I have learned repeatedly that E. J. McGuire was one of the most respected men in all the NHL, and I was his friend.

RIP, E. J.

*****

Mike Kelly was our General Manager that year, and he was the one who gave me the shot to be the strength and conditioning off-ice coach. In the summer leading up to that

1995–1996 season, Mike knew I was training Jamie Wright, Jeff O'Neill, Todd Bertuzzi, Dwayne Hay, Ryan Risadore, and Chris Hajt. The Dallas Stars drafted Jamie, and he was getting ready for his fourth season with the Storm. Todd and Jeff had been drafted in the first round of the National Hockey League and were both preparing for their first NHL training camps, Todd with the Islanders, and Jeff with the Hartford Whalers.

I had asked him if I could join the staff and he told me he just wanted to see what I could do for these three players. I was a football player and wrestler, so he was naturally concerned about how I could train hockey players if I never played the game and could not skate.

Mike was and remains one of the most highly respected men in the Canadian Hockey League, and he made sure he assembled the best staff, coaches, players, and boosters in a "Sports Family" so that everyone would buy into his plan.

It has been an amazing ride being on Mike's "team" over the years, where I could see a very intelligent man, a guru in finding young hockey talent, a man with exemplary core values and inner fire for competition to guide his "sports family" to success. He did, we did, and we all enjoyed the framework that he placed with our organization for the personal, professional, and team success of all involved.

I was the strength and conditioning coach from 1995–1996 to 2012–2013. I stepped away the following year to help train my daughter, Reighan, who had earned a full NCAA Division One Athletic soccer scholarship to St Peter's University in New Jersey. I stayed on the team in an advisory role and the Law Enforcement Mentor. I still serve to this date in that role.

Mike would extend his support to me in the 2012–13 season when I had problems with the head coach. Let us just say we almost come to blows because of a comment he made to me. As I dissected the situation and how to respond, Mike called me up. We discussed my future under this coach and navigated how I would walk away as a coach but remain as a law enforcement mentor and advisor.

Mike showed great concern for my personal and professional reputations as a strength and conditioning coach and police officer. He didn't want the conflict I had with the coach based on my core values to tarnish any roles that I had based on incorrect information. I retired, and Mike released an incredibly supportive news release thanking me for my 18 years volunteering at the team's strength and conditioning coach. Yes, I never received payment for the 18 years of coaching. It was never about the money for me; it was bartering my skills to be part of such a big organization and life experience.

For me, my core values were my bond and promise to others. The incident infringed upon one of those values, and I left the team.

More on core value development and finding your granite later in this book. I will suggest through what is the point of having core values if you don't stand behind them in casual and emergent situations?

With that, I left abruptly in the middle of the season.

In 2015, Mike's years of hard work and sacrifice paid off when the Guelph Storm won the OHL Championship, and seeing him hoist the cup up in the air at centre ice was breathtaking knowing the road he travelled to get there[3].

Headline: Strength and Conditioning Coach Doug Pflug retires[4]
January 4, 2013

In May 1995, Doug met with Storm GM Mike Kelly and offered to help with the Storm's strength and conditioning needs. Now, nearly 18 years later Doug is retiring as the team's strength and conditioning coach to devote more time to his family, other coaching pursuits, and a full-time career as a City of Guelph Police Officer.

"Doug brought the organization a level of expertise that we never had before", Mike Kelly said. Coupled with his energy, drive, and commitment, he was instrumental in the success of not only the team, but also many individual players who received help from his personal one on one training. We have a motto outside our dressing room that states "talented players inspire themselves . . . talented players inspire others". "This very well could have been written about Doug. He is truly one of the most inspirational individuals that I have ever met. We are going to miss him, but his legacy will remain forever as part of the Guelph Storm culture".

In the 2018–2019 season, the team coach and General Manager was George Burnett. George and I had a great working relationship when he was the Guelph Storm Coach for the 1997–1999 season when we won the OHL Championship. I have a great deal of respect for George; he is a very good hockey mind, his preparation for games is excellent, and he truly cares about his players and the organization.

When the team won that year, it elated me knowing that I had a small but significant role with the team. A few weeks after the season concluded, I received a text message congratulating me on my contribution that season and asking what my ring size was.

That fall I would meet with the owners and they presented me with a championship ring. I then received an apology that I only had "only three of the four championships rings" and advised that if they could go back, they had also given me one for the 2013–2014 season.

*****

Jim Rooney was one of the team owners when I joined the team and a high school principal.

Over the years Jim has proven repeatedly to be one of the most caring, positive, and family guys that I have ever met. We have become great friends over the years. He combines his love of family, love of God, love of sport, and love for those around him to provide the best environment all these people in his sphere of influence can succeed. I am a much better man because of Jim's involvement and investment in my life.

It thrilled me to see that Jim was recognized for his outstanding efforts in 2017 and inducted into the Guelph Sports Hall of Fame[5] in the builder's category. Jim not only built teams and athletes; he invested in people, and I am a grateful benefactor of his investment, friendship, and mentorship.

Jim Rooney has been a fixture in the Guelph sports scene for decades—his trademark mustache and positive attitude filling many a rink and sports field.

He was co-owner, president, and governor for the Ontario Hockey League's Guelph Storm from 1991 to 2006. During that time, the Storm took part in four Memorial Cups and won two OHL championships, in 1998 and 2004. He was Chairman of the Board of Governors of the OHL from 1995 to 2001, overseeing the largest league expansion program when they grew from 16 to 20 teams in the 1990s.

Rooney was involved with Storm players on many levels including being the principal at Bishop Macdonell and Our Lady of Lourdes high

Portrait by Robert Howson

schools, where many of the players attended. He believed education was important and ensured the Storm had one of the best education programs in the country, with three Guelph players winning the OHL Scholastic award—Jamie Wright, Dustin Brown (three times), and Manny Malhotra.

In 2001 he became commissioner of the historic intercounty Baseball League, a position he held until 2009. One year later he became owner of the Guelph Royals Baseball Club, keeping baseball alive in the Royal City—a franchise that has existed since the league began in 1919.

"Sport is the fabric of every community", said Rooney. "It reflects the best in people and gives you the opportunity to give back and build community. The relationships you set up in sports are everlasting bonds. They create memories, keep families together, a community together, and generate a sense of 'team' you cherish for a lifetime".

Rooney was not only an executive but coached minor baseball and hockey in the Stanley Stick organization. He was co-chair of the Ontario Winter Games in 2002–2003 and fulfilled a childhood dream of representing his country as a member of Team Canada's first Under 18 (years of age) gold medal winning hockey team in Russia in 2003, as the club's educational consultant.

Jim Rooney was a man that derived great pleasure in helping young people excel in sports and in the classroom, while providing his community with teams of which they could be proud.

Well done, Brother Jim. Thank you for sharing your many gifts with me and the world.

*****

Dr Neil "Doc Wid" Widmeyer was our team sports psychologist and a man I deeply respected. "Doc Wid", as we affectionately called him, was a man of great integrity, wisdom, knowledge, and passion. He and I spent many hours discussing our roles with the team, and he always joked that "he trains the mind and I train the body". Over the years

I worked with Neil, and he had a profound impact on me with how I dealt with my own mental health issues that at times prevented me from being my best. He would walk me through visualization exercises to face my fears, understand them, and use them to fuel my future.

When we won the 2004 OHL Championship and plans were being made for the team to travel to compete for the Memorial Cup in Kelowna, British Columbia, I was asked if I minded rooming with Doc Wid. I was 38 at the time and he was in his 70s, and I welcomed the opportunity of knowing this amazing person and hoped it might also expose me to learn more sports psychology golden nuggets and positive mindset practices for success.

*****

I remember back in 2015 when Michelle called me and asked if we could go to the Toronto Food and Wine show with her friends Brad and his wife, Doris. Michelle had known them for quite some time and other than meeting them briefly at our wedding, I did not really know them. We planned to meet them at their condominium near the venue, and we had a few drinks. I do not know if you have ever been in this position before. Your wife is great friends with another couple, and you are the fourth wheel and need to make friends with both. Over the years of going out with another couple, I have seen some epic fails where not all four people get along, and I did not want this to happen because I was the new guy.

As the night progressed Brad and I bonded on quite a few subjects and relaxed and enjoyed the night. I took time out with Brad and made sure I made the same efforts with Doris because I knew how important this was to Michelle. As the evening progressed, we had an amazing time, the four of us navigating our way around the Metro Toronto Convention Centre, celebrating our simple love of wine.

The event ended around 11:00 p.m., and as we walked back to their place, we decided we would find a place to have just one more drink. As we passed the Ritz Carlton Toronto, Brad suggested we go to the bar there, as he had many drinks with clients there.

We went in and ordered our drinks and recapped the amazing night. At one-point Brad has the look of extreme shock on his face. His eyes lit up, pointed, and mumbled something that I could not understand. I turned around and looked to where he was pointing and saw the Great One, Wayne Gretzky, standing at the bar with several business types. I then remembered hearing that he was appearing in Toronto for the launch of one of the NHL video hockey games in his name.

Brad was so excited to be in the same room as his childhood hero and told me stories of significant memories he had of Wayne. At one point I told Brad that I knew him, and he called an instant challenge. Brad did not know of the many years I was the strength and conditioning coach with the Guelph Storm where, behind the scenes, I have had the honour of meeting so many amazing NHL hockey players like Wayne Gretzky, Bobby Orr, Guy Lafleur, Larry Robinson, Ken Dryden—all my boyhood heroes. I must admit that it is cool to be a guy who skates like an eight-year-old being in the same room with these guys, let alone the same world.

Brad and I chirped back and forth for a few minutes with his challenge and my stating that I knew Wayne.

At one point, I stood up and said "Fine", and I walked over to where Wayne was standing with the business types. After a moment or two, Wayne politely asked if he could help me. He was such a gentleman and genuinely illustrated why all of Canada loves

him. I explained my role with
Guelph Storm and that he had
befriended one of our younger
players, Manny Malhotra, in
training camp, and he said,
"Oh, you are the cop strength
coach that I've heard Manny
talk about with the Storm". We
chatted for a few minutes, and
I let him know why I was there
to prove Brad wrong and further
explained that Brad was like a
small child right now across the
bar. He then called, "Brad!" and
waved for him to come over.
Brad shot over, shook his hand,

and professed his love of Wayne's game. Wayne said that he had to leave and readily
accepted Brad's request for a photo together.

Michelle and Doris had come over at this point and I asked Wayne if we could get a
picture with him and he agreed. The "Great One" was certainly great that night, sharing
these moments in time with four fans. As we lined up for our picture with him, he stepped
in between Michelle and me. I joked he was the safest guy in the Ritz that night because
he was standing between two police officers and he laughed and agreed.

We all expressed our thanks and went our separate ways.

The entire time we walked back to their condominium, Brad continued his boyish
praise of Wayne. The night ended on an incredible highlight, and I won them over.

The next morning, we woke up to the sounds of breakfast in the kitchen. We went
down, and I honestly found Brad quite standoffish. I asked him if I had offended him and
tried to clear the air. He took a sip of his coffee and told me he was extremely disappointed
in me. Extremely shocked, I asked why. He paused, a grin came over his face, and he said,
"Damn, last night you arranged for me to meet my boyhood hero. I'm just disappointed
because I thought you'd have Bobby Orr join us for breakfast". We all laughed and finished
breakfast.

Many times, over the years my role with the
Guelph Storm has allowed me entrance to places
very few have. I have some splendid memories
and friendships because we all worked damn
hard to accomplish our respective goals.

Brad posted the picture with him and Wayne
as his Facebook profile for over two years.

Yeah, I won them over that night.

*****

In 2015 "Doc Wid" fell ill and I went to the
hospital to visit him with Mike Kelly. When we
arrived, we went into his room and were met with

his enormous smile and in his usual energetic voice, said "Hey, Pflugger. how are you, my friend?" We visited for an hour and I presented him a signed copy of *Fingerprints Through Time—A History of the Guelph Police* so that he could pass the time reading, which was another passion of his.

As our visit neared its end, we shared a few more stories, laughs, and a firm hand-shake, and we left.

Over the years, many people have asked me how I can be so positive all the time. The answer is quite simple, Doc Wid always told me "Pflugger, attitude is everything", and I owe my positive mindset, outlook on life, and pay-it-forward practice in memory of this great man.

Little did I know that would be the last time we would speak, laugh, and discuss the world.

Doc Wid, my good friend, trusts in knowing that over the 21years we worked together and shared a friendship, you had a profound impact in both my personal and professional life.

RIP, Friend.

A bit more about "Doc Wid[6]" from the www.exchangemagazine.com

The following is a reprint of an article published in the May 2013 issue of *Exchange Magazine* on Neil Widmeyer, who was affectionately known in the professional world as "Doc Wid". Neil Widmeyer died on December 11, 2015, peacefully at Grand River Hospital.

This posting is a tribute to Neil's life and the many successes he has contributed to the sport psychology and kinesiology disciplines. His obituary follows the article. (Picture source)[7]

"I really love sports". If you are sitting in the room that serves as Dr. Neil Widmeyer's office, training room, and den, this will not come as a surprising revelation. You will already have noticed the auto-graphed pictures of NHL hockey players, swim-mers, and one of Canada's best boxers, among many other mementos.

But these are not simply the memorabilia of a collector—they all say some version of "thanks", because the man known as "Doc Wid" has played a significant role in the development of these elite athletes. Neil Widmeyer is a sports psychologist, although he much prefers the term "mental trainer— it conveys the idea better to youngsters". The more ponderous designation, he feels, carries too much unwanted freight. Whatever his official title, the fact is that "Sports Canada recognizes me and sends top athletes to me".

"Doc Wid" has been involved in this field for a long time. But during his full-time academic career, which included teaching at the University of Waterloo, he tended to focus on the theoretical and classroom aspects of the discipline. Only when he "retired"—an inappropriate word, if ever there as one—did he begin collaborating directly with athletes as their "mental trainer".

> He prefers to be proactive; while some athletes come to him because they have hit some sort of psychological wall, he would rather "use an educational approach".

That alleged retirement came when he took a package from the University of Waterloo, 16 years ago, and promptly started his current enterprise, as well as teaching part-time at McMaster University, and at Resurrection High School.

He is now in his 17th season with the Guelph Storm junior hockey club—a position he took at the request of one of his former students. He and his wife, Lynn, live in Waterloo, and he admits he takes a bit of friendly trash talk for working with the Storm and not the Rangers.

Obituary—"Attitude is everything"
WIDMEYER, William "Neil" Passed Away Peacefully on Dec 11, 2015

WIDMEYER, William "Neil" Died peacefully on Friday, December 11, 2015, surrounded by the love of his family. Neil was an adoring and devoted husband to his wife of 54 years, Elizabeth Roselyn "Lynn" (nee Hipwell). He was a loving and heroic father to children Kim Welch, Kelly (Jon) and Greg. He was the remarkably proud and firsthand "Big Guy" of grandkids: Zachary, Megan, Madeline, and Emily. Neil took immense pride in his family and doted on them all. He was a fun-loving friend with an infectious smile, genuine kindness, and empathy.

Academics and athletes mourn the loss of Dr. Neil Widmeyer, affectionately known as "Doc Wid", who was a pioneer in the field of Sports Psychology. He taught for over 30 years at the University of Waterloo and was an inspiring professor and a valued mentor to countless graduate students.

His research and teachings brought great insight into topics such as team cohesion as well as aggression and violence in sports with both professional and amateur athletes.

Additionally, Doc Wid was part of the Guelph Storm hockey organization for 21 years as their Sports Psychologist, helping players in all aspects of mental preparation. In lieu of flowers, donations to the Canadian National Team boxer and 2016 Olympic hopeful, Mandy Bujold would be appreciated greatly. As Mandy's Sports Psychologist, Doc Wid boasts he is "always in her corner".

Contributions can be made on-line at www.mandybujold.com or at the funeral home with the options of cheque, cash, and debit.

Neil's family will receive relatives and friends on Thursday, December 17, from 1–3 p.m. and 7–9 p.m. at the Henry Walser Funeral Home, 507 Frederick Street, Kitchener, 519–749–8467. The funeral service will take place Friday, December 18th at 1:00 p.m. in the chapel of the Henry Walser Funeral Home followed by a reception. Immense gratitude to our honorary sister, Dr. Alison who helped us all traverse this difficult path with her loving guidance. Thank you also Dr. Stevens and Dr. Hakim, whose bedside manners are professional and caring.

Doc Wid would want you all to remember that "Attitude is everything".

*****

Over the years I have had the privilege of working with over 59 guys who played in the NHL, 40-plus guys who played at the World Junior Hockey Championships and hundreds who have come through our organization. I truly look back at these years in awe. I was a guy who liked hockey, played two sports in University at an elite level, trained like a freak, and because of a dream and belief that I could offer tremendous value, I simply asked to help.

I was given a summer to "try-out" for the team and in the end have been part of 874 Wins, 640 Losses, 63 Ties, and 4 OHL Championships; not bad for a guy who can't skate, eh?

Never be limited by the reality of a situation. Always strive for better and remember that dreams are ideas we just have not tried yet. Once I did, the rest is an amazing history of working hard, playing hard, bonding outside what I knew, and being able to #RiseUpAndExcel.

I challenge you all, think of an idea or goal you would like to conduct in life, and just try it.

The art of doing leads to more opportunities and dreams conducted. Growing up so close to the US border, it exposes us to NCAA Sports, an incredible engine for sports and income.

*****

Growing up, I had always wanted to earn a Division One Scholarship in either football or wrestling. Back in the mid-'80s this was not a reality for a kid from Waterloo, so it stayed a dream.

As my daughter Reighan became to excel in soccer and her team was winning every accolade a team from Ontario could win, her coaches began taking her team to highlight tournaments in the States. As I mentioned earlier, she signed her letter of intent with NCAA Division One St Peter's University in Jersey City New Jersey, to live out her own dream.

I made my big NCAA jump through a University of Guelph Football teammate Jeff Frisbee, who was a professor at West Virginia University (WVU).

He reached out and let me know he was the new General Manager of the school's hockey team and asked for my help. I jumped at the chance and joined the coaching staff. My role was to help set up the off-ice segment of their grassroots hockey development program through their summer camp and to train the guys on the team. They supplied me master's students to function as my eyes and ears while away, and together we trained the players. The best part of this relationship was that I could mentor college students who wished to pursue a bachelor's or a master's degree and set up a career in hockey conditioning. I have the privilege of working with 11 students during my three years with the program.

Headline: Top Strength Coach Joins Division One Staff[8]
Morgantown: June 25th, 2014

The West Virginia University Division 1 hockey team is proud to announce the appointment of Douglas Pflug as Director of Strength and Conditioning

Doug has been a certified Strength and Conditioning specialist for the past 27 years and has trained elite athletes, NHL, OHL, CIS, NCAA and was a National Strength and Conditioning Coach for Wrestle Canada where his athletes competed internationally. Doug has amassed over 35,000+ training hours with his athletes and celebrates that 36 of his clients have played in the National Hockey League and further, 24 of his clients have competed in the IIHF World Junior Hockey Championships.

"We are thrilled that Doug has agreed to join us as the Director of Strength and Conditioning for the Division 1 team. His extensive experience and remarkable professional accomplishments as a coach for the Guelph Storm of the OHL, combined with his additional diverse coaching experiences, clearly demonstrates his appreciation for what is required to succeed at a high level of competition. On a personal note, the strength of character that Doug brings, along with his lifelong commitment to community outreach and mentoring makes him an outstanding role model for the WVU Hockey Division 1 organization. We welcome Doug to the team and are excited to collaborate with him in the future". Jefferson Frisbee- General Manager WVU D-1 Hockey

Doug also holds a University of Guelph Personal Training Certificate and holds his CAN-FIT-PRO Personal Training Specialist Certification. He has completed levels 1, 2, and 3 of the NCCP (National Coaching Certificate Program) in soccer and holds a certificate in Respect in Soccer through the Ontario Soccer Associations ' and Respect in Hockey Certification through the Ontario Hockey League.

Doug specialized in functional fitness, core stability, speed, and agility and 360-degree conditioning.

Doug is a Police Sergeant with 25 years' experience at the Guelph Police Service and lives in Guelph with his wife Michelle who is also a police officer and daughters Reighan-18 and Alexis-10.

"I am thrilled to learn of Doug Pflug's appointment as Director of Strength and Conditioning coach of the West Virginia University D-1 Men's Hockey Program. Doug will bring the same passion, ability, and results to WVU that he brought to the Guelph Storm during his 17-year tenure with the Storm. Many of the former Storm players who went on to play in the National Hockey league owe much of their success to Doug's influence. WVU players are extremely fortunate to have access to such a consummate professional".

—Mike Kelly, VP/GM

Guelph Storm, Ontario Hockey League

Locally the news hit the press as well.

Headline: Pflug joins Mountaineers as hockey strength and conditioning coach
By Rob Massey, *Guelph Mercury* Tuesday, July 8th, 2014[9]

GUELPH—Doug Pflug, a sergeant with Guelph Police Service and the former strength and conditioning coach with the Guelph Storm, will add to his resume.

Pflug has joined the West Virginia University Mountaineers as the strength and conditioning coach of their men's hockey program. A connection from his football days with the Guelph Gryphons led to the position.

"Jeff Frisbee, their general manager down there, played football at Guelph", Pflug said.

A Centennial graduate, Frisbee is a professor in the school's department of physiology and pharmacology. He was a staff adviser for the teams for a couple of years before becoming the team's general manager and president earlier this year.

"We've kept in contact over the years", Pflug said. "He took over the general manager's spot down there and he called me and asked if I wanted to help and jump on board".

The new job does not mean Pflug will leave Guelph or Guelph Police Service.

"I'm going to go down there about six weekends. August 23rd is my first weekend", Pflug said. "I'm going to go down there six weekends and set up a program. I have two pre-med students that want to get into sports medicine. They are going to be my eyes and, as Jeff says, the Doug Pflug down there when I cannot be there for the weekly workouts. Luckily, with technology and stuff like Skype, I can follow all the guys".

Pflug is excited that his involvement with hockey in West Virginia is not limited to the university.

"We're basically going to build the entire program down there", Pflug said. "The neat thing that I've since learned is that there's only about five rinks in all of West Virginia. Their population is about 1.9 (million) so what we are going to be doing there, too, is building a rep hockey program from the grassroots. When I go down there on the 22nd, it has his tryout training camp but there are also camps coming in of peewee kids and bantam kids. We are going to mentor those children.

"Even though you're helping the West Virginia University, it's going to be a community-wide and statewide program that we're going to develop".

Pflug, who has served as the strength and conditioning coach for many local sports teams including the Storm (from 1995 to 2013), Special Olympics floor hockey, Guelph and Waterloo minor soccer, Guelph minor track and field, Wrestle Canada and U of G soccer, will combine some of his trips to Morgantown, W.V., home of the university, with trips to see daughter Reighan play with the Saint Peter's University varsity women's soccer team. She will be a first-year student at the school in Jersey City, N.J., this fall.

The Mountaineers play in the eight-team College Hockey Mid-America conference, one of seven conferences of the American Collegiate Hockey Association. While most of its teams compete in the NCAA, they do not affiliate with that association.

"They won their division last year", Pflug said.

That CHMA win earned West Virginia a berth in the ACHA's 20-team national championship tournament, but they were eliminated following an opening 2–1 loss to Navy. They had been ranked 20th.

"The motto we had with the Storm was, 'Train like a pro to be a pro.' We just want to bring that mentality, that structure and that system into place so we can help them".

AUTHOR'S CHALLENGE

In E. J.'s memory, I challenge you all to fix three things about yourself before you criticize others.

Dreams are ideas you just have not tried yet.

Life is to live, and remember if you can think it, you can work towards it and then do it. What is the worst thing that can happen? You do not achieve the goal? If you reflect, it was not the goal that made you richer with experience; it was the journey you set out on.

In life use the plan-assess-act to solve every problem or plan every personal and professional event you wish to conduct.

For example: I want to lose fifteen pounds:

Plan: How to do it, diet, exercise, lifestyle change.
Ask yourself: What do I need to do to create an environment where I can succeed?
Assess: What do I need to do to fix, do, or find resources to change or implement?
Ask Yourself: How can I implement the plan for maximum efficiency and to work smart versus working hard?
Act: Conduct the plan, always moving, assessing, and acting.
Ask yourself: What can I do to work smart versus hard in obtaining this goal?

Guelph Police Service Chief Ceremonial Unit at the Remembrance Day Parade in downtown Guelph.

NOTES

1. www.buffalosportshalloffame.com/member/e-j-mcguire/
2. www.howlings.net/tag/ej-mcguire/
3. www.google.ca/search?q=guelph+storm+mike+kelly+&tbm=isch&ved=2ahUKEwiJ rJT2uLDwAhUCP80KHY1PBD8Q2-cCegQIABAA&oq=guelph+storm+mike+kelly+&gs_ lcp=CgNpbWcQAzoCCAA6BAgAEBhQyr0EW1POBGCU2QRoAHAAeACAAXalA aIHkgEEMTAuMZgBAKABAAaoBC2d3cyl3aXotaW1nwAEB&sclient=img&ei=_3WRY MmwK4L-tAaNn5H4Aw&bih=657&biw=1366#imgrc=r-MMyNvJp8nLM
4. https://guelphstorm.com/strength-and-conditioning-coach-doug-pflug-retires

5. http://thesleemancentre.com/guelph-sports-hall-of-fame/builders/jim-rooney/
6. www.exchangemagazine.com/corporate-profiles/NeilWidmeyer/
7. https://uwaterloo.ca/kinesiology/news/kinesiology-remembers-neil-widmeyer
8. http://wvuicehockey.pointstreaksites.com/view/wvuicehockey/news-multimedia-1/news-stories-1/news_160237
9. www.guelphmercury.com/sports-story/4621573-pflug-joins-mountaineers-as-hockey-strength-and-conditioning-coach/

My Dream Job

9

It is funny that ever since I can remember, I loved music and found many times that the lyrics of songs seemed written about me.

Whitesnake's "Here I Go Again" came to be a rock anthem to my life, and whenever I faced change because of a negative experience with a relationship, job, position, or coaching opportunity or friendship I would rally around that song. Here are the lyrics and a YouTube link that you can listen to too, rally around and use it to plan your future and work towards personal and professional success. The words from the song personally spoke to me and every time I'd experience adversity, I'd play the song. It's amazing that everything I'd hear, "I don't know where I am going, but I sure know where I have been", a sense of calm and familiarity came over me and I knew that I'd survive. Over the years I have developed the reflective process based on these words and "Who was I? Who am I and who do I want to be?" was born.

Please click on this QRCode to hear the song for yourself and maybe, just maybe it will help you #RiseUpAndExcel.

Source: LyricFind

They then transferred me to supervisor of the Community Relations—School Safety Unit in 2008 and I performed the role of Frontline Media Officer representing our amazing officers and organization.

With this role, I worked for some incredibly special officers who worked in four areas:

1. School Safety—two officers teaching lessons in K–8
2. VIP (Values Influences and Peers)—one officer teaching to grade 7–8
3. HSRO (High School Resource Officers)— four officers that working in and for the schools

DOI: 10.1201/9781003187189-10

   4. Police Service Media Relations Officer and Public Information Officer to the
      Chief of Police

As the Service Media Relations officer, I had the honour to be the voice of our organization in casual and emergent situations. The best part of this job was reporting to the media daily and drawing attention to and highlighting the amazing officers who collaborated with us.

I was coming out of the other side of the chaos and feeling really great about myself. I was practising the skills that it taught me and handled just about everything that had come my way in the past through adversity. I was feeling better about it and moving forward towards living the life I thought I wanted. I had a partner, two amazing daughters, and was coaching several teams. Everyone in my family was healthy, and I had my dream job.

On Labour Day Weekend of 2008, we went to compete at the Henderson Soccer tournament as Reighan and her Waterloo Phoenix competed for the right to an invitation to the Disney Soccer Showcase. It was a great weekend, and we won.

As we drove home, traffic was heavy on both sides of the road, and we shared memories from the victorious weekend. We were going east on the 401 Highway around 5:00 p.m. and then I saw something very odd coming at us in the oncoming traffic. Suddenly a police cruiser shot across the westbound lanes, through the grass median, across our two lanes, through a guardrail, and came to rest on the side of the road.

I quickly parked the car, told everyone to stay there. I ran to see if I could help although I didn't understand what was happening, but I knew this was an emergent situation, and I needed to help a fellow officer. I ran up to the car while trying to take in as much information as possible to Plan-Assess-Act. As I neared the cruiser, I saw a teenaged female get out of the driver's seat. A handcuff hung from her left wrist and she had a police hat in her right hand. She saw me and ran down the embankment. I ran up to the cruiser to see if a fellow officer was in distress and found the cruiser empty.

By this time, the girl was about 20 meters down the embankment, so I ran after her. To my right I saw another male running down towards her. As we ran, adjusting our pursuit angle, we tackled her a brief time later. We placed the handcuffs on her and arrested her.

We walked her back up to the road and saw four to five cruisers flying towards us on the other side of the highway. They saw us and quickly drove through the grass medium and ran to us. Turns out the other male helping me was a Peel Regional Police officer. We gave our names to the officers and turned the suspect over to the police.

I remember getting back in the car and Reighan said, "Dad, that was cool. It was just like TV". I remember smiling and thinking, "I was a superhero to my kids that day", and we drove back to Guelph.

When I got home, I gave my Inspector a call to advise of my off-duty foot chase and arrest to give him a "heads up" in the event he was told about it.

A week later, I was called to attend the chief's office and handed a Letter of Commendation from Waterloo regional Police Chief Matt Torigian.

Dear Chief Davis,
   Re: Sergeant Douglas Pflug #937
   On September 1, 2008, a female suspect engaged in the theft of one of our police cruisers. The suspect was traveling westbound on the 401 near Oxford Road 29, when she lost control of the cruiser. The suspect travelled across the gravel median and onto the eastbound lanes before hitting a guardrail and stopping off the highway. Fortunately,

there were no injuries. Sgt Douglas Pflug was off duty at the time and was travelling eastbound when he noticed the dust cloud and saw the cruiser off the highway.

Sgt. Pflug at once stopped his vehicle to assess the situation and quickly realized that the suspect had stolen the cruiser and was trying to get away. Sgt. Pflug engaged in a foot pursuit along with another off-duty officer and successfully placed the suspect under arrest until Waterloo Regional Police arrived on scene.

We as a police service would like to express our appreciation and gratitude to Sgt. Pflug for his quick and decisive actions which resulted in the apprehension of this suspect.

The accused was charged for Theft and Possession Over, Escape lawful Custody, Flight from Police, Dangerous Operation of a Motor Vehicle, Impaired Operation of a Motor Vehicle and Operation over eighty. Had it not been for the intervention of Sgt. Pflug, this suspect could still be at large and posing a danger to the public.

Sgt. Pflug's involvement reminds us of the crime fighting partnerships we all share as police officers. It is a partnership that goes beyond the boundaries of geography and service affiliation.

Yours sincerely
Matthew A. Torigian
Chief of Police.

I often hear officers state the "Policing is 24/7" and I have serious problems with that because we cannot be on the job all the time. If we do not have time to reflect, refresh, and make ourselves better, we will fall under the weight of years of denial working 24/7. What I agree with in this statement is that although we have off-time, the training that I have gives me a different lens to react to causal and emergent times. I bring the wealth of my training into my private life and when called upon, I am privileged to have those insights and skills to react well. On this day, I was a tired dad and soccer coach driving my family home. When the call to serve came, I could #RiseUpAndExcel in this situation and helped in bringing a dangerous person into custody safely that day.

*****

Professionally, I had the honour of being requested by Chief Bill Blair of the Toronto Police to work for them as a Mobile Media Officer during the G20 Summit. We all saw the chaos when protestors started smashing windows and burning a cruiser, causing extensive damage.

*****

2009: POLICE COMMENDATION FOR MY LEADERSHIP

To Chief Davis from Inspector Maurice Obergan
December 2, 2009

Sir, I know that written commendations usually come from you when it becomes apparent that a member needs to be recognized for their hard work but in this case the situation is a little different. I wish to recognize Sgt Doug Pflug for his efforts with the publication of the first book on the history of the Guelph Police, *Fingerprints Through Time*, and I know you were part of the committee that conducted research for the book.

I was not part of the book committee and feel the need to commend Sgt. Pflug on his efforts with respect to this project. Doug went beyond on the project. He produced the idea after finding some research done by a co-op student in 1984. He spoke to me about having the history of the Guelph Police properly documented and I gave him my blessing. He took initiative and partnered with agencies like the Guelph Historical Society and the Guelph Library for guidance and ability. He then formed a committee involving several retired members as well as current members so that correct information could gather for this project.

Doug worked diligently on this project for more than a year, setting and chairing meetings, assisting with the gathering of thousands of pages of research material, securing writers, editors and finally a printer for the book. Doug spent hundreds of hours of his own time on this project and he never asked for anything in return. The book is not a complete history of the Guelph Police because we would have ended up with a book holding thousands of pages of information. The book is intended to provide some interesting reading with clips about the Guelph Police from its start until now and it does just that. I have read the book and thoroughly enjoy it.

Doug's arduous work on this project did not go unnoticed and I wanted to make sure that you know Doug's leadership and initiative on this project was deeply appreciated by me. Doug's efforts on the project needs to be officially documented and I will be placing a copy of this commendation in his personnel file.

Respectfully Submitted,

Maurice Obergan

2003: PUBLISHED: MANAGING EDITOR— *FINGERPRINTS THROUGH TIME—A GUELPH POLICE HISTORY BOOK*

li

   One thousand copies sold nationwide and $8,000 proceeds from sales were donated to local charities.

   I am also thrilled to have been able to market, promote, and report on the amazing work and members of our police service. They truly made my job easier because of their amazing work and professionalism. Thanks, guys!

   In 2010, they awarded me the prestigious Ontario Association of Chiefs of Police / Ontario Media resource Officers Network (OACP/OMRON) "Media Officer of the Year" Award for Excellence in Media Relations because of a nomination by my organization. This was an incredible honour.

*****

During my years in Community Relations/School Safety and Media, I fondly look back at my four-year stint where I supported the amazing staff that worked for me knowing that they were creating 10,000-plus positive police-youth interactions. I could improve the police-media relationship dramatically, help write the History of the Guelph Police Service Book, *Fingerprints Through Time*, and donated over $10,000 back in profits to local charities.

*****

2010: GOVERNOR-GENERAL POLICE EXEMPLARY MEDAL RECIPIENT[1]

Nominated by Chef Robert Davis for 20 years of full-time exemplary personal and professional service to the community.

   The Police Exemplary Service Medal, created on August 12, 1983, recognizes police officers who have served in an exemplary manner, characterized by good conduct, industry and efficiency. Recipients must have completed 20 years of full-time service with one or more recognized Canadian police forces. Full-time police cadets in training also qualify for the award. Consideration is given only to periods of service for which no other national long service, good conduct or efficiency decoration has been awarded.

In April 2010, my partner told me that she no longer wished to pursue a relationship with me. She readily agreed that she would sign off that I could share custody of Alexis 50–50. I was thrilled because I wanted to stay actively in her life.

We dismantled the life we had shared for eight years, and we sold our house. I found a pleasant house for the girls, and I bought it. Luckily, my ex-partner moved down the street, looking after the best interest of Alexis and schooling.

I was a single dad sharing 50 percent custody with my two daughters to care for.

In reflection, this was such a scary time where I began to practise negative and destructive self-talk on myself. I thought, believed, and told myself daily that I was a loser and not worthy of love or a "normal life". I lost myself in grief and pretended to be normal during that time. When the girls were with me, life was vibrant, joyful, and fun. When I did not have them, it contrasted with being dark, cold, and lonely. I was once again put in a place where I had to revisit the strategies that I learned before to bring me out of the pit of despair and find my light to save my life. I now know that this would prove to be an amazing life-altering change towards the life I had always wanted to win.

*****

Work was remarkably busy, and I was requested to attend the G-20 Summit in Toronto as a mobile media officer, so I jumped at the chance. For a Law Enforcement Media Officer, this was my equivalent to "Grey Cup", my "Super Bowl", and I really wanted to take part.

Leading up to the 20-day deployment, we had to go to the Toronto Police College for two days of intensive training based on the emergent intelligence they were receiving.

This caused me great stress, and I felt vulnerable and did not have my affairs in order. I contacted my financial advisor, bought a policy for $700,000 life insurance, and contacted my lawyer to make sure all my affairs were in order in the event I did not come home. Some may say that this was overkill, but I had a bad feeling about this and yes, through catastrophic thinking eyes, I made the arrangements.

The closure for our house occurred while I was away, and my partner's family really helped me out and moved all my stuff into my new home. Truthfully, that was impressive, and appreciated for those efforts even today. Just because our relationship ended, they continued to treat me with respect.

I then drove to Toronto with all my gear, including riot kit and gas attack kits, and began my 19-day deployment. They assigned me to the Toronto police headquarters in the mobile media unit working 6:00 p.m. to 6:00 a.m. In reflection, this proved to be so therapeutic for me. I was away from my stresses at home, had ample time to think, workout, sleep, and just be Doug for the first time in a long time. I truly began to "repair" during that time and soon discovered myself.

*****

One of the pivotal points in my deployment occurred on Monday, June 28, 2010, 7:45 p.m. I woke up that day around 4:00 p.m. and got ready for work. When I looked out my hotel window, it shocked me to see the chaos that was unfolding beneath me on the streets below. There were thousands of people lawfully marching, protesters mixed in the ranks, there were several public order units in full riot gear, taking up strategic points along the route, and there were two mounted units backing them up. I called Toronto Police HQ, and they asked me to come in right away to help deal with the unfolding chaos. As I ran to the headquarters, I had a tough time processing what was going on. This was Ontario, Canada, and not a country where such things occur. I quickly made my way to work, got kitted up, jumped in our vehicle, and drove towards the chaos to be present for the reports and corresponding interviews. It was around 28 degrees Celsius that day and the full riot gear I was wearing on top of my bullet-proof vest made me boiling and uncomfortable.

We stopped at a point along the route where there were several media vans and offered our help. A young female reporter from CNN-NY introduced herself to me and asked if we could go on camera live and speak about the growing civil unrest, and we agreed. She asked, "Officer Pflug, your prime minister has spent one billion dollars to host this event. Do you think that this is a responsible way to spend this amount of money given the home-lessness issues your country is facing?"

I paused, and answered, "I'm sorry, you'll have to speak with representatives from the Prime Minister's office and . . ." Out of the corner of my eye I saw a darn object coming towards my head at a high rate of speed, ducked, and heard a loud gushy sound or impact. I looked up to see it had hit the young reporter on the side of her head with what looked like a water balloon. She was dazed and looked at me in horror. The water ran down her face and she freaked out and screamed about the water in the balloon. We quickly learned that someone filled the balloon with liquified urine and feces, and when it hit the side of her face, she received the majority. She yelled for the camera operator to "cut" and ran to her news van. She grabbed a towel and tried to clean herself and fix her hair. I saw her grab a cell phone and although I could not hear what she was saying, I could tell she was yelling at the person on the other end, and her body language was extremely aggressive.

She came back to where we were standing and expressed that she was furious that I had ducked, and the balloon hit her. I tried to contain myself but smirked and said, "Sorry, it's my training". I told her we had received intelligence that a few days earlier when the girl made worldwide interest for blowing a bubble in officers' faces that they too were liquified with urine. I asked her if she was going to speak about her experience on camera, and she told me we wouldn't be covering that. I asked why and she said that her news station only wanted answers pertaining to two questions: "Your prime minister has spent one billion dollars to host this event Do you think that this is a responsible way to spend this amount of money given the homelessness issues your country is facing?" and "Why is the police presence so oppressive to people who simply want to march and bring attention to their issues?"

I reminded her about our previous conversation and that I would not answer her question about the Prime Minister. As for her question about our presence being oppressive, I reminded her that the police role was to ensure the fundamental rights to all under the Canadian Charter of Rights and Freedoms of the right to a peaceful assembly. She again asked me the two previous questions and again, I told her to contact the Prime Minister's office and that our presence was not punitive, rather it was to protect everyone that day. She then told the camera operator to turn off the live feed, gave me a dirty look, and said, "Thanks a lot". I challenged her to tell what was really going on, but she refused and told me they did not want that, only answers to the two questions she was asking. I suggested that if she didn't want to report on what was going on, that we were at an impasse and she walked away.

This was truly the first time I experienced what we know as "fake news". The reporter could have easily reported on what was occurring but failed to do so. She and her news agency could have reported on the facts of the day, but they wanted to report on their version of the facts, and my answers did not support their narrative.

When my shift ended that morning, I watched the news and saw a classic shift in what I had known through my media officer experiences with the press. Usually a reporter would in fact check to confirm what they were reporting was true, but this was not the case. What I saw was a massive sprint to get the facts out and many credible news agencies retweeted information quickly. They spread a lot of false information to unsuspecting viewers.

*****

The tour of duty ended, and I drove back to Guelph to my new home with my clean start to my new life.

I continued to get counselling, but it shifted away from PTSI to more basic self-discovery. It was during those sessions and work I truly came to understand one of the huge root causes of devastation and failure in my life.

We discovered that my entire life, because of terrible self-esteem and lack of confidence, that I have placed myself in positions where people needed me rather than wanted to be with me. I only had to look in the mirror and track my life.

- Cop—People need you
- Coach—People need you
- Older Brother—People need you
- Spouse or boyfriend—People need you, but mine had all failed

Once the need was gone in both relationships, they ended because I no longer served a purpose or need.

I went through some very intense emotional sessions after that, and this is where I was first introduced to a positive mindset and how it truly could change the chemistry in your brain. People often laugh today that I am so positive. I am like an Indian rubber ball in a cement room. Well, this happened by chance. It was a very laborious process beginning with each day when I woke up to simply look myself in the eye and say something nice about myself; same thing at lunch, dinner, and before I went to bed.

You cannot lie to yourself or hide from yourself. One day I truly saw the positive residuals of these efforts and now enjoy the happiness in my life.

It is not because I am lucky but rather because I worked my tail off and found my granite. I continue to cultivate and feed it the same way I continue to train my heart, body, and mind.

*****

Looking back, my girls had teased me repeatedly over the years. When we speak of that time they both chime in with "When we were with Dad, it was always BBQ Chicken breast, pastas with sauce, and the three of us would split a bucket of ice cream that we'd each eat with a fork". I also laugh, but it was very difficult for me during those times managing my work, keeping the house clean, and doing a ton of laundry because of the extras of working out and the girls' soccer. It was so easy to come home, turn on the BBQ, boil a pot of hot water on the stove, throw some laundry in, put chicken on the BBQ, put the pasta in the water, homework, dishes, fold laundry, add sauce to the pasta, and eat. The ice cream as a treat for many tasks completed, and then we would begin the girl's bedtime routine. Those days were very tough, and I know I would slide with the chores. Oh yes, we had a dog to care for and I went back to school, so I did my course work when they went to bed.

Wow, looking back I cannot believe I made it through those two years. There was a great deal of blood, sweat, and ample tears of self-doubt and frustration. In the end this did not kill me; it only forced me to focus and be stronger.

FREEMASONRY

With all the change, uncertainty, and feeling that I wanted more out of life, I began to self-reflect and try to figure out who I was, who I am, and move forward to who I wanted to be. I knew at the time that I loved giving back to my community and wondered what my legacy would be when I left this earth. I knew I wanted to be the best dad in the world, one day be loved and respected as an amazing partner or husband, coach, counselor, and mentor but still wanted more.

I also wanted to feel a sense of belonging outside these roles and meet people with a similar mindset of a "service heart".

I had worked for an exceptionally long time and became good friends with Scott Green, who had been my boss often but a good friend. He always wore a gold Masonic ring and one day I asked him about it and what it truly meant to him to be a Mason. It delighted him that I asked him, because they do not recruit people, and we subscribe to 2B1Ask1.

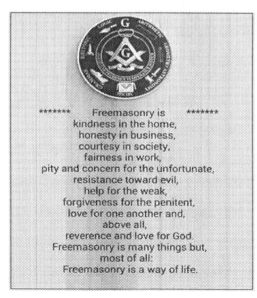

*******   Freemasonry is   *******
kindness in the home,
honesty in business,
courtesy in society,
fairness in work,
pity and concern for the unfortunate,
resistance toward evil,
help for the weak,
forgiveness for the penitent,
love for one another and,
above all,
reverence and love for God.
Freemasonry is many things but,
most of all:
Freemasonry is a way of life.

He further advised that the basic purpose of being a Mason is to make "better men out of good men", better fathers, better husbands, better brothers, and better sons. Masonry tries to emphasize the individual man by strengthening his character, improving his moral and spiritual outlook, and broadening our mental horizons.

I then researched the idea more and found out that the overall benefits of being a Freemason were:

- moral self-improvement
- increased brotherhood
- community
- relief/charity to others
- relief/charity to each other
- leadership skills
- education
- mentors

I was extremely excited to join and asked Scott to aid me in joining his Masonic Lodge 361 Waverly. Our lodge has gold regalia, which signifies that our lodge is over one hundred years old.

As part of this process, I needed to reflect and to ensure that I met the below criteria:

- You must be a man of good repute.
- You must be over the age of twenty-one
- You must believe in a Supreme Being.
- You must be able to support yourself and your family.
- You must live a moral and ethical life.
- You must have a powerful desire to want to be effective in the world.

April 12, 2010, I started and held the position of an "Entered Apprentice".

April 11, 2011, I was "elevated" to the position of "Fellowcraft"

October 3, 2011, I was "raised" to the ultimate position of "Master Mason"

Since that time, I have regularly enjoyed joining over 6 million men in the world as a Freemason and strive to be a "good man making good men better".

Having the support of my Masonic brethren means the world to me. It is a place where I belong and was a piece missing in my life.

*****

When I was the Sergeant in the Media and Community Relations Unit, I was very fortunate to have a great supervisor hierarchy, where I reported directly to Inspector Harry Schnurr, who reported to Corporate Director Shelagh Morris to Chief Rob Davis. The three "bosses" were all nearing the end of their respective careers but remained on the pulse and open-minded towards what the future of policing would be like. With that, the three of them gave me incredible support and latitude to reshape the unit, as I believe would supply better support to the community. This was truly one of the best four years I had with the Guelph Police Service and genuinely gave it everything I could to succeed.

Harry was a popular guy in the police service, and everyone liked him. He had a "surfer dude" haircut, and a balanced life disposition. He was the perfect balance of being the ultimate professional. But do not take yourself too seriously. I look back and I thank him for teaching me this very thing, as it helped me tremendously in the roles both personally and professionally since we worked together.

Shelagh was the civilian equivalent to a Deputy Chief at our organization, and I loved working with her, especially during our weekly chats, where she would share her experience and mentor me on big-picture items. Some men have problems reporting to a female, but I truly enjoyed it because there was no testosterone tension like I've reported in the past and a woman looks at things differently, offering a unique perspective. Gaining Shelagh's respect, confidence, and trust in me through my work efforts and results was especially important to me.

I first really met Chief Rob Davis at my OPC graduation when he held the rank of Inspector and had attended the ceremonies. Over the years I never worked directly under him but was always very impressed that every day he would go to the staff lunchroom, eat his lunch with anyone there, shoot a game of pool or two and chat with our staff. Many leaders distanced themselves from the frontline because of work, responsibilities, duties, and meetings. That was not the case with Rob. Day in, day out, you would always find him having lunch with us.

Through my role in the media, I had the privilege to learn about these three supervisors and not only respect the rank by the person holding it. This lesson would play out to this day, where I always try to sit with people, talk with people and find out their story or their "why" to better understand them and work with them. It is a lesson all leaders at all levels should practise to gain better knowledge during their stay and improve their leadership and organizational credibility.

*****

When I moved into the media, I replaced an officer subscribed to the status quo method of delivery and was also part of the "silo" or "team" that I have referenced earlier. I researched and orchestrated a fundamental change in how we had delivered information to our media partners.

I was glad to work for Harry, Shelagh, and Chief Rob Davis, because they were open-minded and visionaries. They had 100 years of policing experience between the three of them, but they saw the future and wanted our organization as part of it. They gave me free rein to research, plan, and implement a brand new social and conventional media relations strategy. I love this project and promised that I would not let them down. They believed in me and created an environment where I could excel, so there was no way I would let them down.

Sadly, our harmonious working environment opened us up to critics who did not understand it. They were simply jealous of it or did not like me. In retrospect, if they had only asked how we worked so well together for a change and to explain what we were doing, I honestly think we could have prevented such hard feelings.

I just wanted to be left alone so that I could work my ass off on a significant project with my OMRON—Ontario Media Officer Resources Network—colleagues from around the province and potentially to effect dramatic change within my organization, provincially and nationally through law enforcement social media.

The first year, I worked extremely hard to get a system and infrastructure down for the new media relations platform, including a large social media part. This was entirely new, and some people in our organization could not be sure about the benefits. As usual, when people do not understand something, they either fear it or try to shut it down, and some did.

I made some real strides and am enormously proud of what I was doing to promote the fantastic people we had in our organization. With that, I was on the TV and a great deal in the paper. Our goal was to have three to four positive stories per week in the media. With that came some jealousy, and some accused me of being so clear in the media as self-promotion. I laugh because I was not promoting myself; I was promoting others, and I was just the vehicle for doing that. The critics did not understand what we were trying to do or how we were building the new police media relations model in concert with a few other officers in the province-wide committee. Social media was upon us, and we walked.

Harry came to me and said that another Inspector challenged him on my work ethic and devotion to the position.

Harry quickly defended me and suggested I log the hours I was putting into the job and the incredible time I put into it behind the scenes or unpaid at home. Stats do not lie, and Harry used them to fight off this criticism. We found that the average officer works 2,080 hours per year. One year after I catalogued the extra after hours I was putting into media answering the phone calls, monitoring, updating, and responding to our new social media platforms and public appearances, I discovered I had worked 850 extra unpaid hours . . . that was almost half a year's work for free. I would have never recorded this because I was enjoying my job so much under their leadership, but when called to task, we had ample evidence to shut the naysayers down.

I remember this was reported to my police association, and I was called to the task that I was setting a terrible precedent and high expectations for the next officer who'd take on this role. I did not care, so I continued to work on this project with the same passion. The only change was that I did not fill out the off-hours log as precisely as I had in the past. This was not about money to me; rather it was about going at it 110 percent and achieving our desired results. In the end, after one year from the launch, I'm proud to say that we had one of the best social media and conventional media relations platforms for midsize police services in the country.

This later proved valuable when I was selected to attend the RCMP Senior Police Administration Course at the Canadian Police College. We had 24 senior officers (Inspector and above) in our class from all over Canada, Hong Kong, Grand Cayman Islands, and England. This was an amazing course and opportunity for a young Sergeant.

As part of our course of study for the three-week course I was assigned a topic based on an identified organization need from our own service. I then needed to write a business case concerning an issue with our organization. I authored my paper on splitting the Media and Community Relations Sergeants position into two separate roles based on the recorded "lieu time" and increasing demands of the job.

Years after, the unit split, and two sergeants took over.

*****

In the end, Harry had to go to bat for me several times because of similar criticism. It was a positive because it forced me to tighten up my game media, my planning, and documentation of what I was doing.

Our Director of Corporate Services, Shelagh Morris, began stepping in as well. She was getting frustrated that some people were taking runs at her guys. I am very thankful to have such support at such elevated levels in my organization; it prompted me to try even harder. Harry, Shelagh, and Rob created an environment where I could succeed, and I worked my tail off to not let them down.

Near the end of my time in Media, Shelagh did me the honour of nominating me for the Ontario Association of Chiefs of Police and Ontario Media Relations Officer of the year award in 2011, supported by Chief Davis, and I won.

They then invited Michelle and me to the Annual OACP conference at the Deerhurst Inn in Huntsville, Ontario, and celebrated my victory with all the Chiefs and Senior officers in Ontario. It was a fantastic night because I promoted the people I worked with. This further reinforces Robert Ingersoll's quote, "We rise by lifting others".[2]

What caused me grief and caused me to set a higher standard to a new media relations level in Guelph? Thanks for that naysayers; you helped force me to up my game, and now I am enjoying a heightened level of accomplishments and job satisfaction—all because you said that I couldn't and in response, I illustrated to you I could.

*****

I always marvel at the criticism some people have towards others in organization. You see it in every business and government organization. People like to look at what others are doing and in some form of self-imposed version of warped justice complain and if it's not by the same rules or templates as others, they decide you are wrong and that they are right . . . so you become a target.

I have often been the target of people who either do not like me or like how I do things or live my life. I joke that they should spend more time focusing on themselves than focusing on me.

Truthfully, I am not that entertaining and do not know why people waste time focusing on my life.

E. J.'s rule appeared again: fix three things before pointing your finger or attention towards me.

*****

I remember one weekend when I was in the media that they called me out to aid with an industrial gas leak at a factory in Guelph. I quickly went to work, put on my uniform, and went to the scene. When I arrived, I realized that I only had my Guelph Police baseball cap that most uniformed officers wore versus the official forage cap that I normally wore.

I went on camera with the young reporter and answered the questions put to me.

When I got home that night, I received a call from my Grandma Lily, who lived in Waterloo. She always watched the evening news and would repeatedly call me to tell me she saw me. On these occasions, she was a little short with me and I asked her why and if she was okay. She went to state, "Dougie, you looked terrible on TV today. I can't believe you appeared as a representative of the Guelph Police on TV wearing a stupid baseball cap". I tried to explain that this was the average uniform hat we are to wear, but she would not hear of that.

She told me she was going to call the Chief of Police in the morning and I laughed.

I went into work the next day and after some time I was summoned to the Chief's office.

Chief Davis said my Grandma called to complain about the hat I wore. I was so embarrassed because this was not my parents calling my boss, it was my Grandma.

I explained to the Chief that Grandma was very proud of her father, who served in Canadian Military in the First World War and that all her six sons all took part in some form of cadets when they were young. She loved her men in proper uniform. I let him know she felt the ball cap was not formal enough to wear to stand for the organization properly, and she said, "I looked like crap".

We then discussed how our police association had fought for years to wear the ball caps. Now I wanted something different because of my grandma. We discussed the issue for a few minutes, he dismissed me, and I went back to my duties.

The next day, he called back to his office, and I once again feared what Grandma Lily could have done.

He asked me to close the door and come sit down. He grinned and said, "Doug, tell Grandma Lily she's right and you can wear your forage cap for media duties. As far as you are looking like crap, I cannot change that you are ugly". We both laughed, and I was dismissed.

We often joke how the millennials are very coddled in society and they do everything for them, even complaining to their bosses. Here my Grandma Lily took the charge.

Years later, in 2007, when Grandma Lily died at 95 years of age, I let the Chief know. I asked if I could wear my formal dress uniform at her funeral. He quickly agreed and said, "Of course. We don't want to let a fine lady like that down".

Chief Davis headed the Guelph Police from 2000 to 2012, and I greatly appreciate the way he treated me and helped me develop.

Chief Davis served as a police officer for well over 40 years, and one of the most important lessons I learned from him was to have an open mind towards progress. I reflect on the time when I spend hours creating a proposal to create a social media platform for our organization. I prepared an amazing hour-long presentation. When I began, he cut me off 10 minutes in the presentation and said, "Let's do this". I told him I was dumbfounded because I had another 50 minutes of presentation to do. He looked at me and said, "Doug, it's a great idea. I like it. No need to spend more time talking about it. Let's do this".

The embedded lesson: Regardless of where we are in our professional careers or personal lives, we must always stay open to new and innovative ideas.

There is immense pride in knowing that you helped build the bandwagon that others will one day jump onto.

As time has passed, he and I have developed a nice friendship over the years

Thanks, Chief Davis, for going beyond in your leadership role and making my Grandma Lily feel special.

*****

I genuinely enjoyed working for Harry, Shelagh, and Rob, and we have become good friends. They all retired a few years later, and I truly hope they are "living the dream" in retirement.

AUTHOR'S CHALLENGE

The next time you are researching a project I would like you to review and reflect and try using my model:

**Take it,
tweak it,
make it better,
make it yours
and move it forward.**

NOTES

1. www.gg.ca/en/honours/canadian-honours/directory-honours/exemplary-service-medals/ police-exemplary-service-medal#:~:text=The%20Police%20Exemplary%20Service%20 Medal,more%20recognized%20Canadian%20police%20forces.
2. https://www.goodreads.com/quotes/8119455-we-rise-by-lifting-others

Sgt Pflug Goes Back to the Uniform Division

10

In 2013, they told me I would be going back to uniform and joining the supervisory team of two fantastic police leaders.

Our Staff Sergeant proposed to us that her leadership model was that of a flat horizontal triangle. By this, she meant we were all equal, and all had a say in how we were going to run the platoon, and we all had an equal share in the work. She advised that the only time we would make the triangle vertical was when things would come down from our Senior Leadership team. She would function as an umbrella for us and shield us from the weight of command.

About two years ago, I again heard a similar analogy while listening to the Jocko Willink TedEx Extreme ownership YouTube video,[1] where he says that he "would never allow the weight of command to burden his men".

We did a lot of splendid work as a supervisory team together. We had to rise and lead one fateful day when one of the younger officers, Jennifer Kovach, had died working a night shift in a motor vehicle collision. I remember walking in that day and heading to the general office to check in, as I always did with the night shift supervisors. I was quickly brought up to speed and prepared for work and the corresponding lineup.

We met our visibly upset officers, and we tried to navigate this horrific and horrible time. The Chief came in and addressed our platoon that day, and we all set off to work our best that day.

That day was a blur for us as we tried to lead and be strong for everyone that day under the weight that we lost one of our own.

Later that day, I was called by Gloria, her mother, whom I had to know for years, and asked to attend her home. I quickly made my way and sat with her for hours in support.

This would later become the worst day of my career, remembering Jen, but also the proudest as we honoured her memory.

The National Post wrote, https://nationalpost.com/news/canada/guelph-police-officer-26-killed-after-bus-slams-into-cruiser

DOI: 10.1201/9781003187189-11

GUELPH POLICE OFFICER JENNIFER KOVACH, 26, KILLED AFTER BUS COLLIDES WITH CRUISER

Guelph police say Const. Jennifer Kovach was responding to a call when

THE CANADIAN PRESS

Publishing date: March 14, 2013

A young woman who fulfilled her childhood dream of becoming a police officer was killed Thursday when she lost control of her cruiser and crashed into a bus.

Guelph Police Const. Jennifer Kovach, 26, was a vibrant, gregarious, and dynamic woman with a sense of adventure, Police Chief Bryan Larkin said.

"I cannot say enough about what an incredible human being she was", he said at a press conference.

"There are no words to express our sorrow. There are no words to express our sadness".

Kovach was responding to a call when her cruiser hit a Guelph Transit bus shortly after 12:30 a.m.

The bus had no passengers at the time and the driver, who had only minor injuries, provided "significant care" to Kovach, but after firefighters managed to extract her from her cruiser and she was taken to hospital, she was pronounced dead, Larkin said.

There was a light snowfall at the time and investigators are looking into whether road conditions were a factor, Larkin said.

"Const. Kovach was responding to a call for service in assisting another officer with a frontline call", he said.

"Regrettably, we believe [she] lost control of her cruiser and crossed the centre line and struck a transit bus".

Kovach, who loved her dogs and riding motorcycles, was at the start of a promising career, fulfilling her childhood dream to be a police officer, Larkin said.

"I think that from a perspective of the chief, one of the greatest challenges is to see somebody with so much potential, with so much energy, taken from us so soon", he said.

"If you talk to the members of her platoon . . . Jennifer did not come to work; she came to make a difference in the city of Guelph. She came to touch the people of the city of Guelph and she came to actually give back".

Kovach had been with the force for four years.

Her family instilled in her the value of public service, Larkin said. Kovach was the daughter of Gloria Kovach, a long-time city councillor and former president of the Federation of Canadian Municipalities.

Mayor Karen Farbridge expressed her condolences to the Kovach family in a statement Thursday morning.

"There are no words that can adequately express our sorrow over their tragic loss", she wrote.

"We also recognize this is an exceedingly challenging time for our Guelph Police Service, who have lost a member of their service. We would like to express our gratitude for their brave service and assure them that Constable Kovach will always be remembered for her sacrifice to keep our community safe".

Kovach is the third officer to die in the line of duty in the history of the Guelph Police Service, and the only one since 1964.

Ontario Premier Kathleen Wynne said she was saddened to hear of Kovach's death.

"She was so young, with such a promising career ahead of her and her presence will be missed on the job and throughout her community", Wynne said in a statement.

"Ontario owes a debt of gratitude to Const. Kovach and all of our police officers, who do so much to serve and protect the people of this province".

The next day plans were under way for Jen's police funeral. The colour party that I was a member of was released from our frontline duties and assigned to learn how to properly perform the ceremony under a Toronto Police Drill Team Officer's guidance.

As a team, we practised ten hours per day for four days straight with the end goal of honouring Jennifer's life of service, our members, and the organization.

As I reflect, I vaguely remember the funeral that day. We put so much pressure on ourselves to elevate our limited drill skills and honour Jen. I have watched the YouTube video footage from that day and have no conscious recollection of that day's events. Over the years, I have come to the believe that this was a way that my heart, body, and mind tried to protect me.

RIP JK72

*****

Later that summer it was a hot and busy night. We were working nights and I was the Road Sergeant. I remember we were so busy with fights downtown, domestic violence calls, mental health apprehensions—it was a complete gong show.

All our units were tied up and the calls continued to grow on the board—we needed officers freed up to respond to the tough calls that were coming in. I went to the hospital because we had six to eight officers tied up on mental health apprehensions and two officers per apprehension in attempts to speed up freeing the officers up.

I was called to the triage section and met a woman who was six months pregnant, knocked out by her spouse, and then sexually assaulted while she lay unconscious on the floor. I took him to the quiet room and spoke with her about why she was there. A nurse told me that her brother-in-law had arrived to retrieve her, only to find it was the accused. I walked into the waiting room only to learn that he had fled, knowing she was talking with the police already.

We were so busy that night that I called my staff sergeant and recommended that I take the call. Over the next few days, I could get a statement and find out the level of violence she had experienced.

I later found and arrested the male, and they held him in custody.

I remember reflecting that I was nearing my end in policing. It tired me dealing with the multiple levels of violence one person could inflict upon and others I had seen over the years. Here, the violence was inflicted on an unconscious woman, six months pregnant, and her unborn child.

In 2013, I was transferred to the 911 Communication Centre as a sworn supervisor. This initially shocked me. I was a police officer, and what did I know about supervising civilians?

As luck would have it, my stay was short back in uniform, and after nine short months, they transferred me again.

*****

I served on this platoon for eight months and was again called to the Deputy Chief's office and told that I would be reassigned. I protested the move because of my family situation being a 50 percent dad and the disruptions this would cause with their mothers. The transfer was not negotiable, and I was instructed to prepare for the move.

I remember thinking back that my expiry date was coming faster than I thought it would as I lost faith in our organizational leadership and strategic planning.

I asked the Deputy to explain why I was transferred from Media to Uniform to Communications in ten months. I also explained how destructive this was on me professionally and on my family as well.

I have never been the type of person, nor do I respect the person, who idly complains and does not think about problem-solving or action. I have and always will encourage people who had an issue to come to me with three solutions, much like I learned through

E. J. I also discourage people from coming to me to bitch. It is negative, unproductive, and a complete waste of time.

With this third transfer in a few months in mind, I decided I had to practise what I teach and not give an answer. With that, I shifted my focus and mindset for the short term and transitioned my focus from "me to we". In doing so, I refused to complain about a problem and began a process where I improved my education, curriculum vitae, résumé, and interview skills. In the end, I tried several times for Corporate Executive Security jobs, and after each one, I improved my game. I knew I was close because the organizations all received hundreds of applications. I was winning interviews and finished in the top three to four in each case because they respected my experience. The only drawback was that I did not have corporate experience. I always thanked them for the debrief, improved my game, and I took a step closer towards a goal that I had yet to think about or place in my sights.

*****

When I arrived in "Comms", I teamed up with two incredible police leaders, and we quickly tightened up as a supervisory unit. They were both promoted to the rank of Inspector and I am so proud of them and for their families.

Our primary goal was to make this place less toxic, more enjoyable, and a place where people wanted to come to work instead of hated to go to work. I wanted it to sound like a place you would work in.

We actively met with everyone in the unit and asked them what they needed to succeed. We also asked how we could make them want to come into work and focused on their personal goals for their careers.

We received some genuine and harsh feedback, and we made a list to prioritize the top three issues and collectively made our plan and assigned roles within that.

One task I had was to write performance evaluations for every staff member because we found that some had not received one for over five years. For the next year, I reviewed as many calls for service as I could. I wanted to generate a personal inventory of success for each member, so that when I authored the report, it was for them and about them.

In the end, my efforts and those of the other supervisors contributed to a change in thinking, and the unit took a more positive tone that I'm sure increased after I retired.

I went into the unit, and I found that going outside my supervisory zone to this division proved to be a fantastic opportunity for personal and professional growth.

I quickly earned elevated respect for these folks, and they came to learn that they are the first line of police. When you called 911, my staff were the ones who answered the call and not only got information to help the victim but also to the attending officers going to the call. In the end, they tried to get as much information as possible to assist victims of crime and ensure that the attending officers could get to the call and leave the call safely so they could go home to their families.

I served with these fantastic folks for over four years and saw firsthand the stress resiliency and management required to perform such an essential role within public safety. As I further collaborated with them, I was proud to become part of their unit and further advocate for them.

In reflecting, I have much respect for the 911 Communication Centre folks and have become somewhat of an advocate for them in many roles I have.

The biggest revelation I have learned over the years is that the Com Staff are the actual first line of policing—even before the police officer in the car.

Just think, a lady calls 911 because her husband is beating her. Statistically, the average woman experiences domestic violence 35 times before the police become involved. Now, if she gets a caring and compassionate person on the phone and continues to talk, they just possibly saved her. Think about the child who calls 911 because "mommy fell" and again about the caring person who answered the call.

I have heard many uniform officers criticize the Com Staff because they have done see what they do or arrest a person. In defence, a police officer gets a hot call and they have time to draw on training and experience to plan. They get there in adrenaline-charged state. Communication Centre staff deal with the emergent situation and intimately calm things down; officers on the other hand have to opportunity to de-escalate their heightened state by arresting the suspect, processing them and then completing all the necessary paper work. The attending officers arrive with an adrenaline-fuelled involvement, in this case, was respectfully 20 minutes.

In contrast, the 911 call taker is sitting there, receives the same call, gets an adrenaline surge. They hear the woman, crying, speaking, getting beaten; they get as much information as they can to send the officer there and try to help them arrive safely. The officer books out, they stay on the line until the officer tells them it is okay. They hang up, and the next call comes in, over and over during the 12 hours shift.

I think you can respectfully see that in a 12-hour shift, an officer may have 60 minutes of stress but can come down. A 911 call taker may and usually stays in that heightened state for 6, 8, 12 hours, depending on the night. When they get home, they crash and get up the next day and do it all over again.

*****

I was recently interviewed on two podcast episodes on the www.thetacticalbrekdown.com outlining the realities of stress management and resiliency for 911 call takers. I hope in the process I earned their respect and gave some options or tools for a plan to deescalate the adrenaline surges so they can enjoy their downtime.

To further this point, I learned how to call take so that I could better assess their performance and fill any gaps during peak times. That training challenged me, but sitting on the floor during coffee breaks, stress breaks, or filling in when someone wanted a holiday proved precious.

One of my basic tenets of leadership is that influential leaders were great followers first, and you cannot lead if you do not have followers. I honestly believe being trained as a call taker earned their trust, and respect from my staff spoke volumes.

The only side note was that they weighed my usefulness at the time versus all the mistakes I had made in data entry and they needed to fix. This generated many laughs during the time I worked *for them*.

When I received word that I was transferred, I did not fully realize that this experience was necessary for my career development. I genuinely believe that if I had not worked here, then I may not have earned the right to work at the Ontario Police College teaching the Communication Centre Supervisor Course.

In reflection, one incident that genuinely challenged me on multiple levels involved a sudden death that turned out to be a homicide. From the time the call came in, I was in awe at my three staff members' levels of expertise. I jumped on the admin phones to ease that workload on them. I bought them pizza and had it delivered to the station because they worked through their breaks and lunch hours because of the call's severity.

When the call was over, I stayed late and gathered the stats from the increased workload and sent a nomination for the three of them for a Chief of Police Commendation.

Two days later, I was called into my Divisional Inspector's office to discuss the nomination. I thought he would praise the nomination, but instead I received a formally negative document to my surprise. As we talked, I learned that the Deputy Chief took exceptions that

- I sent it too soon
- I listed in the nomination that it was a homicide when it had not been qualified yet
- I did not use the correct form, and that I was on the awards committee and should have known better. I had sent it through an email

I respectfully protested the documentation and left the office. As I walked away, I realized and knew my time with the organization was nearing its end. I was excited, though, as we were hosting the Special Olympics Spring Games and that our past Chief had groomed me and attended four similar past events to be Chair of the games in Guelph.

The organization announced the Games Chair and it was not me. I was upset, but then asked for the opportunity to chair the opening ceremonies committee. I was not given this opportunity, let alone any other significant roles.

I was furious and insulted. I had been a Special Olympics coach for over 25 years, and on three occasions, my floor hockey team won back-to-back-to-back Canadian Championships. They qualified for the World Special Olympics Floor Hockey Championships and won a silver each time, in Boise, Idaho; Japan; and Graz, Austria.

Bearing this in mind, I am sure you can see why I was angry, hurt, and disappointed.

I must give a great deal of credit to my good friend Steve Gill, who was appointed as the opening ceremonies Chair. He knew how hurt I was and asked me to join his team. In the end, we worked together and had an incredible opening ceremony, where I used contacts to have the Mudmen and Suzie McNeil perform in the opening ceremonies. The Special Olympians and their families had an epic time.

The games were an enormous success due to all the amazing volunteers that joined. And as we set up for the closing ceremonies, we learned two hours from the start that the guest speaker was unavailable to attend because of unexpected sickness. I quickly called a friend, Jim Barker, who was the General Manager of the Toronto Argos, a professional football team in the Canadian Football

League, and asked for his help. He told me he would arrange a speaker and asked that we send a cruiser to the university of Guelph football field, where they were hosting their training camp and he'd send a special guest for us. When the cruiser arrived, we found out that Canadian icon Mike "Pinball" Clemmons was going to take over.

This was the beginning for me, realizing that my time with the Guelph Police was ending and that I was nearing my expiry date. I took this exclusion hard but tried my best to make the Special Olympics event epic. I was fortunate to be in a wonderful place in my life and had built my resiliency skills to an elevated level and felt that I could almost deal with anything.

A week passed, and a member of our Senior Team approached and asked me what my retirement plans were as I was in my 26th year of policing. I responded I was unsure yet, and they advised, "Well, you are not part of ours". I walked away angry, knowing I gave everything to the Special Olympics spring games and even saved the closing ceremonies and now I was treated this way.

A few weeks later, there was a ceremony for people who contributed a considerable amount of time towards the games. They did not invite me. Each member received a Special Olympics Gold medal to reward their efforts.

My good friend Paul Turner, whom I have coached within Special Olympics Floor Hockey for many years, was furious. He came to a practice a few nights later where I was training the guys and presented me with his gold medal in protest. Thanks, Paul!

I sat atop the Staff Sergeant's promotional bank, a goal I had worked incredibly hard for, and waited for my turn to come up.

A short time later, I drew deep with my resiliency tools and strategies when I was told that another high-ranking officer told them, "There is no way I'm going to retire so the likes of Doug Pflug can get promoted". I felt the surge of anger, which I quickly diverted to the positive and addressed the guilt I felt for looking for a job out of policing.

A few years later, I heard this officer was retiring and opted out of a retirement func-tion. The person said we could have one for him in a phone booth, and that there would still be lots of room left.

I felt pity for that police leader; our job is to be inspiring, promoting an environment where we have followers and then assisting them in becoming the future leaders that will one day take our place. Instead of developing others, gaining trust and respect, he left and faded away. True leaders transcend the period they lead well past their expiry day; this man did not.

*****

One day in October 2015, I received a call from one of my Gryphon football players who needed help. In training camp each year, I would do the "good citizen" talk with the play-ers and give them all my cell number. I told them I'd be there for them 24/7, but I only had one rule; when you called: don't tell me your name, just say it's one of the players. That way I felt I could speak with them and help as a person with police knowledge rather than as a police officer, which may have put me in a conflict position.

The player said he was inexperienced with alcohol and had too much to drink the night before. As they walked down Gordon Street Hill, they saw a pizza delivery car. The player admitted that he ran to the car door, reached in, and stole a pizza. As he ran off, the driver took chase and then there was an altercation. Police were called and they charged him with robbery.

Given the circumstances, I thought the charge was a bit too much, given the stupidity behind it versus a truly guilty mind. I told him we needed to do some damage repair now regardless of what his lawyer might advise.

I instructed him to:

- abstain for consuming alcohol
- seek drug and alcohol counselling
- write a letter of apology to the driver
- find out from the officer how much the damage was and pay it
- go to the Guelph food bank and donate community service time with 100 hours as our goal
- write a letter to the court for wasting its time and provide them with an in-depth bio on who he was, who he is, and who he hoped to be in the future. Also, to let them know how such a serious charge could affect his future, bearing in mind he is only 18 at the time of the offence
- schedule a meeting with our head coach and throw himself on his mercy in attempts that could stay on the team and keep his scholarship

Then when the case came to court, they would hopefully consider that he was a young man who made poor decisions and apply the mercy of the court.

As we successfully navigated the process when I was called into the Professional Standards Inspectors' office. I walked in thinking nothing of it, only to find that I was being served notification that I was being investigated under the Ontario Police Act for misusing my position as a police officer mentoring the player through this process.

I was the given written notification and treated like a criminal when he put me on the following conditions:

- Not speak with anyone on the team
- Not attend the university of Guelph at all
- I must plan to meet my professor for the course in fourth-year history I was taking off campus
- Not speak to anyone about this
- If I disobeyed this notification, I could be disobeying a direct order and be subjected to an insubordination charge

I was furious with the way he managed it, but he is one of the few senior officers who took many liberties causing me grief.

And again, he was in front of the line.

First, they should have called in an association representative because I later found, this "bail" type document he forced me to sign was against my rights. Further, I said I had holidays to attend a Spring Florida training Camp with the football team as a chaperone, and he did not care. When asked about the course I was taking, again he didn't care and followed up saying that should I breach any of the conditions, that would make up a further charge of insubordination.

They floored me; I was embarrassed, angry, and extremely disenfranchised with my organization.

As I left the office, he told me that my mentoring youth was putting me in a conflict situation and that he would be watching me. I tried to reason with him but he would not agree or see it my way. When I was a Sergeant on the desk, people would call in or people I released from custody would all ask how they could make the courts see them as people who made a mistake. I routinely gave the same information to them and still do since this fiasco as well.

This man did not stay open-minded and illustrated what a poor leader he was.

In February 2016, they again called me into this office and served another notice that showed they had done a thorough investigation and concluded that I did nothing wrong.

He said that although he would punish me, he still felt that my suggesting a specific lawyer in the city was a breach. I was furious and asked him why, and we debated the issue. I would have been extremely honest as I am here, but I sent the football player to a specific lawyer. This lawyer was a good friend of mine who would treat the player fairly, not gouge him for money, and who also played university football himself. Who better to defend my player than a lawyer who understood both university disciplinary processes and the criminal code?

The inspector paused and said, "Well, that makes sense".

A month later the crown attorney and defence counsel made an agreement: they dropped the charge from Robbery to Theft Under $5,000. In the sentencing, the judge commented on all the effort my athlete put into illustrating what a great kid he was and that this one night, although terrible, was not a reflection of who he was. He received a conditional sentence and probation for two years where he was to keep the peace and be of exemplary behaviour. If he did, the charge and conviction would be erased from his record and not affect him in the future.

The justice system truly worked here.

The lesson I truly learned and took forward with me with my staff was mess up, dress up, 'fess up, and move on.

This inspector could have shown me some decency as a police officer and human being, but he chose not to, and that's on him, not me.

As for that Inspector, we would butt heads again in years to come.

A few years later, I met the President of the Ontario Police Association at a social event. He had once been partners with my wife, Michelle. As we chatted about this story, he wished he would have known about it when it occurred. He relayed that this is simple harassment and they had no right to impose conditions on me to abide by from the Professional Standards Division. He further said that it was my fault for not involving my police association but understood given the type of core values I had. He concluded the Inspector took advantage of those.

*****

As I look back, I am so very thankful for the opportunity to collaborate with some terrible leaders who targeted me over the years. I refuse to let them be a negative entry in my memory bank, rather than an opportunity where I was forced out of my comfort zone. I used my resilience tools and experienced tremendous opportunities for personal and professional growth. As you read, you will see this repeatedly. Someone has knocked me down, I stood up, dusted myself off, and moved forward as my only possibility. I have done that, I do that, and I will do that each time I face adversity. That is my promise to myself.

Had I not, I would not have been motivated to #RiseUpAndExcel.

In a warped sense, I would shake their hands today because they did not shoot me down as intended; they elevated me. Thanks, guys.

During my positive self-talk, I often think in the face of adversity, "Next time you try to knock me down, make sure you knock me out cold. You'd better, because if you do not, I am going to get up mad and determined. Success will be my revenge".

*****

As fate would have it, I applied for high-ranking executive positions on two separate occasions. I had made it to the final two candidates for Executive Security roles with Scotia Bank and Manulife Financial. Each time I was told I did not win the job competition, I felt guilt for trying to leave my organization early. After this statement, I never looked back or let that person strip me down. Instead, I used the comments to help me #RiseUpAndExcel and fuel my future.

This did not deter me from my task; it challenged me to better myself knowing that a guy who had no corporate experience finished second twice against all the other candidates. I was motivated and continued to research, learn, and better myself knowing that one day I'd get my chance and when I did, I wanted to bring my "A" game.

Leadership 101, according to Pflug: always focus on the "we" and not focus on the "me".

*****

I don't relay these stories to whine, bitch, gripe, or lay blame. Instead I want to illustrate that in every situation, whether positive and negative, we can learn to from them and experience personal growth. I am simply trying to frame the good and bad leadership I experienced, how I dealt with it, the lessons learned, and how I moved on and hope that you will also.

With these experiences in mind, I became very motivated, knowing my expiry date with the Guelph Police was over and that retirement was fast approaching. I put the resiliency tools I learned from my past and went back to school.

Years later I met Michelle Chamberland on a chance meeting, and we formed a friendship, became best friends, and got married. More on that later. But this is the perfect time to illustrate her wisdom, love, and support for me.

What I thought at the time was an anchor turned out to be a great motivator, and in the end, I earned four certificates from the Cornell University Leadership School in:

- Change Leadership
- Managing for Execution
- High-Performance Leadership
- Executive Leadership

In these courses of study, I learned the concepts of positive mindset and followership concepts. These two simple concepts became a very dominant driving force in my life at the time and set the groundwork for the discovery of my granite and who I am today.

It is easy to look back now, but we always realize that we must always seek learning opportunities in everything for reflection, education, and to move towards personal and professional growth in negative periods.

In 2015, there was a job posting at the Ontario Police College as a Leadership Instructor, and I jumped at the chance. I did extensive research and planned on sending my application, and with the love and support of Michelle, I was called to interview for the position and notified shortly after that I won the position.

*****

The last time I ever saw that Inspector was at my retirement badge presentation ceremony at Guelph City Hall. I left the Ontario Police College and went straight there and had my OPC uniform on. As I stood there with Michelle and several senior command members, he walked in and right past us and sat down. I thought this very odd because he knew I would be there and why. Further he should have at least acknowledged Michelle, knowing that she was a visiting Sergeant from another Police Service, but he did not. When the event was over, everyone but him stood and shook my hand in congratulations as I walked around the room. When I approached where he was sitting, he looked down at his phone and ignored me as I passed by.

Right up to the end he proved what I always thought about him: he was a deficient leader and it was never about the "we" in our organization, it was always about the "he". I truly hope he finds his way one day. The Dash poem reminds that we still have time to change the way we are remembered when we leave this earth.

It is truly incredible to shut my eyes and try to remember the 28 years of my career, and it is blurry. I believe this to in part because we faced and dealt with so much human tragedy seeing how one human can abuse or treat another. It is as if my mind has intentionally created the blur to protect me from myself, my memories, and feelings at the time.

Sgt. Doug Pflug
Badge #937
Sept. 2013 - Sept. 2017
In appreciation of your
service and dedication to the
Communications Unit

My Last Day at Work September 3, 2016
Special Thanks to Chief Jeff DeRuyter, Inspectors Garry Male and Dave
  Pringle, and S/Sgts Tom Gill and Jeimy Karavelus, who bought breaky
  and lunches for me my last week at the Guelph Police Service.

****

The next day I started in the Leadership Unit of the Ontario Police College and have not looked back. This role that I now have with the recruits and senior students is the most rewarding experience that I have ever had my over 33 years in policing. I genuinely love that I have the opportunity to shape the future of policing through the community policing and evidence based policing course I teach the recruits.

On the senior side, I teach the Frontline Sergeant Course and Communication Centre Supervisor Course. It is extremely rewarding to have redeveloped each course with all the positive and negative leadership examples that I have seen over the years. In each case we look to the good and take it, tweak it, make it our own, and implement inspirational leadership. Conversely, when we find poor leadership, we simply try to do the opposite and strive to be the best leaders possible.

*****

It is funny how some popular media today portrays a generalization that all officers are hiding under or covering each other up under the "Thin Blue Line". I have found the opposite, though, over the years, as I was never part of this type of clique and found that once again, you said nothing to anyone about these experiences back in the early 1990s—instead you either sucked it up or moved on. There was no way I would let anyone take my dream, so I put my nose to the grindstone, worked my ass off, and in a few short years earned the right to a transfer to the detective office as Young Offender Detective in 1996.

Ironically, I thanked these guys in my mind for being jerks; their action woke part of me up, and through negative reinforcement, challenged me to be better.

We all need to take what we like, tweak it, make it better, and then make it our own. Conversely, please take what you didn't like, do the opposite because you know how it negatively affected you, tweak it, make it better, and make it your own.

I will be sincere and say that I was very naïve when I started policing; I did not understand or have the tools to deal with all the trauma I'd be part of. In retrospect, I truly wish we had the R2MR[2] training (Road to mental readiness) that the recruits receive today. I genuinely believe that this would have supplied my skills to fend off what I saw, processed, internalized, that woke me up at night in terror.

It is truly incredible to shut my eyes and remember some trauma during my career, some blurry elements. This is our body trying to minimize the trauma we faced. This is impartial because we met and dealt with so much human tragedy and saw how one human could abuse or treat another. It is as if my mind has intentionally created the blur to protect me from myself, my memories, and feelings.

I have found the opposite. Excellent officers strive to hold others accountable, and the bad ones are trying to bring the outstanding officers down as though in a shark tank.

This perceived "Blue line" of absolute protection of all is, in my mind, an illusion.

I was never part of a clique at work and always tried to live by my drumbeat backed by more core values of honour, integrity, passion, and accountability.

Honour: Do the right thing because it is the right thing to do; rules matter

Integrity: What I do when no one is watching

Passion: Life is a gift, so live every second of every day

Accountability: To God, family, self, community, and career

More on these later.

*****

Truthfully, I have no desire to hide or protect a lousy officer under the Thin Blue Line veil of secrecy rhetoric. I will not allow such conduct to put my core values and those associated at risk. There was no way I would let anyone take my dream, so I put my nose to the grindstone, worked my ass off in every role I have.

Ironically, I can now reflect on the negative influences from my past and truly thank them. Their action(s) reminded me of what the right thing in life was to do, woke part of me up, and challenged me to be better through negative reinforcement.

AUTHOR'S CHALLENGE

Do not let someone's inability to focus, strategically plan, or lead impair your ability to lead. Look at every situation as a potential space for you to experience tremendous growth, and after some time and effort, you will achieve it and #RiseUpAndExcel.

NOTES

1. https://www.youtube.com/watch?app=desktop&feature=youtu.be&v=ljqra3BcqWM
2. https://www.youtube.com/watch?v=WyF8RHM1OCg

Who I Am?

Rebirth Out of the Ashes and #RiseUpAndExcel

11

Mary Margret's strategies took several frustrating years to practise—perfect for my specific needs and implementing a plan for future success. I was a single dad with two amazing daughters and kept up my coaching duties because there were positions of stability where people needed me in their lives. I also realized that I wanted more professionally instead of being a complainer or negative entity at work, so I enrolled in the Cornell University Change Leadership Program.

Part of my counselling dealt with the two failed relationships I had and what factors I owned in them.

As I began this internal journey, it came down to "Fatty Pflug". It was that scared little boy rearing his ugly head again, and the associated lack of confidence in myself that had plagued me. I discovered through counselling why I was a police officer, coach, mentor, and why I had failed relationships.

I always put myself in situations where someone may have needed me, not wanted me. Then, when the need was over, so too was my use. Part of my development was to learn to like myself and see "who I was, who I am, and discover who I wanted to be". To this day, I find it remarkable how such a simple formula can reap such fantastic insight, thought, planning and execution for the person and professional success in the future.

Through my story, I hope to provide you with the same understanding and ability to look at your own life, see how a simple and average guy can deal with trauma, learn from it, develop resiliency skills, and plan future work towards that.

The second thing that I learned supported the first; I needed to like myself, work on myself so that when and if I met someone in the future, I'd be giving her my best self. To offer anything less than that would not be fair.

As I have said in the past, I am very impatient. When I invest time and effort into a cause, I like to see dividends like most do. However, that didn't seem to be the case, and I spent many sad and lonely nights alone when I didn't have the girls.

During this time, I grew not knowing what was in store in the future. Let us remember back; life is about growing to be that exact person at the precise time in the correct time.

During the summer of 2010, I was seconded to the Toronto Police Media Unit as part of the thousands of officers who also attended to provide law enforcement presence at the G-20 Summit. I worked as a mobile media officer from 6:00 p.m. to 6:00 a.m.

DOI: 10.1201/9781003187189-13

and, during those 20 days, had much time to reflect on my life under the stress of the situation.

I returned home and moved into a small house I had bought for the girls and me, and we started fresh.

One day in mid- to late-September, I was in a horrible place. It was late at night, and I knelt on the floor, closed my eyes, and threw my arms in the air and asked God what his plan was for me. I recommitted myself to him that night and told him I was ready as tears ran down my face. I asked for a sign, lay down in my bed exhausted, and fell into one of the best deep periods of sleep I had in years.

I woke up the next morning to a new sense of calm and clarity in life, and I knew I was going to be okay.

I explored my new perspective on life. Things tasted better, life felt better, my family and friends meant more to me, and I saw the world through optimistic eyes of possibility. I truly finally felt love and peace and tried to give that to all those I held most dear.

As I progressed, I tried to "live every second of every day" and experience 100 percent of everything I did. I saw this as a second chance, and there was no way that I was going to miss anything from this point on.

Reflecting, this was the last time I have been that low, but I'd instead look at it as that was the starting point of the rest of my life, and I haven't looked back.

Little did I know at the time that my entire life's experiences, both positive and negative, were moulding and shaping me to be a confident person, at a specific time, on a certain date for a meeting of chance.

*****

When I got home from G-20, I received a call from my friend and fellow OMRON executive member Sgt Pierre Chamberland, who worked for the Ontario Provincial Police. He and I had been friends for three years and from time to time he told me he should introduce me to his niece, who was also a police officer. He felt that we would get along great. Each time I declined because I had several bad dating experiences and wanted to focus on my girls and being a dad.

Pierre congratulated me on my work at G-20 and again insisted that I allow him to introduce me to his niece, and again I respectfully declined.

Early in 2010, Pierre and I were at a meeting and on the break. He walked up to me, smiled, and again offered to introduce me to his niece. I told him I had just started dating a nice girl and wanted to focus on that and give the relationship a chance to see where it went. He understood, and the matter was closed.

*****

On December 4, 2010, I went to Niagara Falls, New York, to the Outlet Malls with my friend to Christmas shop for the girls. Having my friend with me immensely helped, so I did not think like a guy when I bought the girls' clothing. It was a fun day just hanging out with a female friend, no strings, just enjoying each other's company.

We got home around 5:00 p.m., tired from the power shopping we did.

My friend called me up and told me to come over because he wanted me to meet someone. I respectfully told him no and that I was used to being alone, and it was best that I continue to work on the "new me". We went back and forth, and I eventually gave in. I quickly showered, threw on some clothes, and cologne. Hell, if I am doing this then I might as well try to make an excellent first impression.

I arrived at his house around 7:30 p.m. and we had a drink or two. He was a police officer and a real estate agent. He told me he would have to break off for a bit because he had a client coming to the house to make an offer on a property up the street.

A brief time later, his client arrived. We had a brief introduction, and then they went into the kitchen to prepare the paperwork. I remember discreetly watching her in awe as they worked. I know it is a cliché, but I fell in love with her that day from our micro-introduction. The young lady was not there to meet a future husband; she was there on a mission to buy her first home . . . and that she did that night.

The next day I called my friend and asked if he would see if she wanted to meet for coffee. I was saddened by the news she was seeing someone else.

I thought, wow, I finally met someone, and she was dating someone already.

Over the next few weeks with Christmas coming soon, I was preparing to take Reighan and Alexis to Disney for Reighan's soccer tournament. Even though I was busy, I could not get the memory of that chance meeting out of my mind.

A few days before Christmas, I saw my buddy was calling me and answered the phone, and he said, "You must have made a great first impression; Michelle has given me permission to give you her number to call her". I called her right away and found that she had a terrible cold. The intention was not for me to reach her that instant, but maybe a few days later, so we laughed.

We spent a great deal talking on the phone and scheduled our first dinner date in Guelph. It is so funny to think back because I was embarking on meeting my best friend, soulmate, and wife . . . and I did not even know it.

She showed up at my front door and looked incredible. I tried to speak with her, but I froze and retreated to the kitchen. Yes, I ran away. She politely let herself in, I regained composure, and we had an incredible night of food and conversations fuelled with hope and possibility.

The next day I spoke to my friend and told her what an amazing time I had. I asked her what the proper time or dating etiquette was before I called her again. My friend pointed out that it was a few days before Christmas and that I might want to wait until after that, so I did not appear desperate. I was faced with a dilemma: let her know I had a wonderful time versus being a stalker. So, I took the plunge and called her, intending to tell her I had a great time, wanting to wish her a Merry Christmas and let her know I'd call after I got home from Florida.

Little did I know that ironically, Michelle was having similar conversations with the guys who she worked with on her shift.

We spoke for about 15 minutes, and the conversation moved to the dating rules or etiquette. Michelle laughed and let me know she had an exciting time and wished to see me again. I then laughed that I was taking dating advice from my two female friends who were single, so what did they know?

Michelle suggested that bearing in mind all the caring and supportive advice that we had received we should do this by "Our Rules" and we readily agreed.

"Our Rules" became the backbone of our relationship; and we have the phase inside our wedding rings. It's the licence plate on our golf cart "Larry", and we have named our 1995 Sea Ray 270 SD boat "Our Rules".

*****

We spent New Year's Eve apart that year because she was with a friend in Toronto and I was at a hotel with a team of 16-year-old girls and their families in a hotel at Disney.

One time early in 2011, near the beginning of a relationship, I told her a story where I perceived I failed. I was extremely vicious, and she asked me to stop and listen. She then asked me one question that changed my life then and to this day, "Doug, would you let me treat you the way you are treating yourself or let me say the nasty things about you like you are saying?" I answered, "No", and she rebutted, "Then tell me why it's okay for you to talk to and about yourself that way?

Bam, ouch, points received and taken.

*****

I have shared this reflective story with many people since that day. They too find direction, compassion, and empathy for themselves because of Michelle's kind gesture towards me.

In 2012, Sgt Ryan Russell of the Toronto Police died in the line of duty. Over 10,000 officers from Canada and the United States attended his memorial out of respect.

I attended with my fellow officers from Guelph and Michelle with her Peel officers. She texted me she had saved me a seat inside where it was warm, and I eagerly sat with her.

As we left the service, she asked me to come with her to meet her father, who was a serving RCMP member. As we arrived at the area where the RCMP bus was parked, we found him. Michelle introduced me as her friend, he turned around, shook my hand, and said "Hello" and turned away to talk with other officers. I thought that I made a bad first impression.

As we walked away, I could see my friend Pierre walking our way and as he got closer, Michelle hugged him and said, "Uncle Pierre".

Can you imagine how I dumbfounded I felt at that moment when I realized the very girl my buddy Pierre wanted to introduce me was Michelle, whom I had been dating almost a month. Now if that is not fate . . . !

Thank God I was not a slimeball and took the number.

Several months later I would meet Sara and Louis when we visited their home in Ottawa. Louis offered me a beer, and as we chatted, he explained he was very embarrassed over our first meeting. He told me that when he returned that day, Sara questioned him on what he thought about Michelle's new boyfriend. He said that he was shocked because he knew he gave me little time and had known I was the "new" boyfriend and not just a friend, he would have been far more inviting. We both laughed and have shared many more over the years as loving son- and father-in-law.

We were married two years to the day we met on December 4, 2012, and inscribed in our wedding bands is "Our Rules" Since that time, we have purchased a boat and golf cart, all having the "Our Rules" name on them.

A dear friend once told me that over the 15 years of friendship we shared, this was the first time she ever saw me genuinely happy.

The wedding party—Playa de Carmen, Mexico

I am genuinely the luckiest person on earth. At 54 years of age, I have two amazing daughters, my parents are both alive, I am in excellent health, and I had the privilege of marrying my best friend, Michelle.

People often ask me what the secret to our relationship success is, especially looking back at my two failed relationships.

The answer is straightforward:

Rule #1: Do want Michelle tells me to do.
Rule #2: If all else fails, go back to rule #1.

But in all seriousness, we have four simple rules that we live by and share with younger couples we co-mentor:

1. Always speak "with" each other and not "to" each other.

Communication is critical, and it must have active listening and active hearing. When a couple cannot communicate, they cannot grow. So, put down your electronic devices, put on some soft music, and have a glass of wine. Please sit back and speak with each other and when you ask about their day, wait, and listen to what they have to say.

Also remember that when you are telling each other about your respective days that it is not a competition. I have counselled many young couples where one or both are police officers.

When you have a difficult day and come home and your loving spouse or partner asks about your day, do not shield them from it; respectfully share it. Once you are done, be sure to ask them about their day as well.

When your spouse relays their day and a bad part of it, do not trivialize or marginalize what made the day bad. One of the best ways to shut them down or out would be to say, "So today someone was rude at work? I dealt with a sudden death. So you are comparing my dead person to a rude person? C'mon!"

Remember that perception is reality. If your partner shares their difficult day, it is not to be competed with. Separate your day and their day as distinct incidents and help each other out. Complete grief or stories will only push the wedge between you further and hopefully not to a point where they decide they are better off without you than with.

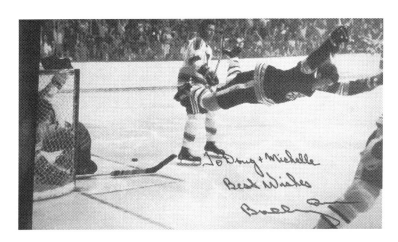

2. Never end the date you are on until you plan the next one.

Life is busy, I get that, but this is not an excuse. Dating is how you met someone, fell in love with them, and decided you wanted to spend the rest of your life with them.

There was a time early in our relationship that we juggled two separate 50 percent child custody schedules on top of two different travel soccer teams going four to five nights per week. My family lives close, Michelle's is in Ottawa, and Michelle has a four-week rotation and I have a three-week rotating shift schedule. Throw in some time for sleep and the other basic needs of life, and that is one hell of a busy "life schedule".

We dated each other for the rest of our lives and have been doing so for ten years now. With that in mind, when we are on that date, we plan the next one and hold each other accountable for it.

This enables us:

- To be accountable to each other. It sucks when you plan a date with a buddy for beer or wings, and if you miss, you both get it, and we have no hard feelings. Michelle and I owe it to ourselves to make sure we keep that date. It allows us time alone and time to remember why we got together.
- Sometimes our schedules would prevent us from seeing each other for seven days straight except for kisses or passes when we got up or got home from work when the other was sleeping. Having the date night made the time away more manageable, knowing we were both fully committed, but it also gave us something to look forward to after the sacrificial seven days we had to be apart.

3. Let each other know the set of ears they should use when you talk with them, so you do not set them up to fail.

One time I came home after experiencing some conflict at work, and as I told her the story, she offered her opinion several times and tried to solve the situation with me. At one point, I politely asked, "Why don't you just listen to the complete story?" She came back with, "Then why didn't you tell me what you wanted before we started?" I blew that one.

We have the following communication rules:

- Do you want me to help you solve this? or,
- Do you want me to listen?

This proves to be a simple but effective cornerstone of our relationship communication, and we never set each other to fail again.

4. Ask What level of detail they wish to know. Know your audience.

We were both police officers and extremely fortunate to have both answered every type of call for service possible. With that, Michelle is the scientist and loves those gritty details, and I am a storyteller and love those.

Sometimes she conveys the gritty scientific facts and loses me much like the old Charlie Brown cartoons. I remember when we went to Chicago for the Annual Blood Spatter Pattern Analyst Conference. The one evening, it was "present a case" during dinner. After about ten minutes, let us say the pasta on my plate was no longer appealing. I do not need that much detail.

On the other side, I must elaborate more to pique Michelle's interest in my stories.

Funny story: One night, Michelle and I were on our "date night" after several days of missing each other. We were understandably happy to see each other and bring each other up to speed with what we had been dealing with at work.

We were at our favourite Italian restaurant, Buon Gusto, in downtown Guelph. I have a slight hearing issue and can get loud.

As we began talking, sipping wine, and eating dinner, our stories went back and forth much like a Wimbledon Tennis Championship Final.

Suddenly, I stopped, looked around and saw that all the people at nearby tables looked shocked in horror. Our stories were not what they had called "proper dinner conversation". We laughed, shrugged our shoulders, and started talking about less work and more about vacation stories.

I am sure our nearby table neighbours appreciated that.

*****

We genuinely hope that this share enables you to experience some of the many joys we have had and plan to have in the future.

This method will later come through introducing your life planning in the Four Cornerstones when I ask you:

"WHO WERE YOU? WHO ARE YOU? AND WHO DO YOU WANT TO BE?"

Similarly, the same model works for relationships; I ask you to reflect and plan your relationship:

"WHO WERE WE, WHO ARE WE, AND WHO DO WE WANT TO BE IN THE FUTURE?"

*****

Over the years, I have spoken with many retired officers, and the most significant piece of information or advice I harvested that I'd like to share is that we all have an expiry date in what we do. With that said: do not retire from something; retire to something.

This small piece of advice motivated me to go back to school and improve myself and prepare for the next step, not knowing what that would be.

I had always really enjoyed leadership and how to inspire people. One day, I spoke with a colleague who said that he had enrolled at Cornell University Online in the Leadership program. I researched the program and found that Cornell has ranked 18th in the World. According to www.CIO.com, the eCornell Leadership Certificate program is ranked in the Top 15 programs along with Harvard, Georgetown, Notre Dame, and Penn State, to name a few.

Cornell University offers several leadership certificates through eCornell, the university's online school. Certificate programs include entry- and high-level leadership programs, including a technology-specific leadership course. You will also find programs for women in leadership and courses covering topics such as change management, digital leadership, business strategy and the psychology of leadership.

The instructor-led courses are held online and take, on average, two weeks to complete. To earn your certificate, you will need to complete multiple two-week courses; certificate programs through eCornell take, on average, two to three months to finish.

There are so many new online universities popping up daily, and I thought that if I was going to invest in myself, then Cornell was the one I wanted to enroll in.

As I began the course, I thrived. It exposed me to incredible material, which genuinely helped form the basis for the leadership style I wished to develop and lead others professionally. This became somewhat of an "academic addiction", and in the end I invested over $20,000 in myself while using my work education allowance to cover $8,000 of that.

We must always invest in ourselves before we can ask others too.

I am proud to say that I earned a certificate in:

2011: Change Leadership
2013: Managing for Execution
2013: High-Performance Leadership
2016: Executive Leadership

In reflection, I am so glad that I had the foresight and drive to go back to school because these four certificates supply academic support towards my real leadership. I completed these courses at night when the girls went to bed to not interfere with being a "dad".

It was also ironic that when I was advised that I was being transferred to the Communication Unit, that I was not happy because it was not on my existing professional plan.

I have always tried to embrace change and promote positively into my next tasks, regardless of how I initially felt about them. Sometimes we just must put faith in ourselves or whatever we believe in and "do the work".

I was not aware that another fork was in my road in 2017, when I saw the job posting for the Leadership Unit at the Ontario Police College.

Trust in knowing that had I not gone back to school or had the Communications Unit's experience, I would not have earned an interview and won the job competition. What is the old saying—failing to prepare is preparing to fail? So always seek opportunities to continually learn, grow, and be ready for what might be around life's next corner.

Teaching the Communication Centre Supervisor Course is one of my primary teaching responsibilities.

AUTHOR'S CHALLENGE

Take some time and sit down with your spouse on a lovely, quiet, relaxing evening and create your relationship plan for success in both casual and emergent times using our model for success.

1. Always speak with each other and not to each other.
2. Never end the date you are on until you plan the next one.
3. Let each other know the set of ears they should use when you talk with them, so you do not set them up to fail.
4. Ask what level of detail they wish to know. Know your audience.

Dash Leadership

12

DOI: 10.1201/9781003187189-14

BACKGROUND

My Aunt Audrey was my dad's youngest sister and a lovely lady who made amazing pecan pies. She teased me, saying that she always sped to and from work in Guelph but that I'd never catch her. This good-natured and loving, teasing session was a ritual when we met at family events. These events usually involved 20–40 people as we had an enormous family on my dad's side; there was Grandma Lily, three aunts, six uncles and spouses, nieces, nephews, girlfriends, boyfriends.

Pflug family chaos organized it, and we all fit in that small pre–Second World War farmhouse on the corner of Erb Street and Bluevale Street, Waterloo, Ontario.

Each time I would go to my grandma's house, I'd see two apple, two cherry, and two lemon meringue pies cooling on the freezer in the back kitchen. We'd go into the small house and squeeze ourselves in amongst all the people, and I would gravitate to where Aunt Audrey was sitting to perform a little Intelligence small fact finding mission to see if there was a pecan pie hiding somewhere.

When she saw me, she would stand up and call me over and give me a big hug. She would then call me out in the family with her loud voice and tease me about being a young rookie officer who could not catch her daily, Monday to Friday, every week, and she sped in and out of Guelph to go to work. She would continue to poke good-natured fun to provoke my many aunts and uncles into thunderous laughter.

As we neared dinner time, I would always discreetly let her know I saw the back kitchen and ask her if she had time to make me a pecan pie, and she'd play our game and let me know she didn't. I joked I wished she had, then she would pull me close and whisper she'd hid one in the back kitchen on the fridge so no one would get it.

We would laugh, and I would eventually eat half the darned pecan pie; it tasted so good.

Aunt Audrey had a hard life. She was young when my cousin was born a few days after me, and back in 1969 the unwed mothers were frowned upon and scorned. She worked her tail off at Imperial Tobacco on Woodlawn Road in Guelph and tried to supply a lovely home for my cousin to grow up in. My uncles all stepped up and tried their best to fill the vacant father role in his life.

DOI: 10.1201/9781003187189-14

In 1996, she was shovelling the snow at her condominium townhome when the shovel hit a sidewalk curb and jammed into her stomach, causing her to rupture internally. Her body had been weakened by years of alcoholism.

In speaking with the attending officers, they said she called 911, and they found her in severe medical distress on the floor beside a bucket of bloody water. They told me she did not want the police, fire, or ambulance to come into a dirty home. She died shortly after because of massive blood loss.

As the family prepared for her funeral, I received a call from Grandma Lily asking me to go to her house.

Grandma Lily was enormously proud of her father, a decorated soldier in the First World War. As my uncles grew up, they all were part of some form of army, navy, or air cadet system because Grandma told me she always loved a man in uniform.

I reflected on my February 1990 Police College graduation and a picture that I still have of Grandma Lily and me and the loving, proud smile as she walked with me in my "Number Ones".

He requested that day that I get permission to wear my "Number Ones" and say a few words at Aunt Audrey's funeral in honour of a hard life lived but with the loving comments from her nephew.

I contacted my Chief the next day and explained this request, and they granted me permission. That is what you did back in those days. They also instructed me to call the Waterloo Regional Police out of professional courtesy and let them know where I would be in my "Number One" police uniform, and for how long.

I spent a great deal of time writing my eulogy piece and met with the minister doing the other half. During this meeting, he introduced me to a new poem that he found that provided people comfort and a plan to bring life from death. That poem was The Dash Poem written by Linda Ellis.

He said that this was a simple poem Linda Ellis wrote one afternoon in 1996 that forever changed her life.

Linda authored the poem when she was working for the top executives of a large and successful corporation with a strict and tense working environment. It seemed to her there were far too many worrying more about making a living than making a life.

Also, words from a letter she had read were resonating in the back of her mind. The wife had written these words of an employee who was aware that she was dying:

Regrets? I have a few. Too much worrying about finding the right husband and having children, being on time, being late and so on. It did not matter. It all works out, and it would have worked out without the worries and the tears if I would have known then what I know now. But I did, and so do you. We are all going to die. Stop worrying and start loving and living.

Her words stuck with Linda and made her stop and think: This is it. This is all we get.

The Dash has indeed affected millions. The poem's words have convinced mothers to spend more time with their children, fathers to spend more time at home, and people to reunite with long-lost loved ones. The words have changed attitudes and changed the direction of life. They have, in their way, made a difference.

That was a very intense day for me, and I had to dig deep down to use my emerging resiliency skills to be an enthusiastic, caring, and compassionate voice at the funeral. I wanted my part to be to bring life back to my aunt's show that was silenced by a premature death. I wanted to give her honour where some thought the addiction was a choice, rather than a mental health disease.

As the eldest male nephew, I wanted to show my family that I was ready to assume some more significant roles and responsibilities in our family.

When the funeral was over, we all migrated to the refreshments room when my uncle came over and told me Grandma wanted to see me right away.

I quickly found her sitting in the corner, eyes full of tears. It devastated her as we all would to have a child die. She told me she was immensely proud of me that day, thanked me, and kissed me on my cheek.

I reflected and was so happy that I could capture Aunt Audrey's joy for life and even made the congregation laugh a few times where she would have demanded laughter.

As we left the funeral home, we were all blown away to see that my brothers and sisters from the Waterloo Regional Police provided a police escort front and back of our long procession that left downtown Waterloo to Memorial Gardens just outside the city limits.

It was a gesture not requested but given out of respect and professional courtesy.

*****

This public speaking opportunity, although quite sad, really speaks to my interest in doing more and exploring the chances of leadership and future promotion at my organization.

I earned my Coach Officer Designation and successfully trained four new officers. In those days, they rode with us for 60 shifts. The first 20 were in observation mode, the next 20 were 50/50 observation and doing police work, and the last 20 days I was the trained observer to ensure we were meeting performance goals and service standards. I enjoyed those roles because I had a passive role in how our organization would look like training officers the way I was trained or should have been. It was here that I began practising the "take what you like, tweak it, make it better, make it your own" and "look at the things you didn't like and do the opposite for success" training theories.

Around 2002, they appointed me as an Acting Sergeant through a chief's order. By this time I had 13 years of policing experience, including ten years on the road, three years in the detective's office, and breath technology. I performed over 150 subject breath tests, was a niche officer who fingerprinted and photographed newly arrested persons, coached four recruits, and was ready for the next advancement.

As an Acting Sergeant, my role was to fill in when needed when there wasn't a road Sergeant working and be a resource to the officers on the road and an experienced set of eyes and ears on the road for our Sergeant or Staff Sergeant who was on the desk as the Officer in Charge.

This was an excellent experience for me in that it allowed me to cut my supervisory teeth, practise the leadership skills I valued, work for my people and my bosses, and work towards the betterment of our team. In this role, I reflected on how important our job was, but equally how vital our home lives were.

Another one of my leadership practices was born, and that was to return everyone home safely to their respective families each night—a goal I hold very close to my heart and instruction today.

This role also made me more resilient as a supervisor as well, and many times I would relay on the many earlier leadership skills I had developed to assist me moving forward.

I have tremendous respect for this role in the police, where it can empower and equally drown. Your organization sees something in you and believes in you to have this chance to earn supervisory experience, which makes you feel quite right. Sometimes your shift has problems because they see you as a buddy, but when you must make hard decisions, they see you as power-tripping and selling out.

As an Acting Sergeant, you fill the role one day, then next you are back with the guys, which can be a tightrope to walk.

The other problem that may arise is from a more senior officer on the shift who has either become disengaged, jaded, was passed over for transfer, or had no desire to lead. When such an officer calls you out in front of the others, do not get into a battle; wait for a quieter time to discuss this. In doing so, people will watch to see if you overreach. When you do not, you will generate respect from them and the experienced officer. Hopefully, you can meet and resolve this. You cannot ignore it because it will fester and undermine your authority, but use your conflict management skills to work through tissue effectively.

I teach all new supervisors on this tightrope walk that you have done an excellent job informing as a constable if they know your core values. If you became a supervisor and are challenged that you are power-tripping or sold out, remind them that the decisions you made were not based on your rank, but instead on the core values they came to love and respect as a fellow worker.

Sometimes when you fill these roles, it is not about your change, the way they see you. Do not take on someone's baggage on the inability to see the difference.

Remember, this is their issue and not yours. Do not let it become one.

*****

I talked to everyone I could from various disciplines, read many leadership books, autobiographies of influential leaders, and anything I could find to better myself and prepare myself as a leader. Please remember that this was 2002 and pre-dated the huge leadership gurus, books, internet, YouTube, etc., we are flooded with today. In retrospect, the funny thing is that even though the volume and means delivered are significant, good leadership traits are still the same.

Lead with a service heart, take care of your people; they will follow you and take care of you.

Several years later, the market was flooded with professional athletes' autobiographies and corresponding leadership stories. While I genuinely appreciate some struggles these people may have made, they are not like me. They were born with some God-given ability to translate into millions of dollars one day.

This is one of my major reasons for authoring this book; I am an everyday person just like you. I was born in an average house, had an average life, but I found it within myself based on triumphs and failures in my life to conduct some cool things.

AUTHOR'S CHALLENGE

How do you want to be remembered? Start thinking about your "Dash".
    More on this later.

Understanding Their "Why"

13

As we have taken this journey through this book, I have shared many examples of times they bullied me, how it affected me, the resiliency learned, and the plan to move forward. You will be asked to do several exercises in the coming chapters to help you define your "why" through a journey of self-discovery under my "who was I, who am I, and who do I wish to be?" model of #RiseUpAndExcel.

As you formalize your process and have a better understanding of your "why," you must then understand the "why" of those who resist us, bully us, or try to push us off our tracks. Do not allow them to succeed as you move towards personal and professional growth and corresponding future successes that you are destined to achieve.

A friend of mine recently shared an article by Dorothy Suskind, PhD, entitled, "Why Are You Being Bullied at Work? Colliding Characteristics of Targets and Bullies That Lead to Workplace Abuse".

I have to say that after reading the article, I truly believed that she was speaking about the journey I have had over the past 54 years of life in both my personal and professional lives.

As I reflect on the article that I have included for you, I genuinely wish I had read it many years ago because I feel that if I were better able to understand the resisters' "why" in my life, I would have been better able to comprehend their action towards myself or even deal with them better. Therein lies a dilemma: I am happy they targeted me, which enabled the growth versus if I didn't let them get to me, I wouldn't have had the opportunity for growth.

The author showed that there are six reasons they may target you in the workplace or life.

- You are well liked by others
- You are non-confrontational
- You are highly skilled
- You are internally motivated
- You are curious
- You are highly ethical

Review the article below and understand their "why". As you better understand your "why", remember that the attacks are not based on what you are doing, but rather what they are not doing. Trust in knowing that you *will* be targeted as you begin your journey towards your own personal and professional growth.

DOI: 10.1201/9781003187189-15

You will be targeted by those who are:

- Less liked by others
- More combative
- Less skilled
- Less motivated
- Less curious
- Less ethical

In the end, it is a compliment when we view this process through optimistic eyes.

I hope you enjoy the article and are better understanding how their "why" is trying to alter your "why". As you prepare for battle, remember the words of Mike Murdock, "Attack is the proof that your enemy anticipates your success".

Why Are You Being Bullied at Work?

Colliding Characteristics of Targets and Bullies That Lead to Workplace Abuse.

Dorothy Suskind, PhD Posted February 5, 2021—Posted with permission.

Targets of workplace bullying are often generous creatives who foster community and search for innovative solutions to knotty problems, characteristics that contribute to the success of the organizations they serve. So why are these top performers sometimes targeted for abuse on the job?

Let us meet the players. The Namies (2009), founders of the Workplace Bullying Institute, use the following adjectives to describe bullies: Unpredictable, controlling, manipulative, and jealous. In contrast, targets of workplace abuse are thought of as innovative, competent, altruistic, and highly ethical. If you were to write these eight adjectives out on index cards and lay them upon the table, the opposing natures of the two descriptions are readily apparent, offering insight into who gets bullied and why.

To dig deeper into the bully's selection process, below is a description of the top six defining traits of targets of workplace abuse, according to research, and why they trigger bullies to pounce. As you read, notice how bullies' need for control and power thread the narratives (Carbo, 2017; Duffy and Sperry, 2014; Namie and Namie, 2009).

1. Well-Liked: Targets tend to exude positive energy. They stop colleagues in the hall to see how they are doing and listen intently as they share. When a peer is chosen for an award, selected to work on a big campaign, or secures a record-breaking bonus, targets are often genuinely happy for their friend's win. Colleagues enjoy targets' company and often comment on their warmth and authenticity.

Bullies may become jealous of targets' perceived social capital and spread gossip to tarnish targets' reputations and get them excluded from work meetings and social events. Bullies often employ the tactic of the "silent army" in which they tell targets how "everybody" was gossiping about them after work but do not supply names or details. These stories are often purposely fabricated in order to shake targets' confidence and make them feel like they do not belong.

2. Nonconfrontational: Targets tend to be community builders, making sure each person feels like he is part of the team. When someone speaks to a target harshly or leaves her out of an important meeting, she makes the most generous assumptions about the behavior. She may think to herself, "I imagine he is just having a difficult day", or "She probably didn't realize I was not on the calendar invite".

Bullies seek power through the path of least resistance. When they make a move and meet with aggression, the bullies will usually retreat and seek out a new victim without claws. Bullies may be attracted to targets' kindness and benevolent worldview and set out to take advantage of their good nature and forgiving spirit.

3. Highly Skilled: Targets tend to be top performers in their field. They have rich content knowledge and others often seek them out for advice. It does not take long for targets' ability to shine through, resulting in well-earned accolades and promotions.

Bullies, on the other hand, may give the illusion of success, pretending to be experts and top producers. A peek behind their masks, however, reveals bullies' tendencies to offload work on others, take credit for colleagues' ideas, and deflect responsibility anytime someone questions their competence or work ethic. Bullies are often intensely jealous of targets' expertise, so in order to maintain their Oz status, they employ manipulative tactics that enable them to hide their lack of skills in the shadows.

4. Internally Motivated: Targets are in competition with themselves, internally motivated to beat their last efforts. The satisfaction of a well-written article, a thoughtfully run in-service, or a successful product launch is a reward. Targets tend not to require a saturation of external praise to maintain their self-worth.

Bullies' fragile ego, in contrast, typically relies on constant validation for a job well done. They are more interested in public praise than personal growth. Perplexed by targets' inward confidence, bullies may become frustrated when they cannot negatively affect targets' level of performance by withholding their admiration and approval.

5. Curious: Targets often have an innate curiosity that calls them to be astute observers of their surroundings. They notice the small problems others have become accustomed to and are not timid about asking questions. Interested in growing their knowledge base and appreciative of diverse ability, they reach out across departments and communities to expand their understanding and perspectives.

Bullies are interested in control and power. Targets' propensity to question often shakes the status quo and calls attention to cracks bullies prefer to keep hidden. Reliant on a steep hierarchy for power, bullies become frustrated when targets make new connections bullies perceive may weaken their role as gatekeepers.

6. Highly Ethical: Targets tend to be altruistic, working to do the right thing even when turning a blind eye would be professionally helpful. If wrongdoing is uncovered, targets first try to work through the designated organizational channels to achieve resolution. Though nonconfrontational by nature, if those attempts are ignored or rebuked, targets' high ethical standards often charge them to become whistleblowers, despite placing themselves in harm's way.

Bullies tend to be interested in appearances. They need the press release to be glowing and the reviews to be solid. If targets point out problems and shortcomings within the organizational walls, bullies may become frustrated by the exposure and shift to blame, shame, and cover-ups. When targets blow the whistle, they will be subjected to bullies' tirades, wrath, and character assassinations, with the most probable outcome of targets losing their jobs.

In closing, it is important to note that it is not the targets' fault they get bullied, for the traits they possess are exactly the ones top companies seek in the hiring process. In contrast, the aforementioned list serves as a call to action to enact protective workplace legislation and adopt strict anti-bullying policies to retain top performers and cultivate work environments where employees are encouraged to be curious, motivated to be kind, and inspired to innovate solutions to problems that hamper growth and stifle the community.

Bullies not only damage targets, they collapse organizations. Everyone wins in a bully-free workplace (except the bully, of course)!

AUTHOR'S CHALLENGE

If a bully sets his sights on you, quickly understand his "why" and use that as confirmation that he is jealous of "who you were, who you are, and who you hope to be" and #RiseUpAndExcel.

The Four Cornerstones of Personal Leadership

14

After my Aunt Audrey's funeral, I reflected deeply on my "Dash" that would one day be on my tombstone and what I wanted it to stand for.

What four words would I want written about me so that when someone passing by could easily read but gain a distant understanding of "who I was, what did I stand for, and how did I make the world a better place than when I came into it?"

During this process, I researched and formalized my four cornerstones of personal leadership that I share with you to assist you in your journey to both personal and professional successes in the future.

Core Values
Community Service
Customer Service
Complacency

CORE VALUES

This journey leads me to show with Honour, Integrity, Passion, and accountability.
Honour:

Do the right thing because it is the right thing to do

Integrity:

What I do when no one is watching

DOI: 10.1201/9781003187189-16

Passion:

Life is a gift, so live every second of every day

Accountability:

To my God, family, self, career, or the rules of any hat, I wear.

I am an enormously proud person and try my best in everything I do. I always try to work on the "we versus me" situation and live my life with others' service hearts.

Sometimes that is not good enough, and I will be overly critical of myself for a host of reasons. Over the years, I develop what I call the "Scoreboard Test" as a reminder to cut myself some slack and make sure the "win" in a situation that I strive for is fair and not setting me up to fail.

When I became a police officer, my mom challenged me to "make everyone's life better that you came into it than worse". I thought this was easy.

As I progressed through my career, it became an incredible anchor around my neck and many times felt myself slip under the water as I tried to stay afloat. This method of practice that I evolved into, frankly, set me up to fail each time. My "win" was so poorly defined that I set a goal that I could never achieve and set up years of failure until I could properly define the "win" in my life.

It was with this spirit and practice in mind I ask you to define what your "win" would look like. Make sure it is not unattainable, like mine was. Using my four core values to grade my win is a far better exercise in reflection than the anchor of a warped definition of the "win" in my life.

For example, some of you may not like me, may hate my guts, or think that buying the book was a waste of time. I cannot change that, nor will I focus on that because you have not earned the space in my brain.

In this situation, the traditional core board may show that I did not "win" and lost 4–3.

My process, in this case, is to reflect on the situation and ask these four "core value" based questions of myself:

1. Did I author this book with the intended honour?
   Yes
2. Did I show integrity in the process?
   Yes
3. Were you able to see or feel my passion?
   Yes
4. Was I accountable to those involved?
   Yes

I further challenge you to explore what your four core values are because once you define them, you can also use them as a measuring stick when you "win," lose," or "draw" in a situation.

Once you apply the evaluation in reflection, hopefully, you will not be too hard on yourself. Cut yourself some slack and dig deeper to move forward and ask:

1. What did I do correctly?
2. What could I have changed?
3. What will I do differently next time?

My core values have come to be the granite for which I stand, my firm footing, my guide in dealing with all situations, and I hope this exercise will help you do the same.

*****

Author's Challenge:
Make a stranger smile.

"Make one stranger smile per day, or mentor a young person. You do not know how those small acts of kindness can unleash some incredible human potential".

Over the years, it exposed me to many forms of a positive mindset, inspiration, motivation, and simply being kind to each other. With that, I produced a solution based on many years and experiences as a police officer, coach, and simple community member.

As a child, I remember speaking with my dad one day about a picture of men in jail for various serious offences. I commented, "Dad, how bad can prison be? These guys are smiling".

He took a moment and instructed me to take a piece of paper and cover the person's smile and look in their eyes. I did that, and as I looked into each of the guys' eyes their false smiles did not distract me. When I told him what I now saw, he said, "Son, don't be tricked by a smile; always look into a person's eyes because they are a gateway to their soul; they will always show you what the person is thinking".

I thought this was a cool father-son magic trick, but that advice at an early age protected me on the street from attacks or provided me with a problem-solving tool when dealing with people in emotional stress.

I often looked into the eyes of people I met. Although they may have been smiling, this father-son simple trick allowed me an extra sense in dealing with a conflict situation.

Just think, you come home one night, or you go to work one day and meet someone. They smile, you leave it at that, and you are saddened the next day to hear they have taken their life. You now live the rest of your life with "I should haves" or "what ifs". I am not trying to burden you with this curse; instead understand that we do not know what is going on in a person's mind.

They could be on a physical, mental, or emotional edge. Your small acts of kindness in offering them a smile could be the slight "pull back" from the ledge where they find hope and realize tomorrow is another day.

The purpose of giving a smile is epic. A face-to-face, eye-to-eye interaction is how we should all strive to communicate. This is becoming exceedingly difficult with the advancements in technology.

In that spirit, I often lecture about Maslow's Hierarchy of Needs[1] and that the model is missing something. It is in fact, missing a basement.

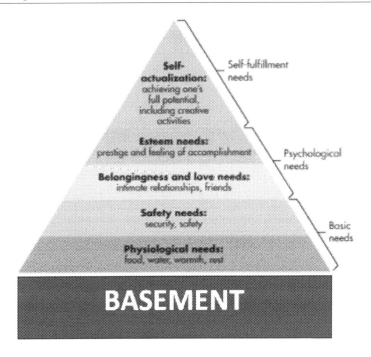

Yes, I have added a basement for several reasons beginning with a story. I have walked the beat many times and always tried to engage everyone, yes, even people sleeping on the sidewalks. In most cases, the people that appeared homeless, for lack of better words, were shocked.

I would ask them why they were shocked, and the majority would say that 25–30 people walked by them and did not even acknowledge they were there, as if they were not existing. This got me thinking, these people had lost hope, and in Maslow's Model, we see the basic need for human life is food, water, shelter, and rest. If these folks did not feel they had any value or hope in life, how could they have a desire to see the basic needs of existence?

Many people's lives are filled with adversity, drugs, alcohol, addictions, psychological or mental trauma or illness, flooding in their basement. We all know that over time if we do not pump the water out, the basement walls can erode and collapse, the structure will fall on itself. We also know that if our basement is flooded, the furnace, electrical, and other utilities will not work.

With that in mind, I have produced a solution based on finding the root causes of this loss of hope. If we can help people "pump out" their basement, the structure will not fall in on itself. They will see the staircase in the corner hidden by the water, and as this analogy, this staircase stands for *hope*. Once they find hope, they may climb the stairs to the necessities of life, again, being food, water, shelter, and rest.

As you move forward with the small acts of kindness, I challenged you about making a stranger smile. That may be all they needed to "pump out" their basement and achieve some fantastic human potential—all because of a simple smile on your face or smile in your eyes.

Just imagine that after you finish reading this book and take on my challenge of making at least one stranger smile per day for the next 30 years.

What starts in this book can change your life and the world

By basic math of 365 x 30, you will personally oversee 10,950 smiles give or take the odd leap year.

If you challenge five people in your life to do the same, the six of you would oversee 65,700 smiles.

If those five people challenged five people in their lives, you will now have 26 people living this challenge and affecting over 284,700.

As you move through the math and challenge more people to become involved, you will find that the math is staggering. Maybe this book will one day change the world.

Am I looking through rose-coloured glasses? Yes, I am, and I would respectfully suggest that someone has to.

I cannot change the world through significant acts, but I believe I can change the world one smile at a time. With that said, in this pursuit of excellence that I know I can enlist all of you to join me and mimic what's known as the "butterfly effect".

The butterfly effect is an often-misunderstood phenomenon wherein a slight change in starting conditions can lead to vastly different outcomes. Understanding the butterfly effect can give us a new lens through to view business, markets, and more.

NOTE: bearing in mind the strict mask-up conditions of COVID, please continue this challenge; a new word has emerged: "smize".

To smize is to *smile* with your eyes, usually in a sexy and playful way.

Whether it is a smile on their face or a smize in their eyes, the impact is the same. Try it one day and reap the simple rewards from your small acts of kindness.

The best part of these simple acts is that they are free, take milliseconds, and require little or no effort other than being aware of your surroundings.

People routinely ask me how they can start positive self-talk and change their belief or lenses through viewing the world. If you start each day and say something to make you smile, build many smiles per day, and create a path like patio stones. If you hit a setback during the path, you can take one step backwards to a smile you are delivered and relieve that positive experience and then take the new action forward.

I have been doing this simple debrief each day. My nightly routine is to pray before I fall asleep and recount my blessing received that day regardless of how big or small. The second part is that I then tell all the gifts through smiles I gave out that day and replay the smile I received from that person. When I add up all the smiles of the day, I know I have earned that day, and I can fall asleep on a positive note, knowing full well I changed people's lives today, one smile at a time.

In times of restless sleep, I refocus on this, and it helps me cut through the stress, refocus on the positive, and usually fall asleep shortly after.

Those small acts of kindness will not only help others, but they are an accumulated step in changing you to a positive mindset, cutting yourself some slack and moving towards the personal and professional successes you dream of.

Are you ready?

COMMUNITY SERVICE

"The best way to find yourself is to lose yourself in the service of others".
—Mahatma Gandhi

We all want to be remembered when we die. Many people have this thought tucked away in the back of their minds, and because life gets so busy, they forget that the more you give your fellow man, the more you will receive. You truly cannot escape the consequences of your actions.

When the Democrats came to power in the last US election, I watched a video by Arnold Schwarzenegger; he spoke about being raised with a service heart[2], [3]. I liked that analogy, and upon reflection I believe that I too have a "service heart".

When I was young, our parents taught my younger brother Don and I that we should always be polite and meet people with a kind hello and firm handshake. My parents told me I should help carry packages, open doors for people, or be available always there to help.

Being raised that way opened my eyes that even if someone may not ask, they may need help but do not ask. Bearing that in mind, I took great pleasure when I received pise for being helpful and seeing the pride in my parents' eyes when they too would receive the praise that we were nice, helpful young men.

I remember many times as children Don and I would race to doors to hold them open for people first, making our early community service a fun competition.

I earlier relayed that my grade 7 teacher called me welfare trash. When I went home that day, I told dad, and it outraged him. We went for a walk, and he told me we are all millionaires. I remember thinking, "What is he talking about? The other kids have way nicer clothes, toys, sports equipment, homes, and food than we do". Dad told me that our name "Pflug" is worth a million dollars and that your name is your bond. He told me that as we go through life, our name will increase in value if we continue to help others. If we invested in ourselves, we would never be poor.

Dad told me that when we invest in ourselves and our name, one day we would receive riches beyond money, but in the respect granted by others. This was quite an in-depth and insightful father-son chat, but looking back on the day, Dad was correct beyond measure.

I have lived a life of service through coaching, counselling, mentoring, policing, and simple volunteerism to many charities and causes. I can walk through town with my head held up high and know I am a respected and valued member of my community.

During my high school years, Mom helped an older gentleman, Reno, who had no one. Looking back, she provided this lonely gentleman with a family in the last two years of his life as he battled cancer. Her acts of kindness helped him with his basic needs of life and provided him with a family and sense of belonging in the last year of his life.

My mom and dad both showed how to help people and sparked an interest in both my brother and me. It is up to all parents or those in positions of authority in a young person's life to share this love and create the spark in their lives.

When my daughters, Reighan and Alexis, were born, I brought them to every event I aided. I wanted to practice what I taught in the same fashion my parents had done for me for so many years, teaching them that a life of service is extremely rewarding.

I used to field so many questions. How could I donate so much time and not at the expense of my family? The answer was straightforward in that I brought my girls with me, everywhere. They got to see their dad first had given, but they also learned the joy of giving, and they too had the community service spark in their lives.

Reighan, my eldest daughter, has done a great deal athletically and academically. One of the proudest awards that she received was her Bishop McDonnell Community Service Award–related bursaries upon graduation. In Ontario, Canada, students must complete 40 hours of community service before they graduate. If they do not do this, then they do not receive their high school diploma. Reighan accumulated well over 300 hours of community service, which was almost eight times what one student was to complete.

Alexis, my younger daughter, also donates much of her time to different community service projects and has discovered a genuine passion for helping at the Special Olympics events. I do not doubt that upon graduation that she will double or triple the graduation requirements.

Community service is one of the best ways to help the public or give back to your community. It has not only positive effects on society, but it will bring benefits to your life and personal development. Why is community service important? There are many texts on the concepts of community service, but I'd like to share four reasons I enjoy and promote others towards community service work as described in the following article:[4]

Volunteerism:

1. It helps me connect with others
2. It is great for the heart, body, and mind
3. Can advance your personal or professional life
4. Brings fun, purpose, or fulfillment in life

"One of the great ironies of life is this: He or she who serves almost always benefits more than he or she who is served".—Gordon Hinckle

The benefits of community service are profound. Wharton professor Cassie Mogilner wrote in the *Harvard Business Review*[5] that her research found those who volunteer their time feel like they have more of it. Further, other research shows that people who donate to charity feel wealthier.

"The results show that giving your time to others can make you feel more 'time affluent' and less time-constrained than wasting your time, spending it on yourself, or even getting a windfall of free time," said Mogilner.

While there are many benefits of community service, here are our top five. Community service:

1. develops an increased sense of social responsibility—a global view of society and a heart for "giving back" and helping others
2. provides an opportunity to apply academic learning to real-life events.
3. builds relationships and "social connectedness" with peers and adults and exposes students to diversity and multiculturalism.
4. improves lifelong communication, interpersonal. and critical thinking skills.
5. helps students find their passions and interests that may lead to a career choice they may not have considered

Community service is an essential way for students to explore their interests, show what they believe in, and define a practical career path. By engaging in volunteer work, students learn experientially. They discover where their passions lie while undertaking "feel good" projects that genuinely are effective. These experiences allow them to make more informed choices about the university and their career while instilling a lifelong interest in giving back.

There is an enormous range of skills you can gain through volunteering, starting with:

- the ability to work in a team
- leadership
- problem solving and adaptability
- 360 degree communicating
- time management
- improved people skills.

AUTHOR'S CHALLENGE

So, I dropped the same challenge that I received well over 45 years ago. Help a stranger out, open a door, say a kind hello, help move a couch, help at a charity BBQ, or support your charity of choice with monetary donations. Invest in yourself, invest in your name, and become a millionaire like my dad told me. You too will receive riches beyond what you can imagine through the service of others with your "new" service heart.

CUSTOMER SERVICE

The world has really been a pretty crazy place the past year under the sanctions and revelations under COVID-19 and how we live life, treat others, and plan to move forward. This change in thinking is a massive time of reflection and I believe we must all reflect and evaluate:

Who we were and how we treated each other
Who we are and how we now treat each other
Who we are going to be moving forward and how we treat each other

We have a choice right now, and I truly hope that our "leaders" help people focus on these three minor questions so that we can have an enlightened future where we focus less on what a person has through material gains. Rather, focus on what a person has done in the betterment of our fellow man. We should not base true worth or value on our bank accounts, but our social wealth earned through kindness towards others.

We must reflect on how we are treating others. This is important given the chains that COVID-19 has placed on us as a society. We have a COVID-19 restriction that has forced us to slow down our world that appears to be spinning out of control and slow down. This induced opportunity and period of reflection is where we can reflect on who we were, who we are, and who we wish to be moving forward.

Earlier, we saw the theory of who we wanted to be or be remembered by; how we treat others is the key to this puzzle, a solution used to create a long-lasting and positive legacy for ourselves and one whom our family may be graded on when we are dead. That said, to assist you in reviewing how you treat people or your "customer service",: I'd like to bring several keys for consideration forward for you to reflect upon in making your plan.

Patience: When being shouted at, insulted, and rudely rushed are all just a part of your day. Keeping your cool is critical to excellent customer service.

Effective Active Listening: It is about taking the time to utterly understand a person's issue and then letting them know you are paying attention.

Attentiveness: You must be present and free of distractions like cellphones, computers, or unnecessary interruptions.

Attitude: Always Be polite and be the type of person you would want to aid your 80-year-old grandmother.

Willingness to Improve: If you make a mistake, mess up, dress up, 'fess up, and move on.

Knowledge: Know what you are talking about and do not bluff people; they will see right through you. Remember, you only have the chance at a good first impression once.

Humility: The ability to admit that you do not have the answer(s): people do not expect us to know everything. They hope we know where to find the right answer.

Have Thick Skin: Not everyone is going to like you. It is an unpleasant fact, so deal with it. My wife, Michelle, says, "Doug, everyone loves pizza, and you are not pizza". How to combat this? Remember your core values exercise earlier in this book.

If you bear these simple tips in mind, you will gain a far better understanding of who you are and what you represent in dealing with others in your personal and professional lives.

Lead with your best self.

AUTHOR'S CHALLENGE

Not everyone loves pizza, and you are not pizza.

Cut yourself a break next time and do not be so hard on yourself.

Judge yourself by the effort you put in and use your core values to determine if you "won" or not.

*****

Dartmouth University recently released a facts sheet entitled, "Kindness Health Facts".[1] I have reproduced the sheet as I believe it provides everyone with reasons for giving back, paying it forward, community service, or just being a nicer person to people. A positive mindset and simple acts of kindness can improve your mental, physical, and spiritual health.

Did You Know That

KINDNESS IS TEACHABLE: "It's kind of like weight training, we found that people can actually build up their compassion 'muscle' and respond to others' suffering with care and a desire to help". Dr. Ritchie Davidson, University of Wisconsin.

KINDNESS IS

CONTAGIOUS: The positive effects of kindness are experienced in the brain of everyone who witnessed the act, improving their mood and making them significantly more likely to "pay it forward". This means one good deed in a crowded area can create a domino effect and improve the day of dozens of people!

Kindness Increases

THE LOVE HORMONE: Witnessing acts of kindness produces oxytocin, occasionally referred to as the "love hormone" which aids in lowering blood pressure and improving our overall heart-health. Oxytocin also increases our self-esteem and optimism, which is extra helpful when we are anxious or shy in a social situation.

ENERGY: "About half of participants in one study reported that they feel stronger and more energetic after helping others; many also reported feeling calmer and less depressed, with increased feelings of self-worth", said Christine Carter, UC Berkeley, Greater Good Science Center.

HAPPINESS: A 2010 Harvard Business School survey of happiness in 136 countries found that people who are altruistic—in this case, people who were generous financially, such as with charitable donations—were happiest overall.

LIFESPAN: "People who volunteer experience fewer aches and pains. Giving help to others protects overall health twice as much as aspirin protects against heart disease. People 55 and older who volunteer for two or more organizations have an impressive 44% lower likelihood of dying early, and that's after sifting out every other contributing factor, including physical health, exercise, gender, habits like smoking, marital status and many more. This is a stronger effect than exercising four times a week or going to church". Christine Carter, Author, "Raising Happiness; In Pursuit of Joyful Kids and Happier Parents".

PLEASURE: According to research from Emory University, when you are kind to another person, your brain's pleasure and reward centers light up, as if you were the recipient of the good deed—not the giver. They call this phenomenon the "helper's high".

SEROTONIN: Like most medical antidepressants, kindness stimulates the production of serotonin. This feel-good chemical heals your wounds, calms you down, and makes you happy!

Kindness Decreases

PAIN: Engaging in acts of kindness produces endorphins, the brain's natural painkiller!

STRESS: Perpetually kind people have 23% less cortisol (the stress hormone) and age slower than the average population!

ANXIETY: A group of highly anxious individuals performed at least six acts of kindness a week. After one month, there was a significant increase in positive moods, relationship satisfaction and a decrease in social avoidance in socially anxious individuals. University of British Columbia Study

DEPRESSION: Stephen Post of Case Western Reserve University School of Medicine found that when we give of ourselves, everything from life satisfaction to self-realization and physical health improves. It delays mortality, depression is reduced, and well-being and good fortune are increased.

BLOOD PRESSURE: Committing acts of kindness lowers blood pressure. According to Dr. David R. Hamilton, acts of kindness create emotional warmth, which releases a hormone known as oxytocin. Oxytocin causes the release of a chemical called nitric oxide, which dilates the blood vessels. This reduces blood pressure and, therefore, they know oxytocin as a "cardioprotective" hormone. It protects the heart by lowering blood pressure.

*****

COMPLACENCY

I see so many people watching life go by. With COVID-19, these numbers are skyrocketing. We all only have a set time on earth and do not know when our expiry date will occur. With that in mind, I want to live, love, and laugh as I navigate my future.

These three lessons came into 110 percent perspective from me when I was one of eight officers who had the honour of carrying Jenifer Kovach's casket as part of the Guelph Police Service Honor Guard in 2013. Jennifer was 26 years old and I remember listening to her close friends talk about how she lived life and her motto of "ride it like you stole it". They then applied that to everyone in attendance and challenged them to live their lives the same way her dear friend had.

I accepted that challenge and, over the past eight years, have not doubted it nor regretted the decision. I have lived such an incredible life since hearing that slight challenge that I am writing this book, hoping my story of trauma and triumph will enable you to draw parallels between what I have experienced and what you have.

Please always remember life is to live, not to watch, and as I earlier wrote, it is better to be a "has-been" than a "never-was". Living a full life is my challenge to you. I would submit that if you decide where you want to be, plan the journey, execute it well, and enjoy the experience. Then hopefully, you will sit back in your rocking chair and say, "That was one hell of a ride; I lived every second of every day".

*****

I had always wondered why God saved me when I was so sick those first three years of life. I now have a purpose, and it is to live every second of every day and make as many strangers smile as I can. My life goal was not to save the world, just my small part of it.

A few months back when I was concluding a five-day training session, one of the course candidates joked about the energy level that I put into the weeklong training and how it exhausted him just thinking about it. He followed up by saying,

> Doug, I have never in my fifty-five years of life met anyone who knew so many people, did so many things in life, has so many projects on the go, and lives such a full life. "You must be a set of 4 cyborgs to get all this done".

I laughed then told him that each morning when I wake up, I look at myself in the morning and tell myself that "I must earn this day". I further advised that throughout the day I constantly challenge myself to live every second of every day with 110 percent energy in everything I do. I joked, "I'll rest one day when I'm dead".

It is hard, but I genuinely try to do this, and when I sleep, my cyborg batteries must charge up.

*****

As I close this section on complacency, I want to draw your attention to the *Bucket List* movie's last scenes. I play these clips at the end of my "Finding your granite through four cornerstones of personal leadership.

The Bucket List—2007

For those of you who don't know the concept behind the movie, it is a story of two men, Carter Chamber and Edward Cole, two terminally ill men who escape from a cancer ward and head off on a road trip with a wish list of to-dos before they die.

Last scene: Brain surgery and funeral eulogy

Morgan Freeman as Carter Chambers while undergoing brain surgery.

Dear Edward, I have gone back and forth the last few days trying to decide whether I should even write this. In the end, I realized I would regret it if I did not, so here it goes. I know the last time we saw each other; we were not exactly hitting the sweetest notes—certainly it was not the way I wanted the trip to end. I suppose I am responsible and for that, I am sorry. But in all honesty, if I had the chance, I would do it again. Virginia said I left a stranger and came back a husband; I owe that to you. There's no way I can repay you for all you've done for me, so rather than try, I'm just going to ask you to do something else for me—find the joy in your life. You once said you are not everyone. Well, that is true—you are certainly not everyone, but everyone is everyone. My pastor always says our lives are streams flowing into the same river towards whatever heaven lies in the mist beyond the falls. Find the joy in your life, Edward. My dear friend, close your eyes and let the waters take you home.

Jack Nicholson as Edward Cole reading his eulogy at his dear friend Carter's funeral.

Good afternoon. My name is Edward Cole. I do not know what most people say at these occasions because in all honesty, I have tried to avoid them. The simplest thing is I loved him, and I miss him. Carter and I saw the world together, which is amazing when you think that only three months ago, we were complete strangers. I hope that it does not sound selfish of me, but the last months of his life were the best months of mine. He saved my life, and he knew it before I did. I am deeply proud that this man found it worth his while to know me. In the end, I think it's safe to say that we brought some joy to one another's lives, so one day, when I go to some final resting place, if I happen to wake up next to a certain wall with a gate, I hope that Carter's there to vouch for me and show me the ropes on the other side.

In the movie, Morgan Freeman's character says to Jack Nicholson's character, "You know, the ancient Egyptians had a beautiful belief about death. When their souls got to the entrance to heaven, the guards asked two questions. Their answers determined whether they were able to enter or not".

Freeman then asks him to reflect on the life he has lived thus far and consider the following two questions, and I will ask the same of you.

Have you found joy in your life?

Has your life brought joy to others?

As you move forward in this exercise of self-discovery to #RiseUpAndExcel, "Lead with our best self, model the behaviour you seek for others and, always create an environment where others can succeed".

*****

I have told you so few times that I am still not extremely comfortable with death, dead bodies, or even worse, death notification. These were times in my career where I had to focus deeply on the task at hand to ensure that I could be as professional as possible. I genuinely believed that when I came into someone's life under these conditions that I owed it to them to be the best officer I could. My challenge was to always try to be the officer I would want to show up to help one of my grandparents.

I am drawn back to a call for service in the fall of 2007, where someone reported finding a person who died by suicide hanging on the slope of a tree-covered hill in Guelph. As I got there, I met up with Constable Mike Gatto, whom I had worked with for many years, and we walked up the steep hill for quite some time. It was fall so the weather was slight rain, and the wet leaves on the wet mud surface made the trek quite difficult. When we arrived at where the call had shown, we found the male died by hanging. We gently followed our procedures and cut him down. We notified our dispatch to have one of the funeral homes contacted to come and help with the body removal. We encouraged them to let the funeral home staff come with boots on because of the messy trek.

A brief time later, the funeral staff showed up—both ladies with nice dress shoes who could not trek up the hill.

It was dark by this point and my partner and I went up the hill with the body bag and we planned to place the body inside and bring it back down the steep, wet, muddy slope to the waiting hearse. Well, things did not go as we planned. We placed the gentleman in the bag, his body still stiff with rigour, and zipped it closed. I was taller so I took the uphill position and my partner took the lower position, carrying the bag. As we gently stepped down the slope trying to navigate the terrain, I suddenly slipped and lost my balance. My feet shot out underneath me and I lifted the bag as hard as I could because I did not want to fall on it or roll down the hill. I landed on my rear end, and my back flattened on the slope and boom; the body landed flat on me, and I slid down the hill a few feet. I was a toboggan for a dead body that day.

No one was around, and my partner and I laughed at my mishap. I picked myself up and we continued down the hill. At the bottom of the hill we met the funeral directors, and we turned the gentleman's body off to them.

I believe it was about 9:00 p.m. and very dark at that point, and I tried my best to clean myself up as my next task as the road Sergeant was to attend the residence and do the death notification.

I jumped in my SUV and drove to the house. I walked up to the front door and noticed there was a large window beside the front door alcove that acted like a mirror. I rang the door bed and as I waited for someone to come to the door; I looked in the mirror and was horrified to see that I had a thick layer of mud all over my back. It went from the back of my head to my heels.

A nice older lady, who turned out to be the gentleman's mother, came to the door and invited me in. I had no chance to clean up and got anxious. I was there sadly to tell her that the son died by suicide and not to make matters worse and spread mud all over her home.

She directed me to the living room and saw a beautiful couch that she asked me to sit on. She knew I had sad news and wanted to make us both as comfortable as possible. I respectfully declined and asked if I could stand. She again politely asked me inside and asked if I would mind sitting beside her.

I was in deep. What could I do? I was there to tell her that her son had died by suicide and I was a mess. My mind raced at how I could navigate this one, and I decided my fate. I politely told the lady that we had found her son and when I was with him, I had fallen. She asked what I meant, and I slowly turned in a circle exposing the incredible mud in back of me and as I wound my 360° turn, our eyes met and she broke out in a huge belly laugh. I looked at her and smiled, and we both laughed for a moment.

She then let me know she suspected that her son, who had battled with mental health issues, had hung himself in the forest where we found him. She was genuinely sad, but my acts of clumsiness made a terrible day in her life livable.

She said that seeing my face, embarrassed as all get-out, and my corresponding spin took some pain away from my presence and we continued our chat about the passing.

She then hugged me and thanked me for making a terrible day a little better and handed me some homemade cookies.

There is a great lesson in life here for all of us. We all have an expiry date; do not take life so seriously that it paralyzes you from being a caring person. Sometimes in crises, people do not need the role you feel, the person you are. Here she did not need Sgt Pflug, she needed Doug.

I hope you all use this story to help focus on what matters and in a time of crisis be the type of person you'd want to deliver that news to you.

NOTE: When I went to the station afterwards to clean up and do the paperwork, I had to walk through the head office. Woody, my friend and Staff Sergeant, stopped me and asked about the call because he knew the family. As I told the story and turned around, he and the officer on the desk broke out in belly laughter as well and I endured my clumsiness for a few days through some good-natured ribbing. Well-deserved, I might add.

AUTHOR'S CHALLENGE

Life is to live. I would like to challenge you to "live every second of every day" and #RiseUpAndExcel. By this I want you to take the challenge and promise yourself that you will wake up tomorrow and begin your day, every day, with a positive mindset.

Look for opportunities each day to write a positive or re-write a negative narrative in your day. Experience each event that you face in your life to enjoy the experience, whether it be a positive or negative one. Try to always see that each experience promoted some growth in your life. You simply just must use a positive lens to see it.

NOTES

1. www.simplypsychology.org/maslow.html
2. https://www-psychologytoday-com.cdn.ampproject.org/c/s/www.psychologytoday.com/us/blog/bully-wise/202102/why-are-you-being-bullied-work?amp&fbclid=IwAR0Jj3fiTwaQjx-AmyEr5Emt5vExVKIs0xsETxSatJ1A6tE2opQgGJAoPfK8
3. https://www.youtube.com/watch?v=vAWvl-g_6rg
4. https://www.helpguide.org/articles/healthy-living/volunteering-and-its-surprising-benefits.htm
5. https://hbr.org/2012/09/youll-feel-less-rushed-if-you-give-time-away
[1] www.dartmouth.edu/wellness/emotional/rakhealthfacts.pdf

.

NO or Next Opportunity

15

Through my involvement in many roles and responsibilities, I have the privilege of coaching, counselling, and mentoring some fantastic young people. I am genuinely grateful that they trusted me and let me help them move forward.

In each of the following stories, we built mutual trust through our shared affiliations, and when life events turned to the worst, they sought me out to help them work through the situation, find their inner light, and move forward towards successes.

I was but a simple tour guide through their respective journeys; they did the work and did #RiseUpAndExcel individually.

About three years ago I was watching the Admiral McRaven Speech for the University of Texas at Austin commencement on May 17, 2014.

TO VIEW THE SPEECH ON YOUTUBE, USE THIS QR CODE

McRaven speaks to his ten points that he has learned through his years as a Navy Seal officer and speaks about starting your day and making your bed so that you begin each day with a task completed. He then goes to expand that as your day progresses, each task completed is like another steppingstone towards success. If you fail, you can always step back to a position of success; at the least, go home to a bed that you made.

In this spirit I have developed, taught, and advised that "NO" means "Next Opportunity".

To illustrate this, think about each day that, like McRaven, you create steppingstones of positivity throughout each day. At one point your past may lead to a wall, and as I stand at the base, you look, and it goes beyond the sky. Do you reflect and say to yourself, "Well, no means I can go further" or do you take a few steps backwards and see the very wall that

DOI: 10.1201/9781003187189-17

is stopping you is only three feet wide. All you must do is step outside your comfort zone by two or three paces and then walk around the wall.

So as you move forward in life remember, when you face a "NO" in life, take a few steps back, reflect, problem solve, create a plan and walk around the wall knowing that your "Next Opportunity" awaits you on the other side.

I have included his speech with an author's challenge in mind. I ask everyone I teach, coach, or mentor to read the speech and take his ten points of success and use them as a template for his own plan of success to move forward. We do not need to waste a lot of time for no reason in most cases in life. We simply need to take a wheel we like, tweak it, make it our own, and use it to move towards your personal or professional success in life.

I hope you enjoy the speech.

President Powers, Provost Fenves, Deans, members of the faculty, family, and friends and most importantly, the class of 2014. Congratulations on your achievement.

It has been 37 years to the day that I graduated from UT. I remember a lot of things about that day. I remember I had a throbbing headache from a party the night before. I remember I had a serious girlfriend, whom I later married—that's important to remember by the way—and I remember that I was getting commissioned in the Navy that day.

But of all the things I remember, I do not have a clue who the commencement speaker was that evening, and I certainly do not remember anything they said. So, acknowledging that fact, if I cannot make this commencement speech memorable, I will at least try to make it short.

The University's slogan is, "What starts here changes the world". I must admit—I like it. "What starts here changes the world".

Tonight, there are 8,000 students graduating from UT. That great paragon of analytical rigor, asks.com, says that the average American will meet 10,000 people in their lifetime. That is a lot of folks. But, if every one of you changed the lives of just 10 people—and each one of those folks changed the lives of another 10 people—just 10—then in five generations—125 years—the class of 2014 will have changed the lives of 800 million people.

Eight hundred million people—think of it—over twice the population of the United States. Go one more generation and you can change the entire population of the world—eight billion people.

If you think it is hard to change the lives of ten people—change their lives forever—you are wrong. I saw it happen every day in Iraq and Afghanistan:

A young Army officer plans to go left instead of right down a road in Baghdad and the ten soldiers in his squad are saved from a close-in ambush. In Kandahar province, Afghanistan, a non-commissioned officer from the Female Engagement Team senses something isn't right and directs the infantry platoon away from a 500-pound IED, saving the lives of a dozen soldiers.

But, if you think about it, not only were these soldiers saved by the decisions of one person, but their children yet unborn were also saved. And their children's children were saved. Generations were saved by one decision, by one person.

But changing the world can happen anywhere and anyone can do it. So, what starts here can indeed change the world, but the question is—what will the world look like after you change it?

Well, I am confident that it will look much, much better. But if you will humor this old sailor for just a moment, I have a few suggestions that may help you on your way to a better world. And while these lessons were learned during my time in the military, I can assure you that it matters not whether you ever served a day in uniform. It matters not your gender, your ethnic or religious background, your orientation, or your social status.

Our struggles in this world are similar, and the lessons to overcome those struggles and to move forward—changing ourselves and the world around us—will apply equally to all.

I have been a Navy SEAL for 36 years. But it all began when I left UT for Basic SEAL training in Coronado, California. Basic SEAL training is six months of long torturous runs in the soft sand, midnight swims in the cold water off San Diego, obstacle courses, unending calisthenics, days without sleep and always being cold, wet, and miserable. It is six months of being constantly harassed by professionally trained warriors who seek to find the weak of mind and body and eliminate them from ever becoming a Navy SEAL.

But the training also looks to find those students who can lead in an environment of constant stress, chaos, failure, and hardships. To me basic SEAL training was a lifetime of challenges crammed into six months.

So, here are the ten lessons I learned from basic SEAL training that hopefully will be of value to you as you move forward in life.

Every morning in basic SEAL training, my instructors, who at the time were all Vietnam veterans, would show up in my barracks room and the first thing they would inspect was your bed. If you did it right, the corners would be square, the covers pulled tight, the pillow centered just under the headboard and the extra blanket folded neatly at the foot of the rack—that's Navy talk for bed.

It was a simple task—mundane at best. But every morning we needed to make our bed to perfection. It seemed a little ridiculous at the time, particularly because we were aspiring to be real warriors, tough battle-hardened SEALs, but the wisdom of this simple act has been proven to me many times over.

If you make your bed every morning you will have conducted the first task of the day. It will give you a small sense of pride, and it will encourage you to do another task and another and another. By the end of the day, that one task completed will have turned into many tasks completed. Making your bed will also reinforce the fact that little things in life matter. If you cannot do the little things right, you will never do the big things right.

And, if by chance you have a miserable day, you will come home to a bed that is made—that you made—and a made bed gives you encouragement that tomorrow will be better.

If you want to change the world, start off by making your bed.

During SEAL training the students are broken down into boat crews. Each crew is seven students—three on each side of a small rubber boat and one coxswain to help guide the dingy. Every day your boat crew forms up on the beach and is instructed to get through the surf zone and paddle several miles down the coast. In the winter, the surf off San Diego can get to be 8 to 10 feet high and it is exceedingly difficult to paddle through the plunging surf unless everyone digs in. Every paddle must be synchronized to the stroke count of the coxswain. Everyone must exert equal effort, or the boat will turn against the wave and be unceremoniously tossed back on the beach.

For the boat to make it to its destination, everyone must paddle. You can't change the world alone—you will need some help—and to truly get from your starting point to your destination takes friends, colleagues, the good will of strangers and a strong coxswain to guide them.

If you want to change the world, find someone to help you paddle.

Over a few weeks of difficult training my SEAL class, which started with 150 men, was down to just 35. There were now six boat crews of seven men each. I was in the boat with the tall guys, but the best boat crew we had was made up of the little guys—the munchkin crew we called them—no one was over about five-foot-five.

The munchkin boat crew had one American Indian, one African American, one Polish American, one Greek American, one Italian American, and two tough kids from the Midwest. They out-paddled, out-ran and out-swam all the other boat crews. The big men in the other boat crews would always make good-natured fun of the tiny little flippers the munchkins put on their tiny little feet prior to every swim. But somehow these little guys, from every corner of the nation and the world, always had the last laugh—swimming faster than everyone and reaching the shore long before the rest of us.

SEAL training was a great equalizer. Nothing mattered but your will to succeed. Not your color, not your ethnic background, not your education and not your social status.

If you want to change the world, measure a person by the size of their heart, not the size of their flippers.

Several times a week, the instructors would line up the class and do a uniform inspection. It was exceptionally thorough. Your hat had to be perfectly starched, your uniform immaculately pressed and your belt buckle shiny and void of any smudges. But it seemed that no matter how much effort you put into starching your hat, pressing your uniform, or polishing your belt buckle—it just was not good enough. The instructors would find "something" wrong.

For failing the uniform inspection, the student had to run, fully clothed into the surf zone and then, wet from head to toe, roll around on the beach until every part of your body was covered with sand. The effect was known as a "sugar cookie". You stayed in that uniform the rest of the day—cold, wet, and sandy.

There were many students who just could not accept the fact that all their effort was in vain. That no matter how hard they tried to get the uniform right; it was unappreciated. Those students did not make it through training.

Those students did not understand the purpose of the drill. You were never going to succeed. You were never going to have a perfect uniform.

Sometimes no matter how well you prepare or how well you perform you still end up as a sugar cookie. It is just the way life is sometimes.

If you want to change the world, get over being a sugar cookie and keep moving forward.

Every day during training you were challenged with multiple physical events—long runs, long swims, obstacle courses, hours of calisthenics—something designed to evaluate your mettle. Every event had standards—times you had to meet. If you failed to meet those standards your name was posted on a list, and at the end of the day those on the list were invited to a "circus". A circus was two hours of additional calisthenics designed to wear you down, to break your spirit, to force you to quit.

No one wanted a circus.

A circus meant that for that day you did not measure up. A circus meant more fatigue—and more fatigue meant that the following day would be more difficult—and more circuses were likely. But at some time during SEAL training, everyone—everyone—made the circus list.

But an interesting thing happened to those who were constantly on the list.

Over time those students—who did two hours of extra calisthenics—got stronger and stronger. The pain of the circuses built inner strength, built physical resiliency.

Life is filled with circuses. You will fail. You will fail often. It will be painful. It will be discouraging. At times it will test you to your very core.

But if you want to change the world, do not be afraid of the circuses.

At least twice a week, the trainees were needed to run the obstacle course. The obstacle course had twenty-five obstacles including a 10-foot high wall, a 30-foot cargo net and a barbed wire crawl, to name a few. But the most challenging obstacle was the slide for life. It had a three-level 30-foot tower at one end and a one-level tower at the other. In between was a 200-foot-long rope. You had to climb the three-tiered tower and once at the top, you grabbed the rope, swung underneath the rope, and pulled yourself hand over hand until you got to the other end.

The record for the obstacle course had stood for years when my class began training in 1977. The record seemed unbeatable, until one day, a student decided to go down the slide for life headfirst. Instead of swinging his body underneath the rope and inching his way down, he bravely mounted the TOP of the rope and thrust himself forward.

It was a dangerous move—foolish, and fraught with risk. Failure could mean injury and being dropped from the training. Without hesitation the student slid down the rope perilously fast. Instead of several minutes, it only took him half that time and by the end of the course he had broken the record.

If you want to change the world sometimes you must slide down the obstacle headfirst.

During the land warfare phase of training, the students are flown out to San Clemente Island which lies off the coast of San Diego. The waters off San Clemente are a breeding ground for the great white sharks. To pass SEAL training there are a series of long swims that must be completed. One is the night swim.

Before the swim, the instructors joyfully brief the trainees on all the species of sharks that inhabit the waters off San Clemente. They assure you, however, that no student has ever been eaten by a shark—at least not recently. But you are also taught that if a shark begins to circle your position—stand your ground. Do not swim away. Do not act afraid. And if the shark, hungry for a midnight snack, darts towards you—then summon up all your strength and punch him in the snout, and he will turn and swim away.

There are a lot of sharks in the world. If you hope to complete the swim you will have to deal with them.

So, if you want to change the world, do not back down from the sharks.

As Navy SEALs one of our jobs is to conduct underwater attacks against enemy shipping. We practiced this technique extensively during basic training. The ship attack mission is where a pair of SEAL divers is dropped off outside an enemy harbor and then swims well over two miles—underwater—using nothing but a depth gauge and a compass to get to their target.

During the entire swim, even well below the surface, there is some light that comes through. It is comforting to know that there is open water above you.

But as you approach the ship, which is tied to a pier, the light begins to fade. The steel structure of the ship blocks the moonlight, it blocks the surrounding streetlamps, it blocks all ambient light.

To be successful in your mission, you must swim under the ship and find the keel—the centerline and the deepest part of the ship. This is your goal. But the keel is also the darkest part of the ship—where you cannot see your hand in front of your face, where the noise from the ship's machinery is deafening and where it is easy to get disoriented and fail.

Every SEAL knows that under the keel, at the darkest moment of the mission, is the time when you must be calm, composed—when all your tactical skills, your physical power and all your inner strength must be brought to bear.

If you want to change the world, you must be your absolute best in the darkest moment.

The ninth week of training is referred to as "Hell Week". It is six days of no sleep, constant physical and mental harassment, and one special day at the Mud Flats. The Mud Flats are an area between San Diego and Tijuana where the water runs off and creates the Tijuana slues, a swampy patch of terrain where the mud will engulf you.

It is on Wednesday of Hell Week that you paddle down to the mud flats and spend the next 15 hours trying to survive the freezing cold mud, the howling wind and the incessant pressure to quit from the instructors. As the sun began to set that Wednesday evening, my training class, having committed some "egregious infraction of the rules" was ordered into the mud.

The mud consumed each man till there was nothing visible but our heads. The instructors told us we could leave the mud if only five men would quit—just five men—and we could get out of the oppressive cold. Looking around the mud flat it was clear that some students were about to give up. It was still over eight hours till the sun came up—eight more hours of bone-chilling cold.

The chattering teeth and shivering moans of the trainees were so loud it was hard to hear anything. And then, one voice began to echo through the night, one voice raised in song. The song was terribly out of tune but sung with great enthusiasm. One voice became two and two became three and before long everyone in the class was singing. We knew that if one man could rise above the misery then others could as well.

The instructors threatened us with more time in the mud if we kept up the singing, but the singing persisted. And somehow the mud seemed a little warmer, the wind a little tamer, and the dawn not so far away.

If I have learned anything in my time traveling the world, it is the power of hope. The power of one person—Washington, Lincoln, King, Mandela and even a young girl from Pakistan, Malala—one person can change the world by giving people hope.

So, if you want to change the world, start singing when you are up to your neck in mud.

Finally, in SEAL training there is a bell. A brass bell that hangs in the center of the compound for all the students to see. All you must do to quit is ring the bell.

Ring the bell and you no longer must wake up at 5 o'clock. Ring the bell and you no longer must do the freezing cold swims. Ring the bell and you no longer must do the runs, the obstacle course, the PT—and you no longer must endure the hardships of training. Just ring the bell.

If you want to change the world do not ever, ever ring the bell.

To the graduating class of 2014, you are moments away from graduating. Moments away from beginning your journey through life. Moments away from starting to change the world—for the better. It will not be easy.

But YOU are the class of 2014, the class that can affect the lives of eight hundred million people in the next century.

Start each day with a task completed. Find someone to help you through life. Respect everyone.

Know that life is not fair and that you will fail often. But if take you take some risks, step up when the times are toughest, face down the bullies, lift up the downtrodden and never, ever give up—if you do these things, then the next generation and the generations that follow will live in a world far better than the one we have today.

And what started here will indeed have changed the world—for the better.

Thank you very much. Hook 'em, horns.

To debrief his ten points, let's see how you can take, tweak, make your own version and #RiseUpAndExcel.

YOUR ASSIGNMENT

1. Start Your Day with a Task Completed

I challenge you to start your day with a positive mindset and compliment yourself as you look in the mirror each day. As the day progresses, find times to continue the positive self-talk.

List three positives: You complimented yourself with today.
One:
Two:
Three:

2. You Cannot Do It Alone

I challenge you to find the three most important people in your day that you need on "your team" to work towards success. List their name and role they have in helping you succeed.
One:
Two:
Three:

3. Only the Size of Your Heart Matters

List three qualities that you feel you need to make yourself successful. Do you use them now or would you like to develop for later?

One:
Two:
Three:

4. Life's Not Fair—Drive On!

What three things or failures have you experienced that hold you back? Write them and let them down and drive on!

One:
Two:
Three:

5. Failure Can Make You Stronger

List three times you failed, which resulted in some tremendous person of personal or professional growth. What do you learn?

One:
Two:
Three:

6. You Must Dare Greatly

List three outside the box thinking ideas that you have that if you took the first step to enact them would lead to successes. What has prevented you from taking that first step?

One:
Two:
Three:

8. Rise to the Occasion

List a time where you were significantly tested, and it really challenged life.

What was it?
What did you do?
What was the outcome?
What did you learn to use next time?

9. Give People Hope

List the names of three people you made smile today. What are their names and under what circumstances?

One:

Two:

Three:

10. Never, Never Quit!

When you are having your darkest day, what three things would you think of as part of your strategy to bring light into your life? Why do you list these three?

One:

Two:

Three:

Take your list and place it in a place where you can see it often. Use it to guide you, use it to reflect upon, use it to focus on the personal and professional goals you have in life.

Do the work, reap the reward.

*****

NO = NEXT OPPORTUNITY

Examples of Ironwill 360° Leadership Excellence
Andrew Yorke
NO or Next Opportunity?

I met Andrew a few weeks before the Summer Olympics in Rio de Janeiro to compete for Canada in the Triathlon. Andrew would be at the University of Guelph track each night training with a group of young sprinters who would run against him, challenging him to run at his full speed. It was fascinating to watch him sprint against one sprinter, then as the lap ended another would take over as a fresh set of legs and run against him in a wall relay fashion: one man versus many. The level at which he was straining was world-class and awe-inspiring as he prepared to live his life dream of competing in the Olympic Triathlon.

I was training my Special Olympics athletes on the track and stairs as I was training them to attend the World Special Olympics Floor Hockey Championships later that year in Graz, Austria.

When I was in the track's corner with my athletes, Dan veered off into Andrew's speed lane, and he yelled at Dan to get out of the way. As he passed, I yelled back that he was a Special Olympian and did not mean to interfere. Both Andrew and I were unaware of what each of us was doing.

When Andrew finished his workout, he came over, introduced himself, and genuinely apologized for his behaviour, explaining the intensity of his training and now understanding what he did.

We both felt terrible for this misunderstanding, and a genuine friendship was born out of this.

We chatted for an hour, and I learned that he one day wished to join the Ontario Provincial Police and follow the footsteps of his grandfather. He knew I was a Police Sergeant, and so we agreed I would help mentor him through the process.

It is incredible how fate puts two people together in a conflict situation, and after a brief time, we entered a protégé-and-mentor relationship.

Over the next few weeks, Andrew would make it a habit to come over to my athletes and speak with them and support their incredible efforts. When Andrew left for Rio, he had his special Olympian cheering section.

We followed the media and saw a terrible headline that Andrew had crashed in his race and awaited the details. I then found the following article outlining what had happened that fateful day.

Headline: The sport is cruel, man': No quit in Canadian triathlete Yorke, who finished 42nd in Olympic event.

"I didn't quit. Ever. That is why I am here", said Yorke, of Guelph, Ont.
Author of the article:

Postmedia Network: Publishing date: August 18, 2016

Rio de Janeiro: Andrew Yorke had tears in his eyes, scrapes, and bruises on his body, and barely any voice for what he wanted to say.

"You work your whole life to get here to race for your life, and you don't quit", he said, trying to keep his composure as his lower lip trembled. "I didn't quit. Ever. That's why I'm here".

Yorke, of Guelph, Ont., was one of two Canadians to compete in the men's Triathlon at the Olympics Thursday, and he wound up 42nd of fifty-five competitors. Just finishing the race was a significant accomplishment, however, after he crashed during the cycling part, blew a tire, and scraped up the entire right side of his body.

"The sport is cruel, man", he said. "There's nothing crueller. It'll break your heart".

Yorke was on a downhill during the 40-km cycle and was trying to conserve energy when he heard a few bikes crash in front of him. With no time to react, he had to guess which direction to go and wound up hitting the tire of the fallen bike and went down at once.

He was able to get up, run with his bike to the next wheel stop, get a new wheel and continue, finishing ahead of 13 riders with a time of 1:52.46.

"I've only crashed twice in my professional career, so it sucks that it happened here", he said. "I just put my head down and rode the bike as hard as I could, and I was thinking of Canada. You are never going to win after a crash. At that point, you know your race is over".

Canada's other competitor in the race—which was won by Great Britain's Alistair Brownlee for the second straight Olympics—was Tyler Mislawchuk of Oak Bluff, Man. He finished 15th, a strong result for the youngest competitor in the field.

"I'm happy with the effort", said Mislawchuk, 21. "I gave absolutely everything I had. It is hard to take in right now. It's a big emotional build-up, and I'm simply happy to be done with the race".

Mislawchuk was 19th after the 1.5-km swim and had a good transition to start the cycling part on 17th. He was just behind the lead group when he started the cycle, but he was never able to catch up, instead spending much of the middle portion of the race as the lead rider of the second pack.

He dropped to 24th after the 40-km cycle but made up considerable ground in the 10-km run, rising to 15th with a time of 1:47.50, two minutes, and 49 seconds behind the gold-medal winner.

"It's the Olympics", Mislawchuk said. "I didn't want to sit back and run for 20th place. I wanted to put it all out there, and that's what I did".

twyman@postmedia.com

When Andrew returned home, he was upset, and we spoke many times over the next few weeks to help him move forward.

I challenged him as he had received a "NO" at the Olympics, but with his greater life plan to become a police officer, this could also lead him to his next opportunity.

As he prepared for his interview, Michelle and I helped him prep expected questions and answers. I suggested how funny it would be when the interviewer asks, "Andrew tell us a time when you faced adversity, what was it, what did you do and what was the outcome?" and he responded, "Well, I was competing in the Olympics . . ."

We laughed, and he could in fact use that story and eventually received a job offer from the OPP.

Several months later, he came to the Ontario Police College, and I could continue our mentorship and taught him a few courses. Andrew set the 1.5-mile record at the Ontario Police College, graduated, and continued in his grandfather's footsteps.

Michelle and I were so proud that Andrew could find the light within him in a bleak period in his life, #RiseUpAndExcel and switch his Olympic "NO" into his Police, "Next Opportunity".

Well done, friend.

Click the QR Code to hear
Andrew Yorke speaks about our mentorship

"NO" = Triathlon Bike crash at Rio Olympics
"Next Opportunity" = OPP Constable Andrew Yorke

Johnny Augustine
NO or Next Opportunity?

During his first year with the University of Guelph Gryphon football team, Johnny and I met through our mentorship program. We at once became friends and started a protégé-and-mentor relationship.

It has blessed me to have this young man in my life. He has an exemplary work ethic, leadership skills, talent, and love for family. He truly is like a son to me.

It's amazing that since the day he started carrying the ball as our running back, he has continued to apply his recipe for success and achieved so many things both on and off the field.

One area I am immensely proud of is that Johnny and I are both Christians and can share our Christ. It is a common theme that has helped us overcome successes, failures, and near misses.

I reflect on the 2017 CFL Draft. They predicted he would be drafted in the first two rounds. At the last moment on draft day, his TV wasn't working, so after a quick call to us, he brought his entourage over to the house, and we started watching the draft. One by one, the players were picked, and as the night progressed, it broke my heart to see the passion in Johnny's eyes lessening; he was not selected.

The draft ended; he slowly stood up, tears in his eyes, and apologies for letting us down. He politely excused himself and left the house. We all stood there in shock, feeling his pain and wish we could have removed it from our friend's shoulder. Johnny received a "NO" that night and trust in knowing it did not deter him. He trained harder, ate better, started Pilates, yoga, and a host of other things to be stronger, faster, and fitter in his heart, body, and mind.

A few weeks later, Johnny called me to say that he had signed as a free agent with the Edmonton Football Team and prepared for training camp with even more focus.

Johnny received a second "NO" when he was released from the Edmonton Camp. Again, this did not deter him; he returned home and put his plan back into place and was signed by the Saskatchewan Roughriders. He received his third "NO" before the 2018 training camp when they released him.

Once again, Johnny had been told "NO", but this did not deter him, and he continued to stay focused, knowing that this would not be the way he ended his CFL professional football dream. I have so much respect for Johnny as we spoke many times during this period, he was told NO so many times, and he never wavered from his goal. It is such an honour to be part of this man's life. I learned so much about myself and my determination because of our friendship.

Early in May 2018, he called me extremely excited and shared some confidential soon-to-be-published news. On May 16, 2018, they announced it that the Winnipeg Blue Bombers signed Augustine. Johnny was so pumped and promised that he would not receive another "NO". He went into training seclusion and looked at who he was, who he wanted to be in the future, and busted his ass to achieve it.

That fall, we went to training camp, and day by day, he got stronger, better, and focused on the task. He was truly living his dream in a place where he could succeed. I remember back when he called me stressed and relieved. He said that they partnered him with a roommate during camp. The process was that if you were being cut, a knock would come at your door, and they would ask you to leave camp. Johnny told me that day there was a knock at their door, but he did not waver, sadly sent his roommate home, and he made the team.

That season Johnny played second-string running back and was on special teams and made the most of his experience. Because of a suspension, as the season progressed, he stepped up to the first string, excelling. He scored his first CFL touchdown on November 3, 2018.

November 24, 2019, the Winnipeg Blue Bombers defeated the Hamilton Ticats 33–12, and Johnny celebrated his first Grey Cup victory.

Here is a man who received several "NOs" in his professional athletic career, and many doubted his ability to live the dream he was working for. If you knew Johnny the way I do, you would have known all along that failure was not in the cards, but his Next Opportunity was, and when it came, he grabbed it and ran with it.

On December 27, 2019, they signed Augustine to a two-year contract extension with the Blue Bombers.

David DiCenzo recently released two articles outlining Johnny's and several other players' journeys. These are must-reads to further provide insight into Johnny's "NO" = Next Opportunity. www.gryphonfootball.com

QUEST FOR THE CFL

Johnny Augustine recalls the precise moment that he wanted to be a professional football player. After his very first game his first year in high school, it dawned on Augustine that playing football for a living should be his goal. The former star running back of the Guelph Gryphons realized that dream last year when he made the Winnipeg Blue Bombers' roster.

It has taken an incredible amount of work to get there but Augustine never shied away from putting in max effort.

"I used to do crazy things growing up", says the 26-year-old from Welland, ON, while riding the bus with his Blue Bomber teammates as they prepare for a Friday night matchup with the Edmonton Eskimos. "I would do 1,000 pushups and 1,000 sit-ups every day. I was in karate and that helped me develop discipline and a work ethic. And I always had people around me who supplied motivation.

"It's been a relatively smooth transition (to the CFL) physically and mentally because I prepared myself for this".

Gryphon Football has a long tradition of sending athletes to the next level, beginning all the way back in 1925 when Joe Cook joined the Toronto Argonauts. And over the decades, several players wearing the red, black and gold have swapped their jerseys to make a name in the CFL, like Gerry Organ, Jed Tommy, Jeff Volpe, Parri Ceci, Frank Marof, Mike O'Shea, Kyle Walters, and Rob Maver, just to name a few.

In recent years, the number of Gryphons off to the league has been impressive. The program's extended period of success, combined with the first-rate facilities and coaching, has produced a squad of players who were ready to join the pro ranks. Names like John Rush, Curtis Newton, Cam Walker, Ryan Bomben, Jeff Finley, Curtis Newton, Jacob Scarfone, and Andrew Pickett are among them. And just these past couple of years, decorated Gryphons Luke Korol, Royce Metchie, Nick Parisotto, and Gabe Ferraro have joined Augustine in the CFL.

Like his long-time teammate Augustine, Ferraro knew he wanted to be a pro at an early age. The 23-year-old from Mississauga grew up an Argos fan and remembers players like Jeff Johnson speaking at his high school football banquet. Ferraro even got to try on Johnson's Grey Cup ring and is quick to point out that he was in the stands at the 100th edition of a big game at Rogers Centre.

"It was always more than a dream—it was a goal", he says. "I thought it was always attainable and something that I was working towards. It never left my mind".

Ferraro's journey to the CFL was not easy, having been drafted by the Calgary Stampeders and released. But Ferraro kept training in Guelph with his brother Daniel, waiting for a call. Earlier this summer, it came, and the Saskatchewan Roughriders were ready to give the Gryphon kicking legend a chance.

"They called me on a Wednesday and asked, 'Can you fly out tomorrow morning?'" says Ferraro from his new in-season home, Regina. "I flew in and was playing on Saturday. It happened so quickly I was not even thinking. Then suddenly, it was game day.

"I've been enjoying the experience. It is a wonderful team and the locker room is formidable. It reminds me a lot of Guelph—they really preach family, loving your teammates and playing for your teammates. I love it here".

Ferraro, who credits the Calgary organization and specifically Maver for helping him realize what it ultimately takes to be a pro throughout the past two CFL training camps, got his first action against the Stamps. He was glad that it was a whirlwind because he did not have time to dwell on what it all meant. When it came time for his first kick off, the U SPORTS legend experienced a new sensation.

"I could feel my body shaking", he says. "It was nice to get the butterflies out right away and it was just another football game at that point. A lot louder but another football game".

Ferraro has settled in, making seven of his first nine field goal attempts as a pro, including a longest make of forty-eight yards. Augustine is also finding his groove. The second-year pro kept two mementos from last year that sit in his Guelph home—a touchdown ball from the 2018 exhibition season and another from the regular season, each coming against the Eskimos.

"It was a confirmation that I could actually do this", says Augustine. "That was humbling. If you put forth the effort and drive, it is possible. To score a touchdown at the highest level was an accomplishment".

Now the next crop of Gryphons who have shown the talent to play beyond U SPORTS is preparing for their season. Quarterback Theo Landers and offensive lineman Coulter Woodmansey opened eyes at the East West Bowl. And some of the elite fourth-year players in their draft year include receiver Kian Schaffer-Baker, linebacker AJ Allen, and defensive back Dotun Aketepe.

"My whole focus is Guelph football", says Aketepe, who stays in touch with his former teammates now in the CFL. "You don't get this time back. That is something I have heard of and learned. I have seen a lot of people whose football careers ended in high school or ended with an injury.

"I understand that there could be a future in football, but I have to enjoy this time right now. When that time comes, I'll face it head on".

And those are exactly the words of advice those players already at the next level have for the current Gryphons.

"Don't look too far ahead", says Ferraro. "Enjoy the moment you're in, every meeting, every practice. The guys you go to university with are your brothers, your lifelong friends. That is the most fun you are going to have. As great as it is to play pro, and that is our goal, when you are playing with your brothers at school, that is the best.

"It goes faster than you think. You don't know how good you have it until you're gone".

Augustine continues to stress the importance of work. The Blue Bomber players are expected to arrive at facilities about 8:30 in the morning but like most of his teammates, the former Gryphon gets there at 6:30 a.m. The days are long and the hours, as he says, are sometimes "ridiculous", but Augustine understands the more work put in, the better the results.

"Hard work, dedication, heart and having a vision", Augustine says. "It's one thing to just say it. Action speaks louder than words. You must take the steps. Not just in football but for life in general. If it means waking up an hour early to be prepared, then do that.

"Do not put things off. You have to have a clear path and act on it".

GRYPHON GREY CUP WINNERS

There is a razor-thin line between being pumped up for a championship game and being out of control. Johnny Augustine found that balance critical to success on Grey Cup Sunday. The former Gryphon Football running back legend was more than fired up when his Winnipeg Blue Bombers took the field against the Hamilton Tiger-Cats in the 107th Grey Cup last month at Calgary's McMahon Stadium. Augustine had been in big football games before but nothing like the CFL finale, where the Blue

Bombers were looking to end a 29-year drought for a city desperate to celebrate a winner.

It was the last stop in a campaign fueled by the mantra "On to the next". This was, as Augustine puts it, a business trip.

"We weren't going to be satisfied with just being there", says the 26-year-old Welland, ON native, who played in the backfield and on special teams this season.

"The locker room was initially pretty quiet. You could tell guys were getting ramped up. It just continued to get louder and from the get-go during warm-ups, I was jacked up. I felt that much faster, that much quicker. I was embracing the whole moment.

"As much as we had the emotion, we had to control it on the field and find that balance, so we were aware, able to look at schemes, and compute everything.

"Opening kickoff, I got the first tackle of the game. I was jumping and on a high".

Winnipeg set the tone early in the game with a big interception. And after taking a 21–6 lead at halftime, the hungry Blue Bombers closed the deal and defeated Hamilton 33–12.

The city finally had its Grey Cup. And a contingent of all-time Gryphons—Augustine, John Rush, Winnipeg head coach Mike O'Shea, and General Manager Kyle Walters—once again tasted what it was like to lift a trophy.

"It was pretty surreal to be part of something that big", says Rush, a former President's Trophy winner, who has been known to reminisce about the university days with Augustine in the Blue Bombers' special teams' meetings. "The whole time I was just thinking, 'We're really doing this!' It was crazy.

"After the game, all I could think about is how much we had and overcame to get to that point and how happy I was for everyone involved because I knew how much it meant for them. It's impressive to be able to share experiences like that with guys you love to play with".

Rush says there is a brotherhood, culture, and love for one another in the Winnipeg room. He saw it before, with comparable results. Five years ago, to the day, Guelph came out on top in an emotional 23–17 victory over the Western Mustangs in the 108th Yates Cup.

It is like that meeting with a guidance counselor or in a job interview when you are asked, 'Where do you see yourself in five years?' Augustine might not have answered 'Grey Cup champ' but he was certainly confident that he would be highlighting his skills as a professional football player.

"When you're young and trying to make it, you don't think about championships", says Augustine, who got to spell the Grey Cup MVP running back Andrew Harris at various points through the season. "It's one step at a time. I knew in five years I would be playing in the CFL but for me to win that Grey Cup in only my second season, it's definitely special".

A central theme to both Guelph's Yates Cup win and the recent Grey Cup victory was overcoming adversity. The Gryphons had to come back to win in London and put their demons to rest after earlier attempts at securing the OUA banner fell short. Winnipeg was in control of the Grey Cup out of the gate but the challenges they faced came in a different form—a tough road in the playoffs (wins over Calgary and Saskatchewan) before a matchup with a dominant Hamilton team that pundits thought would be difficult to beat but more importantly, a championship drought almost three decades long.

"They were pretty similar in the sense that in both places, we'd been deprived for years of a championship and for at least the four years I was on each team, we had worked towards and gotten closer to the goal," says Rush. "So, to see it come to fruition in both circumstances has been pretty incredible".

That Rush and Augustine did it under the guidance of Gryphon Hall of Famers O'Shea and Walters made it even that much more special. Augustine says at the beginning of the year, players introduce themselves and tell the group where they played in university. O'Shea, whose Grey Cup win was his first as a coach after experiencing three in his playing days, has acknowledged those Gryphons with a "Go Guelph!"

"I have the utmost respect for Coach", says Augustine. "He has done so much for the league.

"It was very humbling afterwards; we all got together and took a Guelph pic. We did it, we are proud Gryphons".

"I don't think I can say enough good things about this man", Rush adds of O'Shea. "He has helped mould me not only into a better football player, but a better man. He has a personal connection to each of his players and takes the time to get to know you and how you learn.

"Every time he talks in a meeting, whether it's to you or someone else, you're learning something new because he's so intelligent".

The former Gryphons have been thrilled with the Grey Cup win. But they are not satisfied. Augustine says that the story could not have been written better this season, though he has envisioned what a future championship might look like. He has worked hard to get where he is, and that effort was rewarded as his role on the team behind the workhorse Harris expanded over the course of 2019.

Augustine takes pride in his preparation. It is what helped make him Guelph's second all-time leading rusher and what got him to the CFL. The goal next time is for him to be the main man leading his team to a title.

"I've been through ups and downs, not getting drafted, bouncing back and forth", Augustine says. "That's why we all have a special bond in the locker room—it's not easy to be a professional athlete. Guys go through a lot. It is a business at the end of the day. To be able to hold that trophy, it shows all the demanding work I put in and believing in myself paid off.

"Going forward, I want more. I am enjoying the win, but I want this feeling as much as I can.

"I just want to be ready for that moment".

I am honoured to advise that Johnny and I are such great friends and know we will share many more great times in the future.

**Click on this QR Code to hear
Johnny Augustine speak about our mentorship**

**Johnny Augustine
"NO" = CFL Draft
"Next Opportunity" = 2019 Grey Cup Champion**

**Orion Edwards
NO or Next Opportunity?**

I remember sitting at the University of Guelph Gryphon Football Charity Golf Tournament at Guelph Lakes Golf club chatting with Orion in 2016. Orion had torn his ACL and was awaiting surgery to repair it. We chatted about his goals and I let him know that I would be there to aid if I could get in any way. We say we set up the athlete and our protégé mentorship.

I was so impressed that Orion did not allow this "NO" to shut down his spirit. I elevated it, and after surgery and during his 16 months of rehab, he became the team's Chaplain. It has been another tremendously rewarding experience for me knowing that I can aid Orion in any way possible.

Orion worked so hard the next year and a half, and I know he made dramatic advancements as an athlete, Christian, student, and teammate. In reflection, we have chatted, and this was "God's plan for Orion and his subsequent growth".

While he has had significant successes athletically, I am equally proud of winning the McKendry-Baker Memorial Scholarship at the University of Guelph. The award honours my first Deputy Chief, Harold McKendry. The award is given annually and recognizes students registered in the Criminal Justice and Public Policy major who are interested in pursuing a career in police services, have completed a minimum of 8.0 credits, and have taken part in extracurricular activities to support families within the community.

Selection is based on the most significant impact made to support families in the community through positions held, extracurricular activities, and involvement on campus and in the community, as evidenced by a letter of application and one letter of reference supporting the impact. It honoured me to attend the event with Orion and his family as it tied in my Guelph Police world and my Gryphon Football world through this amazing young man's outstanding accomplishments.

I joined Orion and his family in my dress uniform to celebrate the award ceremony. Orion won this on back-to-back occasions in 2017 and 2018.

Orion continued his studies, rehabbed his knee, regained his starting defensive back position, and played his senior year of University football in 2017.

Rob Massey, January 1, 2021

www.guelphtoday.com/pursuit/former-gryphon-turns-to-bobsled-and-hopefully-a-trip-to-the-olympics-3226087

FORMER GRYPHON TURNS TO BOBSLED AND HOPEFULLY A TRIP TO THE OLYMPICS

Orion Edwards has gone from the gridiron to the icy track as a member of the Canadian bobsled team's development squad

If not for an injury in his second season with the Guelph Gryphons football team, former defensive back Orion Edwards might not be pursuing a dream of competing in the Winter Olympics.

Edwards, who turned twenty-six this month, is a member of the Canadian national bobsled team's development squad.

"The seed was planted in 2016, actually, when I tore my ACL", he said during a talk on Zoom.

"My sister's a nurse so she came to Guelph. I had my surgery in Guelph at the hospital, Guelph General, and she came and helped me out and made sure everything was good in the recovery process. The day of the surgery after I woke up from surgery, a couple of hours later we watched *Cool Runnings* together on Netflix while eating dinner and just hanging out that night. I had short locks at that time and Sanka, one of the main characters, had short locks as well. She looked at Sanka and looked at me and said 'Well, your hair's the same length' and I was like 'OK'. 'Well, you should bobsled'. And I was like 'That's a weird deduction.' "

Of course, that was not the only reason.

"No, no, not just that", his sister said to him. "I think you're fast and powerful and strong and I think that's what you need to be a great bobsledder".

The seed sat dormant for a couple of years until after he finished his time with the Gryphons, winning the Ted Wildman Memorial Trophy, an award that takes into consideration the player's athletics, academics, and community service.

After graduating from the University of Guelph, Edwards moved to Seattle.

"I was working for Athletes in Action, which I was part of in Guelph, and I was with Athletes in Action at the University of Washington and Seattle Pacific University", he said. "I was a campus missionary which was a wonderful experience. Some of the athletes I worked with there I still talk to now".

But Edwards soon discovered he could not quit competitive sports cold turkey.

"I was still working out and I felt like I still had a lot of athletic potential so let's see what else I can do with it before it's too late", he said.

Another visit from his sister and another conversation about bobsledding turned Edwards into a winter athlete, something that no one at the U of G would have foreseen.

"I don't think I would've struck myself as a guy who would be a winter athlete if you asked me this about five years ago", he said. "I'm actually born in the winter, but I've never really been a big wintertime fan. Snow is beautiful and stuff like that, but I thrive in the summer. I like summer weather a lot".

With his mind made up on giving bobsledding a shot, Edwards reached out to Neil Lumsden, the former running backs coach for the Gryphons whose son Jesse had been on the national bobsledding team. Lumsden put Edwards in touch with Morgan Alexander, the high-performance manager of Bobsleigh Canada Skeleton (BCS) and Edwards' journey to becoming a bobsledder started.

He had to attend a BCS combine where the biggest thing would be to run a 30-metre sprint in 3.90 seconds.

"I actually did (the combine) in Guelph in July of 2019", he said. "I ran the standard and if you run the standard, you get invited to the national team tryouts in Calgary. I went there last year in October. You have to do the combine tests again, plus on top of a power clean and a bench press test, you have a push test".

The weightlifting and the running were things Edwards had done with the Gryphons. But a push test?

"To be honest with you, my push assessing my first year was absolutely horrible", he said. "Essentially what happened is that we had our combine testing around October 2 or 3 and then on about the fifth or sixth, we had some learn-how-to-push camps—three or four days of it. And then we had a push assessing the week after that. You are pushing testing with everybody there, the top-level guys who are past Olympians like Ben Coakwell and Cam Stones and Justin Kripps and all those guys.

"I'm pushing super slow as I'm still learning and all that. That first push testing was hard, but I've improved a lot from last year to this year".

Now Edwards does both two-man and four-man bobsled with the development team and as the brakeman, he's the guy at the very back of the sled, the last to load.

His first actual run down a track came last year and it was not in Canada.

"My first run down the hill, we went from a lower start—corner three. It was in Lake Placid, N.Y., and our pilot was Pat Norton", Edwards said. "I remember in the truck going up to the top of the hill he asked me how I was feeling and I said that I was a little nervous, but I thought it was going to be fun and I thought it was going to be cool".

Another one of the crew asked him what he would do if he got scared and decided he did not want to do it. He had a reply ready.

"I'm too deep in the cut, meaning that I'd already put a lot of work and time and a lot of energy and even some finances behind it to get to where I am", he said.

"My first run down, it was fun. There is no feeling like it. There are a lot of turns, twisty and pressure. Feeling G force for the first time was different as well. It is fast. Sometimes it can be a little scary, but it is fast, and it is fun. It is a ride. It's a very thrilling adrenaline rush".

Now he is on a holiday break. The Canadian team did not take part in the 2020 part of the 2020–21 World Cup season but is expected to travel to Europe to join the tour early in January. Edwards, though, will be among those who will not be going.

"I decided to opt out of the second half", he said. "I did have the choice to go, but I didn't feel that for me personally it would be the best choice for me to go to Germany at this time".

That decision came because of the coronavirus pandemic and with a thought of his mother and grandmother. He lives with them when he's in Ontario and he didn't want to jeopardize their health and he's not the only member of the squad to turn the offer down.

While training this season in Calgary and Whistler, B.C., the Canadian team adhered to COVID-19 protocols. It was split into several nodes of up to ten athletes and two coaches and those groups stayed together throughout the training period.

"Hopefully in the future I'll get to go overseas", Edwards said.

He will get to compete in North American Cup events early in 2021, a series he raced in during the 2019–20 season. In North American Cup four-man events at Lake Placid and Park City, Utah, last season, Edwards was a member of the crew that recorded three fourth-place finishes and a fifth.

Thinking back on his time with the Gryphons, three things stand out—the 2015 OUA championship Yates Cup win, the years leading up to that title win and his ACL injury.

"I think adversity shaped success", he said. "They had lost the Yates Cup final to (McMaster) the year before I arrived. My first year there, we did not get to the Yates Cup. We lost to Queen's in the semi-final. The next year we went back to Mac and lost by five points (in the Yates Cup final) and neither defence let up a touchdown. And then finally winning it at Western against Western, that grind and growth as a team to get there, my experiences with my teammates, the guys I call my best friends today.

"The staff and all the efforts put in by the coaching staff, the assistant staff and therapy".

And then there is the ACL injury.

"It was one of the hardest things that happened in my life, which is minuscule with what we're looking at today with the pandemic going on", he said. "But it was (also) one of the best things that happened in my life. It shaped me. Adversity shapes you holistically as a person, physically, mentally, spiritually, and academically— all of it if you will allow it to.

"My years at Guelph were very formative years and I think the vision of the past head coaches, especially coach (Stu) Lang, was for it to be your formative years and that you wouldn't just leave a champion, but you'd leave like a champion in life and that you'd be shaped into a great man.

"I learned a lot and I confirmed a lot about myself. Sometimes you've got to go through that".

And if the ACL injury had not happened, he would not be riding on the back of a bobsled with the goal of competing in the Winter Olympics.

"I don't know what would've happened".

A few months ago, Orion reached out to Michelle and me through a Zoom call, and he let us in on his big secret; he showed us the engagement ring that he was going to give his girlfriend, Samantha Griffin. She said yes a few days later!

Congrats to this amazing young couple. May they be blessed with good health, laughter, and love and enjoy God's love.

NOTE: In 2016 and 2017, Orion was presented the U of G Gryphon Football "Pflug" Family Community Service Award.

GUELPH—Orion Edwards Wins this Year's Award for his Outstanding Service to the Community

I have known Orion Edwards for 4 years now through our mutual involvement with the University of Guelph Gryphon Football team. Quite frankly, he is one of the most amazing young men I have had the pleasure of calling a friend. Orion's maturity level is beyond his years and he seeks every opportunity to better his life while balancing his Christian beliefs, academic pursuits, elite athletic endeavours, two part-time jobs, friendships, family commitments, S.A.M. (student mentorship), community service and his duties as our team Chaplain for more than 100 players and coaches.

Orion suffered a season ending injury last spring when he tore his ACL during the East-West Bowl, a game for the best university football players in the country. This did not deter him from his lifelong goals. He embraced his rehab after reconstructive surgery with passion and sought out more opportunities to aid his teammates, thus becoming team chaplain.

Orion is currently pursuing his degree in Criminal Justice and plans to complete a master's degree in Social Work so that he can further aid others. I know he will be successful in both endeavors and I will continue to stand beside him as reference and mentor should he need.

It is with extraordinary pride that I announce that he is this year's winner!

Orion is a young man I truly respect, and I am sincerely excited to watch him reach his full potential over the coming years.

Criteria for the Award

• involved in community work on a volunteer basis in Guelph or abroad

• be a positive male influence /role model and promote the core values of the University of Guelph Gryphon Football program through community service work

• has created a significant difference in the quality of life in the community and shown a high degree of willingness to help others

• focused on improving the quality of life of an individual or group of individuals where they volunteer

Orion Edwards
"NO" = ACL Injury
"Next Opportunity" = Canadian Bobsled Team

Scott Raso
NO or Next Opportunity?

I have been friends with Scott Raso for 30 years, and he illustrates NO equals your Next Opportunity better than most people I know. Scott once weighed 425 pounds. During his annual physical in 2013, he was given a near-death sentence by his family doctor and told that he would succumb to premature death if he didn't make changes in his lifestyle and health.

Scott was not satisfied nor deterred with this death sentence and began a journey that saw him lose pounds and make the bariatric surgery target date of pounds. The surgeon would not perform the surge unless he got to that weight. Scott had the surgery and continued his new life.

Guelph Mercury reporter Vik Kirsch wrote an excellent piece published in the paper on June 9, 2015, outlining Scott's incredible story that I would like to share. www.guelph-mercury.com/news-story/5669288-from-425-to-175-pounds-one-guelph-man-s-journey-into-a-new-life/

From 425 to 175 pounds: one Guelph man's journey into a new life
Vik Kirsch—Guelph Mercury
Tuesday, June 9, 2015

Guelph: Scott Raso is, in one sense, less of a man than he once was. But in another, he is so much more.

At his peak weight two years ago, the Guelph man tipped the scale at 425 pounds, while today he's down to 175, and with a diet and exercise regimen accompanying bariatric surgery at Guelph General Hospital, he sports a lean and fit body—and a healthy attitude.

He has a new lease on life. He feels full of energy and is becoming a fitness and aqua fit trainer and offering his personal story at bariatric centre orientation and information nights at the hospital. He is proud of turning his life around. "It's been a godsend," Raso, 35, said Tuesday in an interview. He wants to help others on the same journey. "I like sharing my story: the ups and downs, the struggles," Raso said.

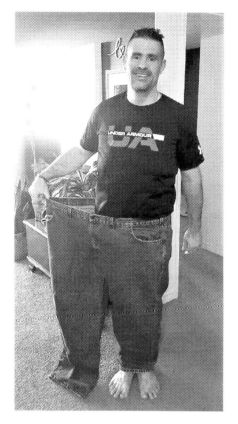

The hospital much appreciates such testimonials. "It's just such a wonderful opportunity for patients thinking about or planning for bariatric surgery to understand what the journey is," said hospital patient services senior director Joyce Rolph. "It's a lifestyle change, and it is a huge commitment . . . to be successful. And we want patients to be successful".

Her hospital performs 370 bariatric operations a year, using a multidisciplinary team for pre- and post-operative care and continued guidance. "We have a fabulous team," Rolph said.

Julia, a young niece Raso looks after, made a T-shirt he is proud to wear. It reads: "One mission, one goal. Failure is not an option. Believe."

Raso had been heavy-set since childhood. "As my mom said, I always liked my meals," he recalled. Murray Miller, a neighbour who has known Raso for many years, has seen him struggle with weight growing up. He said he had watched him blossom into an inspiration for others while still being close to his family and caring about the community.

"He's just a remarkable young man," Miller said.

A senior food worker at the University of Guelph, Raso, noted a history of colon cancer in his extended family. So, he took it seriously when two doctors advised him to reduce his risk by losing weight, even consider an operation at Guelph General, a regional centre of excellence in bariatric surgery since 2009.

"I had tried all kinds of other things. It hadn't worked," he said, referring to approaches like crash diets.

Being morbidly obese with a 58-inch waist made it challenging to do simple things, like putting on a pair of socks or riding his mountain bike. "Everything just hurt". He loved sports but could not play.

The weight caused such sleepless nights that a doctor threatened to have his driver's licence taken away. It was the final straw. "That's my means of transportation," Raso said. On a January day last year, he had surgery.

It reduced his stomach to between the size of a golf ball and racquetball, cutting his food intake and his desire to eat. It was accompanied by a new healthy eating and exercise regimen he is still committed to.

He overcame two complications (a little internal bleeding and a hernia that was corrected) and today feels fit and fine. He has energy "and then some". He is in a good relationship, he said, with an understanding woman, and that is a welcome bonus.

Bariatric surgery, he stressed, must come with a pledge to make positive changes in a person's lifestyle.

"It's not a quick fix," Raso said.

He is proud of the acknowledgements he received for the charitable work he takes part in, seeing them as reaffirming his commitment. They include a children's cancer fundraising event in April for which he climbed the 660 stairs of the Skylon Tower in Niagara Falls—no easy feat for anyone.

Before his life turned around, the idea of becoming a fitness trainer "never crossed my mind". Now, he sees it within reach.

vkirsch@guelphmercury.com

Scott recently spoke at a bariatric support group to lend his support to potential surgery clients. His speech,

"Just a little over six and a half years ago, I had a massive health scare. I was 425 lbs and was diagnosed with a really severe case of sleep apnea and was told I stopped breathing 166 times in one hour and was threatened that they would take my driver's license away if I did not get help and get my sleep apnea under control. But not only that but with Colon cancer also runs in my family, my risk was extremely high in the possibility of having that as well.

Both doctors had suggested seeking my family doctor in the possibility of bariatric surgery. I went in to see my doctor, and she put it very bluntly. 'Scott, if you keep going the way you're going, you will not live to see your 40th birthday.'

I went home in shock with that news and called my mom. As a nurse of over 30 years, she did some research into what bariatric surgery entailed, and we started the process.

In December of 2014, it all came to a head with being approved for surgery early in January of 2015. Since then, I have taken this incredible tool and ran with it.

Now do not get me wrong, by no means was it the effortless way out. I have had my share of ups and downs, good days and bad days but knowing I had my family and support team behind me pushed me every step of the way to never give up and always believe in myself.

My sister Julia who was eleven, produced a saying that went on all my workout shirts, 'One mission, one goal. Failure is not an option. Believe.' This was one of the ways she felt would keep me motivated. Knowing that she was always with me every time I worked out and to look at that face and hear her voice say it to me every time I put on my workout shirt, others that have helped my journey my best friend Phil who no matter what was going on never left my side even in the most downtimes and my buddy and motivator when forming my workouts pushing myself to the limits when training for charity events and great role model Doug.

My mom Bonnie and brother Brent also played a huge role with an abundance of support, coming with me to my appointments and getting more education on how and what will make me successful in this journey.

Since bariatric surgery, I have met some fantastic people, especially my wife. She has been a huge part of this. She has been my rock and the brains behind meal planning and has made life easy by joining me in the bariatric diet. I have since taken such a huge liking to healthy lifestyle living and exercise. I have put myself through school and become a personal trainer, aqua fit instructor, swim instructor and lifeguard.

I have taken part in many charity events in the community. With that also, I enjoyed my love for golf, hockey, skiing, swimming, baseball, and other various sports. As I look back now through all the good and rough times, I would not change, and the thing I have done today I went from 425 lbs to as low as 170 and up to a healthy and fit 205 where I sit today and am very blessed that not only did the bariatric clinic in Guelph help me and give me the tools for a second chance at a healthy, life but they gave me a new lease on life.

Not everyone gets a second chance to do this and to take it to embrace it cause the sky's the limit. All you have to do is take it and run with it".

Recently Scott was married, and part of his wedding day speech, he said,

To my good friend Doug, thanks for everything you have done for me and helped me through some dark times and helped me become the person I have become today.

I needed to lean on for being there at any time through my colossal lifestyle change and being my guide and mentor.

Your love and support that you have given me outweighs any kind of friendship I could ask for, and I am very blessed to have you in my life as I walk this new pathway with my wife and knowing I can lean on you to guide me and give me the best advice to becoming an amazing man and husband.

Scott Raso

"NO" = Weighed 425 pounds
   and given a death sentence
"Next Opportunity" = New life

175 Pounds
Certified Aqua fit
Certified Swim Instructor
Certified Lifeguard
Can Fit Pro Fitness Instructor
Married and soon to be a dad.

These are but a few protégés that I have had the honour of aiding over the years. Always remember, when the world tells you "NO," do not accept the finality of this small word, expand it, and let it stand for:

Next Opportunity.
NO = Next Opportunity

_____

Your Name
NO = _____
Next Opportunity = _____

Time to Practise What I Teach

16

UNDERSTAND THE "WHY" IN ALL PEOPLE

As a leadership instructor and executive leadership mentor, I love studying what other leadership instructors, theorists, and leading-edge people are doing, saying, and teaching. In my studies, came across Simon Sinek, who has a tremendous leadership mind. I recently watched a TedEx video of Simon, explaining his Golden Circle concept and understanding a person's "why".

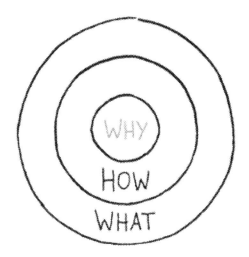

The Golden Circle

WHAT
Every organization on the planet knows WHAT they do. These are products they sell or the services

HOW
Some organizations know HOW they do it. These are the things that make them special or set them apart from their competition.

WHY
Very few organizations know WHY they do what they do. WHY is not about making money. That's a result. WHY is a purpose, cause or belief. It's the very reason your organization exists.

"The 'Golden Circle'", he states, "is a naturally occurring pattern, grounded in the biology of human decision making, that explains why we are inspired by some people, leaders, messages and organizations over others". In the lecture, he explains the concept.

I would encourage you to watch the TedEx link I have supplied to understand better the theory from the man who indeed describes it best. In the end, he concludes that most

DOI: 10.1201/9781003187189-18

people communicate by starting with the "what" they do aspect and eventually work their way back to talk about "how" and "why" they do what they do. According to Sinek, "People don't buy what you do; they buy why you do it".

I have watched the video many times and read text on the theory. I love the simplicity, so this is why I am drawing reference to it. Through this exposure, I hope that you will also take a journey of self-discovery and understand your "why". Once you do, assess, plan, and act on your personal and professional goals and learn the "why" of those around you. I genuinely believe that knowing you and others will better enable you to work together. Once we are all on the same page, where we have a shared and inspired vision, we understand and use each other's goals and skills, solidifying the team, and the journey as we embark on together.

As you begin this understanding of the "why" journey, I want to provide a brief background to assist you in framing the concerns, language and thought processes of the Golden Circle. I feel it is prudent for me to help you on the journey and share what mine was, and better understand who I was, who I am, and who I want to be.

I recently came across a blog entry on www.smartsightings.com that I found breaks this down wonderfully, and I am happy to share their post with you.

START WITH WHY

Sinek explains that "Why" is the most important message that an organization or individual can communicate as this is what inspires others to action. "Start with Why" is how you explain your purpose and why you exist and behave as you do. Sinek's theory is that successfully communicating the passion behind the "Why" is a way to communicate with the listener's limbic brain. This is the part of our anatomy that processes feelings such as trust and loyalty, and decision-making.

Successfully articulating your "Why" is a very impactful way to communicate with other humans, define your value proposition, and inspire them to act. Sinek's theory is that communicating "Why" taps into the part of the listener's brain that influences behaviour. Therefore, the Golden Circle model is considered such an influential theory of leadership—at an organizational level, communicating your "Why" is the basis of a strong value proposition that will differentiate your brand from others. He gives the example of Apple in the video clip at the end of this article.

HOW

The organization's "How" factors might include their strengths or values that they feel differentiate themselves from the competition. Sinek's view is that "How" messaging is also able to communicate with the limbic brain—the important part that governs behaviour and emotion. But his opinion is that organizations would do better to improve how they articulate their "Why", in addition to "How".

WHAT

It is easy for any leader or organization to articulate "What" they do. This can be expressed as the products a company sells or the services it offers. For an individual, it would be their job title. Sinek argues that "What" messaging only engages with the neocortex—the part of our brain that is rational. His argument is that this part of the brain is less of a driver of decision making than the limbic brain: the part that "Why" and "How" reach better. Successful people and organizations express why they do what they do rather than focusing on what they do.

Some critics argue that Sinek's Golden Circle model is just reflecting passion. Enthusiastic leaders and passionate organizations express their commitment and enthusiasm authentically, and this is what inspires others rather than the way they express themselves.

Other critics argue that Sinek's theory implies humans do not use their reason at all when making decisions, which is debatable.

I genuinely hope that you explore your "why" so that once discovered, it will better enable you to know "What, How, When, and Where" to move forward to achieve your personal and professional goals.

Always remember that your "Why" is found within you. It is a feeling, goal, drive, or conviction that compels you to do the work you want to do, even if it requires short-term sacrifice. We will all struggle through periods of self-doubt, confusion, lack of will, fear or fatigue. Trust in knowing that through those sacrifices, you must still move forward guided by your "Why" to pursue the work you want to do because it gives you meaning.

For more information, please check out:

*****

On January 17, 2020, I would have to put all my previous years of experience, trauma, resiliency, and coping mechanisms to the ultimate test.

NOTE: Out of respect from the family, I will change the actual names to "Mark" and "Mary" to relay this story.

A few weeks earlier, on New Year's Eve, Michelle and I attended a party with our dear friend Mark. As the evening progressed, we went to our condominium for one last drink. Mark and I were born in 1996; he liked the same music, movies, and TV shows as

I did growing up. We spent a great deal of time together with Michelle and his lovely wife, Mary. We had been spending time together with the two of them, watching the World Junior Hockey Championships that year in their home and at a few pubs. Go, Canada, Go!

Rarely do you find another couple where all four parties genuinely enjoy friendship, and we were so blessed to find this couple to hang out together.

We had planned to fly out of Detroit on January 18, 2020, to Florida, where we'd be meeting Michelle and my parents, and the six of us would be going on a Caribbean Cruise.

We went to the store that week and bought the last of what we needed for the trip when we came upon triangular knee pillows for sale. Michelle was having back problems, and this was just what she needed. The week before, Mark joked Mary caught him with her pillow between her legs and gave him grief. We bought one for Michelle and Mark.

When we arrived on January 17, 2020, at our condo on Boblo Island, Amherstburg, we placed the knee pillow in Valentine's Day bag and left it on their condo door and went back to our condo, laughing in anticipation for those two of them to find our gag gift.

A short time later, I received a call from Mary, who had found the gift, and she was laughing hysterically at our gesture and joked she couldn't wait until Mark got home that night to see the fun.

Around 8:30 p.m., we got ready for bed knowing we had a long day ahead of us. We had an appointment in Detroit at 9:00 a.m. for our Nexus card interviews, then would go straight to the Detroit Airport, and fly to Florida. The plan seemed simple, seamless, and well thought out.

My cell phone rang, and I saw the caller ID was Mary, and thinking it was Mark, I answered and said, "Hello, dumbass. How are you?"

I heard a male voice speak and knew it was not Mark. Shocked, I asked the male caller to repeat himself, and he said, "This is Windsor Homicide. Could you please come down to Mary and Mark's Condo Unit, right away?" I yelled to Michelle, and we got our clothes on as quickly as possible and ran down to their unit, unaware of what we were walking into.

As we ran out our second-floor condominium to their first-floor condominium, it was such a weird experience. As we ran there, both Sgt Michelle Pflug and Sgt Doug Pflug came out of retirement as we arrived at the front door . . . our professional selves took over.

When we got there, we were met by two friendly faces; two Windsor Police detectives that I had taught a lesson on youth crime legislation two weeks earlier. I was processing things in slow motion, trying to get as much information as possible, when the one officer said, "Do you know Mark White?" I said, "Yes, I do". The officer then told me they had come to the condominium checking in on Mary and thinking they were investigating a murder-suicide. I was dumbfounded and asked what he meant.

He told me that officers were at the Libro Center in Amherstburg with Mark's pickup truck, and he had taken his life with a shotgun. My knees buckled momentarily, and I quickly gained composure. A massive rush of adrenaline went through my body and Sgt Doug Pflug, who had been retired for three years, returned as if it was yesterday. The officers gave Michelle the information and little did I know, but Sgt Michelle Pflug returned that night as she had been retired for a year. Michelle and I ran into the unit and found Mary on the kitchen floor, absolutely devastated and in shock.

Michelle comforted her, and I went to get more information from the officers to grasp what was going on.

A million things went through my brain, and I was having a challenging time processing that my friend was dead, let alone by his own hand. I thought back to how a few weeks prior; we joked that we'd run the Detroit St Patrick's Day road race as two couples, we'd go out for drinks when we returned from the cruise, and we even talked about Mark and Mary coming with us later in February to our favourite resort in Cuba. We had plans, and my experiences locked me.

For 28 years that I was a police officer and dealt with people with suicidal thoughts or ideologies, no one had actually made any plans. They all struggled to see the next day, let alone the plans we had four weeks later.

In my mind I experienced self-doubt and assessed myself some blame thinking, "I just talked to him; how could I have not seen this? I failed my friend and his family". I then tried to make sense of this and ate some of my stress; I needed to be very professional at all involved, and I would not fail now.

I went back into the condominium to help Michelle and Mary go to her daughter's home in a nearby town. We told the officers that we would take Mary to her family and do the death notifications for them, given we knew the family.

Both officers were very thankful.

We drove Mary to her daughter's house, a 30-minute drive that seemed like hours given the stress everyone was going through. What made matters worse was that Mary's daughter kept texting that she heard there was a shooting and wanted to make sure both her parents were safe, and we knew that wasn't the case.

When we arrived at the home, I knocked on the door, and her daughter answered and said, "Doug, what's wrong?" and her face sank.

It transported me back to the massive burden of earlier similar stresses, and the weight of those sat on my shoulders. When I retired, I thought that all would go away, but this was not the case. I "tightened up" up my composure, reminding myself of what I was about to do and that I needed to be the type of officer that I would hope showed up to my home in a similar situation. I then told her that her dad was gone and that he had taken his own life and her face sank, and she cried. Mary pushed by me and hugged and tried to comfort her daughter while managing her disbelief and grief.

After a brief time, we strategized how to get Mark's son to the residence to let him know and took the steps. When the entire family was there, we took a step back, experiencing our grief and shock, but suppressing it as we tried to be "strong" for the family.

This was a balancing act, I did not think I would have to assume for quite some time, but we were.

It was also weird during the event because Michelle slipped into her Sgt Pflug role and mine. We have been together for ten years and never saw that version of each other in an emergent situation.

The coroner called the home, and the family asked me to speak with her. I answered all the questions that I could and as she tried to verify that it was, in fact, Mark that had died.

It was about 12:30 a.m., and the family was grieving so we quietly left home so that the family could grieve in private. The drive back to the condominium was tranquil as we both went about our Sgt roles trying to get back to our "normal".

We went to bed knowing that we had to get up at 6:00 a.m. As we lay in the darkness, we did not talk much; we hugged each other, and we fell asleep.

The next day, we woke up still in shock at what had happened the previous 24 hours. I again questioned how I, as a trained officer, did not see this coming. I had chatted with Mark a few days before he took his own life, and I never noticed anything . . . nothing.

I got angry with myself, wondering if I could have prevented such a terrible situation and prevented the family's grief. I became stuck in those thoughts.

I looked outside and found that we were in the middle of a full winter storm, and it said that the water level was very high, and the vehicle found it very hard to navigate the height from the ferry onto the island. We quickly packed up and drove to the ferry dock, which runs every 20 minutes round the clock.

As the ferry pulled up, we tried to board it, but the angle was too steep to accept the length of our minivan. We were stuck on the island, sad, shocked, and worried we would miss our trip.

A few minutes later, I received a text from our dear friends Stacey and Pedro, telling me to have a great vacation. We explained we could not get on the ferry, so they offered to take us over on their large 4 x 4 pickup.

We gratefully accepted, and they took us off the island and advised they'd take us across the border to our Nexus meeting, wait, and then drop us off at the Detroit airport. We were so lucky and thanked our "holiday angels".

As they drove us to the border, we chatted about Mark, and the four of us tried to justify his actions, understand, and debrief our respective sadness and grief. The next few hours were incredibly stressful given the weather, road conditions, and aggressive itinerary. Michelle and I felt relieved when they dropped us off at the airport well before our departure time.

God sent us two angels that day through our dear friends when we needed help. Thank you, Stacey, and Pedro.

I remember sitting back at our boarding gate, and we tried to talk and rationalize what we had just experienced the earlier 24 hours. We were shocked at the events, how we felt, the aggressive itinerary that got us there, and we tried to "tighten up" and enjoy our trip.

Sadly, over the years, "tighten up" is a term I use, which means suppress how I am feeling to perform a task, and we were tight after that.

We boarded the plane, sat back, and slept the entire way to Florida. We were exhausted, defeated, sad, and on the other side, so thrilled to leave the freezing weather and go to paradise. That was quite the dichotomy of emotions.

When we arrived in Florida, my in-laws met us, scanned our faces, and asked what was wrong. On the way to their home, we relayed what had occurred the earlier 24 hours and they comforted us. That night we went out for dinner to a relaxed beach-type bar and loosened up and enjoyed our surroundings.

The next day we boarded the cruise ship and found my parents, who had arrived on a different flight that day. Dad came to me a while later and asked what was wrong as he could see the stress in my face, and I broke down and told him the story.

Michelle and I processed what had happened slowly and worked together to listen to each other, support each other, and help each other to "loosen up".

Fate was not on our side that cruise as it rained the first three days. We battled the suicide under cloudy, rainy skies on what was supposed to be a beautiful experience with sunny weather. Over these days, we stayed with each other and tried our absolute best to be healthy while dealing with our growing grief.

We functioned those days but did not experience life or the intended joy. Sadly, our parents were distressed because they tried to help us, but the recent nature of events prevented their intentions from helping. This was a process that we would have to go through, one day at a time.

We had the pleasure of running into a gentleman one day. We were sitting under an enormous umbrella, and he was in the seat next to us. I have a bit of a hearing issue these days and sometimes forget about it, and I can get loud. In this state of grief, I saw that he had heard part of our story recounting the suicide. I got his attention, and they met us with a smile. I apologized for being loud and ruining his time on the cruise. He laughed and pointed out we were under an umbrella with torrential rain and our story was not that bad compared to his. He let us know he served in the US Army and had completed seven tours of duty and taught post-deployment post-traumatic stress to returning soldiers. Over the next three hours Michelle and I spoke with him, and we helped each other heal.

The next day he ran over to us with his wife and introduced us and, said, "Honey, this was the delightful couple I spoke to you about last night".

We sat down with them for a while and shared non-work-related stories and genuinely enjoyed the time we spent with them. It was in the end very therapeutic, as she also had served in the US Army, and we drew many parallels as a couple with them. Secondly, we talked couple-to-couple about adversities faced, resilience used, and tools incorporated to move forward from our respective trauma.

On Thursday, January 23, 2020, we woke up to beautiful sunshine as we docked in Cozumel, Mexico. It was a beautiful day; the sun was shining, there was a warm breeze, and we left the ship and walked around and enjoyed the day. Leaving the ship and walking around was a very therapeutic experience for both of us, and we returned to the couple we usually are. We laughed, joked around, enjoyed the weather and sights.

We then went back on the ship, and I told Michelle that I had been surveying out the two water slides on the ship and today was the day. We changed our clothes and went on deck. Michelle walked with me and felt my joy; I was her child for the moment.

I'm sure Michelle thought, "Great, I get to be the parent to a six-one, two hundred forty-five-pound child right now" but encouraged me nonetheless to have fun.

I walked up the stairs, waved to her, she took a pic, and I launched myself down the slide. The water was warm, and the ride had many spins, turns, and velocities. As I neared the end, I positioned my body in a seated position and came down the final ramp. I slid the entire length and came to rest as my feet hit the stainless-steel diamond plate grate at the end of the slide, and I felt a large "thump". I paused and thought, "Oh great, I broke something in my foot", as the extreme pain shot up my right leg.

I then used both arms to lift my body, jumped out of the slide and stood on my left foot. I lifted my right foot, and the water beneath my feet became saturated with blood. I asked her if she saw anything, and her face grimaced with fear.

I looked at her face, then down at the steel grate. I had severely lacerated my foot. I saw that the top corner had bent towards riders when the steel screws had snapped. What I quickly found was that my foot had been impaled on the jagged piece of steel, resulting in a huge gash to the bottom of my foot from the middle of my baby toe to my arch. We quickly called for the staff, and they summoned a medical staff.

They arrived with a wheelchair and wrapped my foot up in my towel, which became heavily blood-soaked. Several staff members that were onsite told me they had been putting in maintenance reports on damage to the grate, but they had not fixed it. I also learned from the attending staff members that the other slide was down, so the cruise left this one open to stop complaints that both were not functioning that day. Michelle and I took several pictures of the area to illustrate what had happened to the doctor. We then took the staff names, and we left the area.

As we were taking the pics and gathering names, a shift supervisor came over and saw what we were doing and called someone on his phone.

They took me to the ship's doctor and told me I would need seven stitches to close the wound. The doctor told me that the gash went through my skin layers, exposing open flesh on the bottom of my foot. The doctor told me to hold the railings as he needed to freeze the area and put freezing between my toes with a two-inch long needle. As he entered between all my toes, I could feel the needle hit the many bones in my foot, and my stomach flipped, and I became nauseous.

The doctor finished the stitches, did his paperwork, and bandaged me up, and they released me two hours after the injury occurred.

Michelle and I went back up to the deck and moved to the water slide. I was so angry that this happened. There had been maintenance slips in for days, but they did not act, and I was seriously injured.

When we arrived, we found the slide open, which surprised us. We looked at the diamond steel plate and saw that they had repaired it with large steel screws, and the damage was no longer visible. We took more pictures as one manager curiously looked on. The manager came over and asked what we were doing, and I showed him there before-and-after pics of the diamond plate and said the cruise line was negligible here. He politely excused himself and went to the phone station on the deck.

For the next few days, I was treated poorly; they ignored me, knowing that we had taken the pictures and several staff members who were very kind to us before the injury no longer treated us the same. We guessed they were under a gag order.

The night before we left, I hobbled up to the service desk in the main lobby and asked for help to disembark the next day, given that I could not put any weight on my foot. The young lady I met was rude and abrasive. At one point, I asked her to be more polite and understand my situation. She blurted out in a condescending and rude voice, "Sir, you should be lucky that we didn't charge you for the emergency medical assistance".

I was shocked and told her that my best friend took his life the day before we left, that along with the injury and associated pain and the way she was treating me was placing me in similar territory when I suffered the Post-traumatic Stress Injury (PTSI) so many years ago. She looked at me, asked for my sail and sign card, and walked away. She returned a few minutes later and handed me her phone, and said, "Here, talk to our mental health counsellor". It infuriated me about her insensitivity and marginalization of my situation and mental health. I was the victim here, and she made me feel like it was my fault.

I refused, telling her I did not know who the person was on the phone nor where they trained, and I certainly would not bare my soul to them with the 400 other people standing nearby. She pulled the phone back and said, "Make sure you document that he's refusing to speak with you".

I again asked if they were going to compensate me for their negligence and my several lacerations and she tilted her head and said, "Ah, no" like a belligerent teenage girl.

I thought to myself, "You idiot", and forced myself to take a breath and calm down.

I then asked for wheelchair help for the next day to help us without luggage and to leave the ship. I was the one who usually carries the bulk of it and could not even support my weight, let alone several suitcases.

They told me they would send me a deckhand and wheelchair the next morning. As we completed the plans, I confirmed I had several bags and two one-litre bottles of Grey Goose we bought in their duty-free store. They assured me," Sir, don't worry; we will treat your luggage as if it were our own". She spoke to me as though she was scolding a child and further said, "Wrap the bottle in all your clothes, and I guarantee we'll treat it nice".

The next day the deckhand arrived with the wheelchair and took us off the ship quickly and without incident. They then wheeled us to the luggage section and could not find one of our bags. We had to navigate the area with hundreds of people running to retrieve their luggage. Out of the corner of my eye, I saw a large suitcase wrapped in a large clear garbage bag.

We navigated to the spot and saw that it was my bag. When they took it off the ship, they smashed one of the two-litre bottles of vodka. I had wrapped it inside all my clothes, which supplied a six-to-eight-inch buffer so I am not sure how this could have happened. One can only imagine the force it took to break it. As we opened the bag up, I found my entire clothes were vodka-soaked, and my expensive leather shoes and belt were soaked, and the shoe dye spread over all the Calvin Klein suits and clothes. I lost about $3,000 that day, as it ruined everything.

We then made our way to the transport buses and the airport, stinking like vodka.

As we sat at the airport, my foot throbbing in pain, we could not believe what had happened. They say that "bad things happen in threes". That was so true: a best friend dies by suicide, foot impaled and they received seven stitches, and they destroyed all my clothes. It still shocked me that the cruise line did not compensate me, which frankly blew my mind. The previous year we had been on a cruise with the same company, and when they backed out of Puerto Rico, they damaged a prop. They could not make the other ports of call, and we limped back to Miami. The cruise line stepped up then and gave us all a 50 percent off discount on our current travel, a 50 percent off voucher for future travel, free Wi-Fi, and a bottle of wine at dinner.

That time we thought it was an exceedingly kind gesture. In this situation, they treated me like a criminal.

When we were going home in the taxi, my stepmom opened a letter that was left in their cabin by the cruise line. She read it and asked Michelle to read it and clarify what she thought it meant. Michelle read aloud," Dear guests, thank you for patronizing our onboard casino. As a valued customer, we would like to offer you and your guest a free seven day cruise that included room, board, meals, and casino credit. "

I was enraged and thought, "Are you bloody kidding me? You maim me, marginalize me, blame me for the injury, and offer me nothing. My parents win money in the ship's casino, and you offer them a free trip".

A week later, I hobbled back to work with my foot heavily bandaged. I struggled, slipping down a slope, and was unable to free myself from "tightening up" or being "stuck". I was so proud that I did not self-medicate during this very traumatic time. I called my counsellor, Mary Margaret, and after about an hour I felt much better about myself and healed.

*****

In the end we sued the cruise line for negligence and were forced to settle 12 months later. The COVID-19 impact on the cruise lines has been devastating the past year, and I did not want to gamble and receive nothing.

We signed a nondisclosure agreement but trust in knowing that it did not even cover my loss in clothes.

*****

This memory was horrific for all involved. While I did not experience the life-altering trauma that Mary and her family did, this put me in a dark and devastating place.

I teach resiliency and strategies to overcome trauma. My story illustrates we must all find the light in the darkness. I found mine and it was within me.

Sadly, Mary sold her place on the island and moved away. She told us they had bought the condominium to "be their retirement castle and now it was her prison". She also recommended that she did not mean to offend us, "But seeing you two so happy together is very difficult for me and makes me uncomfortable". Sadly, I understood and was very empathetic towards her comment. Truthfully, I would feel the same if I were in her shoes.

*****

As I reflect on Mark's life, his suicide, and our friendship, I have realized that I cannot change what he did. I know and admit that sometimes I try to see the good in everything and have even told myself I sometimes miss seeing reality. That said, I genuinely believe in the power of a positive mindset. If I believe that I can do something, how is that different if I believe I can't do something?

As I grow older, wiser, smarter, or with more insight, I try to focus on everything towards what I can learn out of this. That takes tremendous effort, having been raised through my life experiences to never give up and have the pride associated with that.

I have learned that the easiest way to get help is to put my pride and ego aside and simply ask for it. I do not live this life in isolation; I have so many wonderful friends and family that want to help, I just need to ask. I bet you have the same.

*****

This reminds me of Michelle's and my second Christmas together.

I love giving presents and watching the excitement of everyone opening them, the energy level ramps up, there are smiles and laughter. That Christmas as she handed out presents, I discreetly placed mine one-by-one behind my back and fully took them for the joy everyone displayed. Our conversation went as follows.

M: Hey what did you get for Christmas?
D: I don't know, I put all mine behind my back so I can enjoy seeing everyone else.
M: So, you like watching people open presents?
D: Yes, big time.
M: Does it make you feel good?
D: Oh yes, it's my favourite part of Christmas.
M: Does it make you feel great inside to provide joy to others?
D: Yes, it really makes me happy to see the joy in people's faces and see how happy they are.

M: Doug, why did you rob me of that same feeling seeing you open your presents today with everyone else?

Ouch, I will say it repeatedly, Michelle is someone I love, respect, learn from, and look up to.

Her wisdom won that discussion.

Lesson learned and trust in knowing that ever since, I open my presents in sequence with everyone else.

I will never see the "me" again in a comparable situation. I will focus on the "we", and I challenge you to do the same.

*****

AUTHOR'S CHALLENGE

Need help, please ask for help.

If you find yourself in darkness, look within yourself and find your light.

Know that you are not alone and please do not place a finite solution to what could have been a temporary issue.

What's Next? Actionable Goals for You to #RiseUpAndExcel

17

Here are goals and objectives to better serve those in his life and extend sphere of influence through the lessons learned through adversity.

"WRITE YOUR STORY AND MAKE IT A BESTSELLER"

"Your Rough Draft for Your Plan"

We must always create a simple plan. I have found that this plan assists me because it provides an opportunity to learn from the past, balance the present, and work towards a future of personal and professional successes.

Think and reflect on the following question of yourself, fill them out to the best of your abilities, be honest with yourself in reflection because that will be your backbone towards success.

"WHAT'S NEXT? ACTIONABLE GOALS FOR YOU TO #RISEUPANDEXCEL"

Goals and objectives to better serve those in his life and sphere of influence through the lessons learned through adversity.

DOI: 10.1201/9781003187189-19

FINDING YOUR GRANITE EXERCISE

Moving forward, write your four core values down:

1.

2.

3.

4.

POST-SITUATION REFLECTIVE
QUESTIONS TO ASK YOURSELF

1. What did I do correctly?

2. What could I have changed?

3. What will I do differently next time?

USING THE NEWFOUND GRANITE THAT YOU HAVE CREATED BASED ON YOUR FOUR CORNERSTONES OF PERSONAL LEADERSHIP APPLY TO THE FOLLOWING QUESTIONS TO DEVISE YOUR OWN PLAN

What I Have Learned in My Journey?

Step #1

1. Define what your four core values are in life and why.
2. Write them down and post in a place you can view daily.
3. Make a data entry in your Outlook or similar computer every six weeks.
4. These appointments with yourself enable you to review, reflect, and refocus on your core values, why you chose them, and how you can use them to give future goals.
   a. This breeds accountability for your future.
   b. Helps to remind who you were, who you are, and who you want to be.
   c. Slows down your process to reflect, review, and plan when life gets busy. Paying yourself and taking time for yourself is necessary. You must always be "good to yourself" before being useful to others.

Step #2
Review, Reflect and Plan Who You Were, Who You Are, and Who You Want to Be

1. **Who was I?**
   a. What were my goals in life?
   b. What did I do to achieve them?
   c. What could I have done to achieve them?
   d. If I could change one thing, what would that be?
2. **Who Am I?**
   a. What are my goals in life?
   b. What am I doing to achieve them?
   c. What do I need to do to achieve them?
   d. If I could change one thing, what would that be?
3. **Who do I want to be?**
   a. What are my goals in life?
   b. What will I do to achieve them?
   c. What lessons from the past can I learn to achieve them?
   d. If I could change one thing, what would that be?

Step #3

1. Celebrate and journal all successes toward your goal.
   a.   We often ignore the small foundational learning and growing opportunities and
   b.   never deeply appreciate or enjoy the journey.
2. Conversely, journal situations you did not feel that you reached your full potential.
   a.   This supplies time for reflection and the opportunity to "cut yourself some slack" and not be overly harsh on yourself.
   b.   Judge the effort you put into this, not always focused on the result
   c.   Reflect on what went well, take it, tweak it, and make it better
   d.   Reflect on where you did not achieve, analyze, create an alternative plan, and implement
   e.   In the end, both these points are where you will experience the most significant personal growth
   f.   Do not focus negatively; be inspired that you have room to improve, act and enjoy
3. Celebrate and review all the positives and negatives and learn to from them.

COVID-19 and #RiseUpAndExcel

18

WWW.RISEUPANDEXCEL.CA: Blog post August 12, 2020
COVID "DASH LEADERSHIP" PLAN
August 12, 2020

Recently I was asked by one of my friends, "How do I move forward and grow after COVID?" They further showed that they and many of their friends have been stuck over the past months and need a jump-start to life. They needed a way to move forward, get back on the tracks of life, and improve both their personal and professional lives.

The cloud of COVID reminds me of the old saying that "We must hit rock bottom before we can rebound".

In that spirit, I would like to suggest that many of us have hit rock bottom because of the isolation and lack of personal engagement with friends and family because of COVID. This bottom does not scare me, though; rather, it is a place where I can experience self-reflection to redefine my "granite".

My "granite" is where my core values provide me a firm place to stand upon and a place where I hold those dearest in my life and those who I never want to let down and want them to be proud of me.

Family and Core Values are my rock.

I have an exercise that I run called "DASH Leadership" based on the Dash Poem by Linda Ellis (https://bit.ly/2PIjEB1) and corresponding YouTube Video of Senator Bob Dole reciting the poem at his acceptance speech for the 2008 World Food Prize. Dole spoke to the audience at the Iowa State Capitol in Des Moines on the importance of making the most out of one's time and the value of helping others (https://bit.ly/3amy2bt).

I invite you to read the poem and then watch the video with one question in mind: "What are my core values and how can I change or write my dash moving forward?" Then reflect on your answer(s). Then ask yourself, "Who was I, who am I and who do I want to be?"

I would like to share that sometimes in life, I realize that I may fail in a task or personal interaction with someone. As I reflect on those failures, or periods where I can experience the greatest personal growth, I try to focus on the effort I put into the situation based on my core values of honour, integrity, passion, and accountability. In reflection, they are my actual measuring stick, and if I have used those in every relationship, although a conventional scoreboard may say I failed or lost 4–3, I accept the "loss" but take great pride and confidence in knowing I stayed on my tracks and I applied my core values.

As we conclude this blog, I challenge you to reflect and define who you were, who you are, and who you want to be moving forward, Post-COVID?

DOI: 10.1201/9781003187189-20

Author a remarkable story, make it a bestseller always bearing in mind, stay on your tracks and trust in your DASH.

I TURNED 54 THE OTHER DAY

September 25, 2020

It is simply amazing to think that I turned 54 on September 23, 2020, and frankly cannot wrap my head around that. The fact is true that my body may be 54, but my passion and brain still seem to be in their early 20s. The past ten years have seemed like a blur of beautiful experiences, projects, friends, family, giving through charity work, significant job change, and having the honour of coaching, counselling, and mentoring thousands of young people in the hope they all reach their potential.

While some of my friends and a past colleague are retiring and winding down their incredible years of service, I have just begun.

I genuinely know that there is a "drive" coming from deep within that is challenging me to make the most out of every day. I am living every second of every day and trying to make the world a better place, one smile at a time.

My blog post is going to be brief, but with two pieces of homework, I will assign and would be honoured to hear from you once completed:

1. Make at least ten strangers smile today and follow:

2. At the end of this task, ask yourself: "Who was I, who am I, and last, who do I want to be moving forward?

We do not know when we will die, but man-o-man, let us have one "helluva" productive way to live every second of every day until then. Life is a gift, so let us earn it, one smile at a time.

Always strive to be #StrongerFasterFitter in heart, body, and mind, and you will always #RiseUpAndExcel.

Multimedia Resources: Where Else Can You Find Doug?

19

Media:
- Queen's Sovereign Medal Award, https://bit.ly/3kz2brP
- Guelph Mayor's Award Speech, https://bit.ly/36v6u21

Podcasts:
Start-up Instinct: two episodes:
"You Are a Millionaire"   "Life Is Not guaranteed"

Tactical Breakdown
"Stress and Resiliency"

Thrively Leadership Canada
"Vulnerability in leadership is a SUPERPOWER"

DOI: 10.1201/9781003187189-21

Website: www.riseupandexcel.ca
Instagram: Ironwll360

Twitter: @Ironwill360   @SgtDPflug

2020 THE *GRYPHON'S LAIR* ISSUE #34
GRYPHON'S COMMUNITY
INVOLVEMENT FEATURE

Gryphon Football players wear many hats. They are athletes, students, and mentors. But one of the common denominators among all of those that come through the program is the role of community ambassador. It is a job that is as important as the one they do on the field, and in many cases, makes a much bigger impact. Any player on the Guelph team understands this responsibility well before they ever wear the red, black, and gold jersey. It is discussed in the recruiting process, and community service has become an ingrained part of the program's distinct culture.

Doug Pflug is one of the people responsible for that. Pflug was a U of G player from 1986 to 1989 but he made one of the most important decisions of his life when his playing career was done, taking a job as a Guelph police officer.

"The program helped define and create the core principles that I learned through football, which were characteristics the Guelph Police Service wanted", he says.

Pflug was always intent on giving back to the community that was so good to him. About 20 years ago, then Gryphon head coach Tom Arnott asked Pflug to come to talk to the players about getting involved in volunteering. Each training camp, he would pay a visit to talk with the team, mentoring those who wanted to pursue a career in law enforcement, police, fire, ambulance, or corrections.

And Gryphon Football's commitment to the community went to a new level when Stu Lang joined the program.

"Stu always says, 'We're going to take good, young men and make them better,' " Pflug explains. "Our legacy, once football is done, can be to transcend these young men into really giving back to the communities and making an impact".

The football program and its players are now fixturing throughout Guelph. The team does work with several organizations including Big Brothers, Big Sisters and many women's charities, while also raising awareness for critical campaigns like the Think Pink Game, where YWCA Women of Distinction are honoured, or recognizing those doing work in the city with Gryphon Football Community Heroes.

Pflug helped develop the Salute to Service game at the Gryphon Home Opener where those members of the local police, fire, ambulance, and correction branches are hosted in the Gryphon's Nest.

"We want the community to support us in our athletic endeavours, but it can't be a one-way relationship," says Pflug, noting that Gryphon Football has produced 25 members, among the players, staff, and coaches, who have embarked on careers in those areas of service.

One of the truly gratifying aspects of Gryphon Football's commitment to the community is when the players make trips off campus to see the people. Grace Pereira, an employee at the Guelph YMCA, hosted a community event in the summer where second-year defensive back Uriel Kalenga and third-year quarterback Brayden Lassenba came to visit and teach camp kids football skills.

"It's important for these student-athletes to be involved in events like this as it gets them out, not only as a promotion for the team but also because it allows them to be around a community, they may not be familiar with and interact with children," says Pereira.

"It reflects upon the values that are important for a team to be successful by creating a space where these boys work together to teach the future generation of football players the knowledge and skills they have acquired. It was a fantastic opportunity for the children to be able to take part in this event, and they responded. When it was time to leave, the kids were quite upset and mentioned how much fun they had. Even throughout the rest of the summer, I had parents and children remarking how much fun it was and if another event could be scheduled.

"It was a day filled with excitement and joy and it really spoke to the heart of these players, taking time out of their off-season training schedules to help coach and educate the next generation of players".

Giving back is not limited to the boundaries of Guelph, however. Kicker Jared Fernandez-Brown went to Ecuador last May as part of the ME to WE program, helping with the construction of a building at a school in Chimborazo. The experience made an impression on the young Gryphon.

"We don't realize it, but our community has done so much for us, providing us with better opportunities", says Fernandez-Brown. "When we give back, it brings everyone closer together. I have always said that everyone in the world is just one big family and we must help each other and those in need.

"That's why trips like this are a wonderful way to give back to not just your community, but to the world, we live in".

The strong character among Gryphon players is obvious. Pflug, along with his wife and fellow officer Michelle, also thought that a community service award presented at the annual Gryphon Football Gala would be a great way to recognize those who went above and beyond. This season will mark the fifth year the award is presented with Matt Nesbitt, Orion Edwards (twice), and Nic Mirijello the earlier recipients.

Pflug considers community service as medicine for the soul, a gesture that helps both those in need and the individual reaching out.

"I love seeing people who have realized they had some opportunity in their life because of their athletic ability and that they want to pay it back", he says. "Anyone who will be successful in life has to one day learn that 'me' does not supersede 'we'.

"We want these guys to look beyond their own personal interests and the team's interests and say, 'I want to make my community better.' "

2019 THE *GRYPHON'S LAIR* ISSUE #28
FEATURED ALUMNI

This month, we feature Gryphon Football alumni Doug Pflug!

Doug was a running back with the Gryphons, making appearances at a few Yates Cup finals, before graduating in the late eighties with a degree in Sociology. He was a two-sport athlete also competing in wrestling.

Thinking back to his playing days, he tells a great story about his favourite memory being when he was asked to fill in for an injured teammate during the 1986 Yates Cup final against Western. The play was a fake field goal attempt deep in Western's red zone. "It was my rookie year, I was a second-string tailback, and I was absolutely scared to death to have such a prominent place in this game", he says. The play was successful, and Doug ran about 15–20 yards before being tackled on the 2-yard line. "I was so happy because our team scored on the next drive as I watched from the sidelines. That play taught me to always be ready and regardless of the role we have, we must always rise to the occasion and give it our absolute best for the team. Knowing my efforts set my team up for the score on the next drive is exhilarating still to this day". Stories like this that are described with so much detail nearly 23 years later brings a unique sense of family and nostalgia to our Gryphon alumni.

After leaving U of G, Doug started a career with the Guelph Police, fulfilling the dream he has had since he was 9 years old of being able to make a difference in society. While working as a police officer, Doug coached with the Our Lady of Lourdes Football team to get his football fix. "This was very important to me because I was able to share my love of football, police a great community, and be a positive male role model to the young men and other students as a coach and a police officer". Doug continued to share his expertise and guidance as a police mentor with the Guelph Storm since 1995, as well as serving as the Strength and Conditioning Coach for 17 years.

Like many of our alumni, Doug's passion for the game and the Gryphons are just as strong today, and he plays a huge role in our Gryphon Football community with multiple volunteer efforts that help to make our program the best.

In 2001, Doug was contacted by former head coach Tom Arnott to join the team as the law enforcement mentor to provide guidance and ensure our players are great citizens as well as football players.

Doug then took on a formal mentor role for two former Gryphon players, Johnny Augustine, and Orion Edwards, from 2012–2017 supporting them on and off the field to become the stars they are today.

In 2012, Doug sought to increase his involvement with the team, starting up multiple social media initiatives including a fan-based Facebook page and Twitter (@GryphonsLair) where he tweets the games and posts some sideline shots, as well as all Gryphon Football updates.

In 2015, Doug and his wife, Michelle, set up the Pflug Family Community Service Award to be presented at the Wildman Trophy Dinner to recognize the outstanding community service efforts of a player. The winner this season was Nicholas Mirijello, who received his name on the trophy, a $200 gift certificate, and a letter of reference.

In 2015, Doug set up a partnership with Avalon Group Homes for at-risk-youth and created the opportunity for Gryphon players interested in working with youth to earn a part-time job. Players that have

worked for this group include Johnny Augustine, Orion Edwards, Dean Yaromich, Akeem Knowles and Elijah Walker.

Doug's involvement with the Gryphons has also consisted of creating multiple community-based endeavours including honouring Community Heroes of Guelph before every home game and the annual Gryphon Football Special Olympics Powerlifting meet hosted at Alumni Stadium.

The list of ways Doug has contributed to help make Gryphon Football and our athletes successful off the field and in the community is more extensive than can possibly be described in a short newsletter feature but is definitely deserving of the recognition.

"Being a Gryphon is, simply put, paying it forward to make the lives of our community and younger members better. We have an incredibly special organization", he says. "As a young man, it helped me channel my energy in a very productive way. It taught me about elite teamwork, brotherhood, honour, integrity, passion, and accountability. All these traits assisted me in transitioning into law enforcement where the same traits are held so dear".

Thank you, Doug, for all you have done and continue to do to help advance our Gryphon Football program! You are truly a great Gryphon alumnus!

University of Guelph Gryphon Football Pflug Family Community Service Award Winners
Presented annually at the WILDMAN Awards Dinner

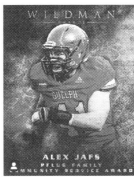

2020

N/A due to COVID-19

2019

Alex Jafs

2018

Nicholas Mirijello

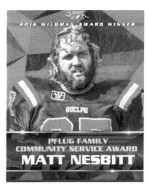

2017

Orion Edwards

2016

Orion Edwards

2015

Matt Nesbitt

Significant Career Achievements

20

2020: SOVEREIGN MEDAL FOR VOLUNTEERS

On July 1, 2020, Doug was named one of Canada's "123 Exceptional Canadians" by the Governor-General of Canada's Office and awarded the Queen's Sovereign Medal for Volunteerism.

Headline: Special Olympics coach giving back everywhere he goes[1]

They have awarded Douglas Pflug the Governor-General's Sovereign Medal for Volunteers

By **Devan Mighton,** *The LaSalle Local*

Claim to Fame: A former university athlete, Douglas Pflug has spent the last three decades serving his community.

The former University of Guelph Gryphons football player was hired by the Guelph Police Service in 1989. At that time, he was introduced to the Special Olympics' Law Enforcement Torch Run.

He has been a high school football coach, a university football mentor and liaison coach, a girls' soccer coach, a fitness coach in the Ontario Hockey League, and the coach of the Guelph Buns Master Rollers Special Olympics floor hockey team.

He has his own mentorship business called Ironwill 360° Leadership, where he also conducts coaching and motivational speaking. For his efforts with the Buns Master Rollers and Gryphons, Pflug has been named a 2020 Governor General's Sovereign Medal for Volunteers recipient.

His list of additional personal achievements is long: The Queen's Diamond Jubilee Medal in 2012, and the Governor General-Police Exemplary Medal in 2010; he was twice awarded Chief of Police Commendations for two separate life-saving efforts. In 2016, he was awarded the City of Guelph Mayor's Award for outstanding and ongoing commitments to Guelph in both a personal and professional capacity.

Background: Pflug grew up in Kitchener-Waterloo. In 1986, he enrolled at the University of Guelph where he wrestled and played football for the Gryphons.

DOI: 10.1201/9781003187189-22

He jokes that he also somehow walked away with a history degree in the middle of the sports he was playing.

In 1989, he became a police officer with the Guelph Police Service. Policing led him to the Special Olympics. "Immediately, I was introduced to the torch run and the Special Olympics", he explains "It sparked an incredible 35-year passion".

He coached high school football for five years before becoming the strength and conditioning coach of the Ontario Hockey League's Guelph Storm. He has been with the team for 25 years, is still a peer mentor with the team, and has three championship rings to his credit despite barely knowing how to skate.

Who are the Buns Master Rollers? "About [a decade] ago, my buddy asked me if I wouldn't mind helping his Special Olympics floor hockey team get ready for the Canadian championship in 2012", he recalls. "They won the Canadian championship in 2012 and they also won the opportunity to go to Boise, Idaho for the Worlds. I had the privilege of coaching the guys there". Pflug says that he is not just their coach, but also their counsellor and mentor. "It's not just the physical", he explains. "I always say that I train their heart, their body, and their mind".

The Buns Master Rollers went on to take the silver medal in Boise.

"In 2014, they won the Canadian championship again and they went to Japan and, again, won silver", says Pflug. "In 2016, they three-peated as Canadian champions and then went to Graz, Austria and they won a silver medal. It is an incredible journey of working with and for these young men with intellectual and some physical disabilities".

He says that collaborating with Special Olympians is both gratifying and inspiring.

"My two hashtags are #StrongerFasterFitter and #RiseUpAndExcel and it's probably been the most rewarding experience I've had in my life, dealing with the Special Olympics, because I challenge anyone to go there in a bad mood and leave in a bad mood," he says. "With the Special Olympics, if you put five lb. of love in, you get 50 lb. back".

In 2017, after 28 years with the Guelph Police Service and working his way up to sergeant, Pflug retired. He and his wife, Michelle, also a retired sergeant and CSI with the Peel Region Police, came up with a way to give back to his former football team and created the University of Guelph Gryphons Football Pflug Family Service Award in 2018. It is given out annually to the Gryphons' graduating football player that gives the most to his community.

"With the Special Olympics, if you put five lb. of love in, you get 50 lb. back". — **DOUGLAS PFLUG**

That same year, he created the Gryphons Football Special Olympics Powerlifting Competition, which allowed Special Olympics athletes to work out in the Gryphons' weight room and mingle with the players. "This was a fantastic opportunity for me to share my love of the Special Olympics with my love for the Gryphons football guys and from there a relationship was born", says Pflug.

Sponsored by Big Kahuna Sports, the athletes get use of the stadium, as well as free food and shirts. For his efforts with both the Special Olympics and Guelph Gryphons, Pflug is named a 2020 recipient of the Governor General's Sovereign Medal for Volunteers. "Sometimes people will look at a Special Olympian or some-one who might be different and they'll discount them without even having a conver-sation with them and finding out what their core values are, who they are, who they were, and who they want to be," he says. "That's where relationships and friend-ships are formed when you just sit down, and you talk with people as opposed to talking to them".

Life in Amherstburg: The Pflugs have started to plan for retirement on Boblo Island. He and his wife spend about a third of the year there.

He says that he has already been contacted by Windsor Police Service Const. Cealia Gagnon about coaching in Windsor once they move to Amherstburg full-time.

Five years ago, after checking out Orillia and Wallaceburg, the Pflugs looked at a home on Boblo Island at the recommendation of friend and realtor Shawn Leblanc.

"The thing that impresses me most is that the whole area, people are so absolutely wonderful", says Pflug. "People of means don't have the attitude like you find in the GTA area and it doesn't matter what your bank account is, people grade you on your core values".

Leading by Example: "Knowing that we all have an expiry date in our [polic-ing] career—I started when I was 21—there was no way I was going to retire at 50", states Pflug. "I went back to school about five years ago and earned my executive leadership certificate from Cornell University knowing that I always wanted to go back to police college and teach".

He is now a leadership instructor for the Ontario Police College's sergeants' course in Windsor. "I want to mentor young officers on what you're supposed to be", he says. "I've had the privilege of meeting 100–150 LaSalle and Windsor officers and even when I come back to town they say, 'Hey Mr. Pflug, how are you?' and it's up to those who have done to mentor those who want to do it".

"I challenge people to define their core values. Mine are honour, integrity, pas-sion, and accountability. I promote that in every aspect of everything that I do". He has served at the Ontario Police College for three years and recently signed on for another three. "I have some unfinished business to do. I have been in the pit of dark-ness. I've got some horrific memories that I still grapple with and have nightmares about, but I wanted to end it on an extremely high note where I could potentially change policing one smile at a time".

*****

2020 WWW.GRYPHONTFOOTBALL.COM

Doug Pflug: A Remarkable Canadian

When Doug Pflug graduated from the Ontario Police College over 30 years ago, his parents Paul and Joan, asked him to make a promise. They asked that their son try to always improve the lives of the people he would meet daily. The 22-year-old Pflug, full of energy and enthusiasm for the job that lay ahead, thought nothing of it.

He did not realize how challenging the journey would be. Three decades later, the Waterloo, ON native has kept his word to his parents. Pflug has devoted his life to helping others, not only as a career officer, but also as a mentor, volunteer, coach, father, husband, and friend. And the office of Julie Payette, the Governor General of Canada, has taken notice.

Pflug was recently honoured by being named to the Governor General's list of 123 Remarkable Canadians.

"This may have one person's name on it but there are hundreds of people through my life who have loved me, supported me, and assisted me," the retired member of the Guelph Police Service says in a humbled voice. "This is a culmination of all of it. This is not about me.

"It's about the wonderful friends, family, and colleagues who have always helped me".

Pflug's choice for the prestigious honour is far from surprising. He has been a fighter since birth. Pflug showed resilience as a newborn when he overcame Pyloric Stenosis (a dangerous condition that causes babies to become dehydrated from excessive vomiting) and then at the age of three, also dealt with Immune Thrombocytopenia, a blood disorder leading to easy bruising and bleeding.

They were mere setbacks in a life devoted to giving, which Pflug felt was his calling. In addition to his years of service with the GPS, he has been relentless in trying to make a difference in the lives of others, be it through his volunteer work with Special Olympics, coaching, personal training services, or work with the Ontario Police College, where he currently acts as the coordinator for the Sergeant Course and the 911 Communication Supervisor Course.

One of Pflug's greatest passions is his deep connection with Gryphon Football. He wore the red, black, and gold as a tailback from 1986 to 1989 and came back to the program he loved almost 20 years ago at the request of then coach Tom Arnott to fill the role of community liaison. Five years ago, the Pflug Family Community Award was created to recognize those Gryphons who go beyond to impact others.

That experience as a Gryphon made all the difference for a young man with a desire to leave his mark on the community. When his Ontario Police College colleague Mike Souliere nominated Pflug for the Remarkable Canadian award, he asked, "How the heck do you do all of these things?"

"I told Mike that Gryphon Football taught me how to be a man", says Pflug, adding that Stu Lang's influence on him has been a blessing. "It's about core values, standing up for people, about giving a voice to those silenced by whatever the adversity they may face in life. It is my calling. I am a Christian. I want to be who I can be and help as many people in the world so that I can earn the life given to me by my god.

"Honour, integrity, passion, and accountability—those were taught to me through the vehicle of football".

"Doug has been a great example of what we as coaches hope all of our student athletes achieve here at our program: to become a good man," says Gryphon Football head coach Ryan Sheahan, who has gotten to know Pflug this past year. "His countless volunteer hours and his leadership with the Special Olympics program has been inspirational and has created a fantastic opportunity for our players and coaches to give back to our community.

"We are proud to have him as a friend of the program".

Pflug notes that sports are a great precursor for law enforcement. There are common principles among them, and he says that of the 2,500 Ontario Police College recruits over the past three years, 50 per cent have experience in U SPORTS athletics. The U of G has been an excellent recruiting ground, as well. Including Pflug and offensive line coach Mike MacDonald, a retired RCMP officer, there have been twenty-five former Gryphons who have pursued a career in policing.

Pflug, who also teaches media relations and the contents of the Youth Criminal Justice Act, is an incredible resource for Gryphon Football graduates entering that world. He is adamant about sharing his experiences and principles with these young men before they start their first day of work.

"As an officer, you often go into people's lives on their absolute worst day", says Pflug, a believer in being strong in both mind and body. "You can't become part of that chaos. You must supply the calm.

"That's when you can truly serve the communities you've been asked to assist".

Those former Gryphon players entering police forces are learning valuable lessons from Pflug, who instructs with both energy and compassion.

"Doug is a kind-hearted person who will always go out of his way to help anyone", says a recent Gryphon Football grad, who must remain anonymous for safety reasons as he prepares to begin his policing career.

"He is a genuine individual. And he wants to see people excel in everything they undertake.

"Doug will provide as many tools as needed for them to do so. He wants our society to be a better place and he works hard to achieve this goal by the people he helps on his path".

But Pflug's words are not reserved for just future officers. Gryphon standout and recently crowned Grey Cup champion Johnny Augustine says that Pflug has been an incredible role model.

"Since my second year, Doug mentored me, guided me", says Augustine, a U of G legend and current member of the Winnipeg Blue Bombers. "He's like a second father because he really gave me great advice. I can say that I am the man I am today because of him. He has humbled me in so many ways. Just the relationships I have with others, I am a big believer in treating people the way you want to be treated, show respect.

"Because of Doug showing me those little things and how far they can go, I want to thank him for that".

Pflug never shies away from a conversation. And he is understandably outspoken about the current views around policing in 2020. He openly denounces bad officers and is a staunch supporter of Black Lives Matter.

"There's a bad narrative out there and rightfully so", Pflug says. "I get it. George Floyd was murdered. There are police officers who don't have the ability to do their job and they shouldn't have their job".

Pflug was exposed to racism in high school at Waterloo Collegiate Institute. He had a young friend named Ram Tumkur, who was of Indian descent. Ram was constantly bullied because of his race and Pflug took it upon himself to defend the boy. Ram would attend Pflug's wrestling, football, and track practices, before their daily walk to the bus stop to ensure his safety from the predators.

On June 23, 1985, Ram, and his sister Chitralekha were among the 329 people killed when terrorists planted a bomb on Air India flight 182, which went down in the Atlantic Ocean off Ireland.

Pflug, who was eighteen at the time, realized then that life was sometimes unfair. He had always tried to protect Ram, but this catastrophic event was out of his hands.

"My heart still bleeds", he says.

Recognition for the 123 Remarkable Canadians honour is on hold because of the pandemic. Pflug has opted to have an in-person visit to Ottawa's Rideau Hall, which could take up to two years. He will wait patiently and focus on the chance to celebrate the award with his daughters Reighan and Alexis, and wife Michelle, a blood spatter expert who also teaches at the Ontario Police College.

Most importantly, he can be proud that he honoured the demanding wish of his parents 30 years ago.

"Everyone owns a piece of it", Pflug says of the honour. "I want to share it with my friends and family".

Written by: David DiCenzo

2016: INDUCTED INTO THE CITY OF GUELPH SPORTS HALL OF FAME[2]

1997–1998 Guelph Storm OHL Champions: Strength and Conditioning Coach

1997-1998
GUELPH STORM HOCKEY CLUB

The 1997–1998 Guelph Storm was an incredibly elite group of players under the leadership of coach George Burnett and general manager Alan Millar. They finished the Ontario Hockey League season in first place overall, just one point ahead of the Ottawa 67's—the team they would eventually meet in the final.

"(Previous GM) Mike Kelly had left a strong base—a team with lots of versatility and discipline", said Burnett. "They had great leadership and could play the game lots of different ways".

Led by defenceman Chris Hajt and centre Manny Malhotra, this team didn't have a scorer in the top ten, but they were bursting with character players like Nick Bootland, Brian Willsie, Bob Crummer, Jason Jackman, and Kent McDonell.

The Storm would march through the playoffs knocking off Sudbury and Plymouth in four straight games. However, a near tragedy struck when the Whalers Jesse Boulerice viciously swung his stick at Guelph's unsuspecting Andrew Long leaving him unconscious on the ice and unable to play the rest of the season.

"That was so emotional for our team", said Burnett. "We had not only lost a good player (second in team scoring during the regular season) but just seeing him laying on the ice was terrible, but we stayed strong".

In the final they would beat Ottawa in five games on a series-winning goal by Willsie to win their first OHL championship and advance to the Memorial Cup. There, Malhotra would lead the club in scoring, but it was goaltender Chris Madden who stole the show. He had a .947 save percentage and was named the tournament MVP. They met the Marian Hossa led Portland Winterhawks in the final and lost a 4–3 heartbreaker in overtime.

You could argue this is the greatest Storm team to represent our city. Six players would go on to play in the NHL (Malhotra, Willsie, McDonell, Hajt, Eric Beaudoin, and Brian McGrattan).

"It was a team of character and great skill", summed up Burnett.

Inducted into the Guelph Sports Hall of Fame—Team category—May 18, 2016

2016 CITY OF GUELPH MAYOR'S AWARD[3]

For his outstanding and ongoing Guelph commitments in my personal and professional ability.

Each year, the Mayor of Guelph presents Mayor's Awards to honour Guelph's difference makers—people who make our city a better place through volunteer service. 2016 marks the 20th year of the Mayor's Awards.

"Sergeant Doug Pflug is a 26-year member of the Guelph Police Service who, outside the uniform, has given thousands of volunteer hours to an extensive list of local organizations.

Over the past 14 years, Doug has served as a coach for the Guelph Buns Master Rollers Special Olympics Floor Hockey team, which capped off its tremendous record by winning the National Championship this winter. Collaborating with the athletes weekly, Doug is a mentor, motivator, and lifelong friend to the team.

Through the Guelph Police Service, Doug has been a leader and champion for many community initiatives and organizations— including Guelph Wellington Crime Stoppers; the Special Olympics Torch Run; and the Police Service's #no more bullies campaign. For many years he organized the Cst. Jay Pirie Memorial Hockey Game, where the Guelph Police "No Stars" took on the Guelph Storm to raise funds for Guelph and Wellington Special Olympics.

Doug also served as the community outreach coordinator for the Ontario University Athletics champion Guelph Gryphons football team this past season. He is currently a mentor for eight players who wish to pursue a career in policing and is leading the football program's youth outreach and mentoring initiative.

For more than 17 years, Doug was the strength and conditioning coordinator for the Guelph Storm, and served as a mentor for many young hockey players who called Guelph home. He is also the strength coach for the University of West Virginia Men's Hockey program, part of the American Collegiate Hockey Association.

Sgt. Pflug has dedicated countless hours and touched thousands of lives in our community. He exemplifies the Guelph Police Service credo of "Pride, Service, Trust".

To watch the award presentation and Doug's Acceptance speech click:

2015: GUELPH POLICE SERVICE COMMUNITY SERVICE AWARD

*****

2012: QUEEN'S DIAMOND JUBILEE MEDAL RECIPIENT

Queen's Diamond Jubilee Medal Recipient for service to the community in both his police and personal ability. Nominated for my exemplary personal and professional community service by a community member to our MPP Liz Sandals. A committee of three local Order of Canada recipients reviewed and approved the nomination and sent it to the Governor General of Canada.

POLICE SERGEANT RECEIVES JUBILEE MEDAL[4]

Web posted on June 28, 2012:

The final award presentation scheduled for the Guelph Police Service Awards Ceremony, held June 27, 2012, was intended to be Sergeant Douglas Pflug being awarded the Queen Elizabeth II Diamond Jubilee Medal by Guelph MPP Liz Sandals. Unfortunately, MPP Sandals' arrival at the ceremony was delayed, and the presentation did not occur during the awards ceremony. MPP Sandals arrived about a half-hour after the end of the ceremony, while the reception was still taking place. So, a small group watched and celebrated as Pflug received his well-deserved award. The Fountain Pen was there, and here is what you missed:

CHIEF BRYAN LARKIN

I am immensely proud of Doug, as are all the members of the Guelph Police Service. On behalf of [Guelph Police Services] Chair Judy Sorbara and Deputy Chief De Ruyter, I congratulate the Pflug family on this great honour.

Now, after travelling around with Liz as she presents these medals, I am pleased to welcome her to our house, the Guelph Police station.

MPP LIZ SANDALS

I am delighted to be here, and I am deeply sorry for the timing getting messed up. I am sure you all have heard about the Queen Elizabeth II Diamond Jubilee Medals. This is the 60th anniversary of Queen Elizabeth's ascension to the throne, which makes her the second-longest serving monarch in the entire history of Great Britain. Only Queen Victoria reigned longer, and if you ever visit Queen's Park, the queen at Queen's Park is Queen Victoria, you can see her sitting on her throne there. I imagine if this queen reigns as long, they would put up a matching statue there.

Queen Elizabeth has been a real model of devotion to duty and a leader who has fulfilled her role no matter what obstacles have been thrown at her throughout her life. In honour of that, Queen's Jubilee medals were struck. Ontario is presenting two thousand medals: each of the 107 MPs handles handing out fourteen and can choose how to hand them out. The way the process worked here in Guelph was, we asked for nominations, and received the nominations. I had two local people who are members of the Order of Canada, Bill Winegard and Ken Kasha, aid me with reviewing the nominees and selecting the final candidates. Then the candidates were submitted to the Ontario Minister of Citizenship, and then up to the Governor General, because ultimately, it is the Governor General, acting on behalf of the Queen, who approves all candidates.

So, as you all know, Doug is being honoured here tonight. So, here is a little bit of information about Doug, which you all know but it does not hurt to hear about it again.

Doug Pflug takes an innovative approach to his role as the official spokesperson of the Guelph Police Service, and in overseeing the School Safety, High School Resource Officer, and the Values, Influences, and Peers programs. He is passionate about kids, organizational success, and keeping the community safe.

On a personal note, some of you, particularly Judy, know that I have served as a school trustee for 15 years. I also served as [Minister of Education] Kathy Wynne's parliamentary secretary, and as the chair of the Safe Schools Action Team, so the programs that affect school safety are programs that are very near and dear to my heart. In particular, the High School Resource Officer program that is here in Guelph started before it was provincially mandated. We at Upper Grand and Wellington Catholic were among the first boards to do it anywhere in Ontario, and it has been a very successful program, both from the point of view of the schools and of the police here in Guelph, for building good relationships amongst the students and between the students and the police.

Doug also generated a total commitment of $100,000 from Win-Mar to create a Youth Crime Prevention and Education Programme which focuses on Guelph schools and the community. He also spearheaded the local planning committee for the Ministry of Education's police school protocol design—again something that started here in Guelph before it became provincial policy, and something I had the pleasure of reviewing from the provincial policy side as part of Safe Schools.

Doug has also served as an executive member of the Committee of Youth Officers for the province of Ontario [COYO], and Wyndham House for Boys. I am often a guest speaker at COYO's annual conference, and I think it is one of the best organizations in Ontario dealing with issues around youth violence and drugs and the general various problems where youth intersect the criminal system. It is the only conference I know of that has all the players involved: it has the police officers, the school administrators, it often has school social workers, and it also has the community social workers.

And finally, Doug is active in coaching with all sorts of organizations. He works with Special Olympics, but also with lots of local sports organizations.

So, you are very, very deserving of this Queen's Jubilee Medal, and we are all enormously proud of you. Congratulations.

*****

2011: OACP/OMRON "AWARD FOR EXCELLENCE IN MEDIA RELATIONS"

Nominated by Corporate Manager Shelagh Morris for outstanding efforts in Law Enforcement in conventional and social media strategies.

Award Information: In Ontario, police officers and civilian personnel are dedicated to professional media relations and corporate communications. They are committed to ensuring the public face of their service is well represented in print, radio, television, and social media. The Ontario Association of Chiefs of Police and the Ontario Media Relations Officers Network (OMRON) are pleased to present The Catherine Martin Award for Excellence in Media Relations.

This award recognizes the dedication and commitment of an individual in an Ontario police service who has improved the relationship between media and police. The award will be presented to a sworn or civilian member (or team) who has demonstrated consistent dedication and professionalism in the strategic use of media and/or social media—either individually or as part of a campaign—to educate and showcase the profession of policing in the community, supporting public safety or advancing investigations. The individual/team is valued by their commands as an advisor, recommends strategic positions for police leaders, and produces corresponding messaging in the Province of Ontario.

YouTube video created for the award ceremony

2011: INDUCTED INTO THE CITY OF GUELPH SPORTS HALL OF FAME[5]

2010 Guelph-Wellington Special Olympics Floor Hockey Strength and Conditioning coach

For the Guelph Buns Masters Rollers Special Olympics Floor Hockey team, it was a four-year journey to the World Championships in 2009.

Guelph has always had an active floor hockey community, winning the national championship back in 1986. It began in 2006 when the Rollers won the Regional championships, then in 2007 they captured the Provincial championship in Toronto. The following year they represented Ontario at the National tournament in Quebec City.

They entered that event on a winning streak and their only blemish was a tie with Quebec during the opening game of the nationals. They would not lose again, winning the gold medal and berth in the World championships in Boise, Idaho the following year.

At the World's, with seventy teams present, Guelph was seeded in the top pool with teams from Jamaica, Trinidad-Tobago, and Hungary. After beating all three teams in the round robin, they would face Jamaica in the final. Things looked good with the Canadians holding a 5–2 lead heading into the third period, but some untimely penalties opened the door and Jamaica stormed back to win the gold 8–7.

The Rollers featured a father and son coaching team with Paul and Shawn Turner (along with Mark Cullen) and even a father and son amongst the players with captain Paul McTaggart and son Andrew. Many of the veteran players had said this would be their final season but after settling for silver, all but one player from the roster is back gunning for another shot at world gold.

Paul Turner was honoured as the longest serving volunteer in the Ontario Special Olympics with thirty years behind the bench. "Guelph is known throughout the country as a dynasty" said his son Shawn. "We have developed an excellent program".

Inducted into the Guelph Sports Hall of Fame—Team category—October 26, 2011.

NOTES

1. www.thelasallelocal.com/life/special-olympics-coach-giving-back-everywhere-he-goes/
2. http://thesleemancentre.com/wp-content/uploads/2016/05/1997-1998Storml.jpg
3. https://guelph.ca/city-hall/mayor-and-council/mayors-office/mayors-awards/2016-mayors-awards-recipients/#sgt-douglas-pflug
4. www.thefountainpen.com/cgi-bin/showstory?id=9385
5. http://thesleemancentre.com/guelph-sports-hall-of-fame/teams/2009-guelph-buns-master-rollers-team-canada/

Final Thoughts

21

As I reflect on the past 54 years of life on this earth and 35 years in law enforcement, I genuinely sit in awe at the life I have lived alongside all of you.

The most dominant fact that I've come to learn is that I too have focused over the years on some negative experiences and forget to focus on the positive that came from them. The pursuit of a positive mindset is what I teach, but also follow to achieve the fullest life possible.

Over the years as a police officer, I have had the real privilege of working alongside some incredible and remarkable officers—I would respectfully suggest some of the best in the world.

My goal in this book was not to criticize or point fingers of blame. It was to highlight and frame the context of the adversity I faced in my life, celebrate the opportunity of the experience, learn from it, and look for the Next Opportunity.

To my colleagues, thank you for your individual part in my past, present and future. I am so genuinely thankful to have fought in the trenches with you. We have laughed, cried, and worked extremely hard trying to make the world a better place, one call at a time, one smile at a time.

Thank you all for being part of my story.

To all those who allowed me to enter your lives in the many roles I tried to fill, I would also like to thank you for your trust. Trust in knowing that I know your faith is precious. I know I hold it deeply from our experiences together.

Dad once told me that a person will always be a millionaire when they hold their name and word up high and continue to invest in themselves. I welcome your respective trust, friendship and experiences in the same values and esteem, and I am therefore a wealthy man.

I hope as the weeks turn into months and months turn into years, you all challenge yourself to a similar journey of reflection, self-discovery, and periods of healing. We all have the light within us. Please take steps to find yours.

I am immensely proud of my contributions and know that I have left the world a better place than I found it through my efforts. I can now sit back and enjoy retirement knowing I was a "has-been" versus "never-was".

We owe it to our families, friends, colleagues, and yes, ourselves to take pride in our sacrifices of "serving and protecting" and enjoying the next 40 years of happy, healthy, and inner peace.

Thank you for believing in me, for picking me up when I fell, and for believing in me. I have learned precious lessons from you that enabled me to move forward and then celebrate our collective successes.

DOI: 10.1201/9781003187189-23

I always joked that I wanted to retire one day, "healthy, happy and sane, not insane".

Trust in knowing that I will because this journey has allowed me to "Find My Granite through my four cornerstones of personal leadership".

I sincerely hope that my "vulnerability as a superpower" has inspired you to reflect, do the work, and "Find your granite and four cornerstones of personal leadership".

I must go now . . . I have some mountains now to climb until next time.

I love you all. May God Bless you and your families.

—Doug

I Can—I Must—I Will—I Did

Who Do You Want To Be?

"NO" (your name here)

_____
Your Name

NO = _____

Next Opportunity = _____

It's now time to book the book down and to reflect and write your plan to move forward and #RiseUpAndExcel. Always remember the fuel to accomplish this will be found through three small phases to guide you, "I Can, I Must, and I Will". Once completed you can follow up with, "I Did".

Your author's challenges that were assigned throughout this book—it's time to #DoTheWork.

APPENDICES: AUTHOR CHALLENGES

1. Think of someone that you have let earn headspace and evict them.
2. Do not let past events in our lives hold us back from life's experiences in the future. #RiseUpAndExcel.
3. Sometimes the best compliments in life are never given. We all have an expiry date, so make sure you reach out before it is too late.
4. Take some time to reflect on your "pivotal moment" and write it down to capture it as I have done mine. Focus on the positive you have learned from it because it shaped you. In this process find three to four people who helped you navigate the time and moved forward #StrongerFasterFitter. Call them and tell them the lasting impact they continue to have in your life and celebrate your successes with them.
5. Try to give back to someone or something.
6. I challenge you to give what you can in mentoring youth; they need us to help plan, find, and seek their paths. When you mentor a young person, never lose sight that you will help in the release of some exceptional human potential.
7. Your challenge is twofold:
8. Thank a frontline worker for their service

9. Create an email folder and store all the positive comments you receive. Then, on a difficult day, re-read those comments and appreciate, respect, and need them.

10. My challenge is to seek the resources you may need one day. Know how to access them and get the help you may need.

11. Use the plan-assess-act to solve every problem or plan every personal and professional event you wish to conduct.

12. The next time you are researching a project I would like you to review and reflect and try using my model: Take it, tweak it, make it better, make it yours, and move it forward.

13. Do not let someone's inability to focus, strategic plan, or lead impair your ability to lead. Look at every situation as a potential space for you to experience tremendous growth, and after some time and effort, you will achieve it and #RiseUpAndExcel.

14. Take some time and sit down with your spouse on a lovely quiet relaxing evening and create your relationship plan for success in both casual and emergent times using our model for success.

15. Start thinking about your "Dash".

16. "Make one stranger smile per day, or mentor a young person. You do not know how those small acts of kindness can unleash some incredible human potential".

17. Help a stranger out, open a door, say a kind hello, help move a couch, help at a charity BBQ, or support your charity of choice with monetary donations.

18. Cut yourself a break next time and do not be so hard on yourself. Judge yourself by the effort you put in and use your core values to determine if you "won" or not.

19. Life is to live. I would like to challenge you to "live every second of every day" and #RiseUpAndExcel.

20. Need help? Please ask for help. If you find yourself in darkness, look within yourself and find your light.

21. Ask yourself, reflect, and write down your answer. Who were you? Who are you? and Who do I want to be?

CHAPTER #24 FINDING YOUR GRANITE EXERCISE

Moving forward, write your four core values down:

1.
2.
3.
4.

Reflect of a time when you were very happy with the end results of a project, situation or adversity faced. Reflective questions to ask yourself:

What was the situation?
What did I do correctly?
What could I have changed?
What will I do differently next time?
What do I need to do to achieve them?

"Write your story and make it a bestseller"
"Your rough draft for your plan"

We must always create a simple plan, and I have found that this plan assists me because it provides an opportunity to learn from the past, balance the present, and work towards a future of personal and professional successes.

Think to yourself and reflect on the following question of yourself: Fill them out to the best of your abilities, be honest with yourself in reflection because that will be your backbone towards success.

"What's next? Actionable goals for you to #RiseUpAndExcel"

Goals and objectives to better serve those in his life and sphere of influence through the lessons learned through adversity.

Finding your granite exercise:

Moving forward, write your four core values down:

1.
2.
3.
4.

Think of a project you must begin and to ask yourself:

What skills, knowledge or controls can I bring to the situation?
What positive and negative experiences have I gained from this initiative?
What needs to occur for a successful outcome?

Using the newfound Granite that you have created based on your four Cornerstones of Personal Leadership apply to the following questions to devise your own plan.

What have I learned in my journey?

Step #1

1. Define what your four core values are in life and why.
2. Write them down and post in a place you can view daily.
3. Make a data entry in your Outlook or similar computer every six weeks.
4. These appointments with yourself enable you to review, reflect, and refocus on your core values, why you chose them, and how you can use them to give future goals.
    a. This breeds accountability for your future.
    b. Helps to remind who you were, who you are, and who you want to be
    c. Slows down your process to reflect, review, and plan when life gets busy. Paying yourself and taking time for yourself is necessary. You must always be "good to yourself" before being useful to others.

Step #2

Review, reflect, and plan who you were, who you are, and who you want to be?

1. Who was I?
    a. What were my goals in life?
    b. What did I do to achieve them?
    c. What could I have done to achieve them?
    d. If I could change one thing, what would that be?
2. Who Am I?
    a. What are my goals in life?
    b. What am I doing to achieve them?
    c. If I could change one thing, what would that be?
3. Who do I want to be?
    a. What are my goals in life?
    b. What will I do to achieve them?
    c. What lessons from the past can I learn to achieve them?
    d. If I could change one thing, what would that be?

Step #3

1. Celebrate and journal all successes toward your goal.
    a. We often ignore the small foundational learning and growing opportunities and
    b. never deeply appreciate or enjoy the journey.
2. Conversely, journal situations you did not feel that you reached your full potential.
    a. This supplies time for reflection and the opportunity to "cut yourself some slack" and not be overly harsh on yourself.
    b. Judge the effort you put into this; do not always focus on the result

c. Reflect on what went well, take it, tweak it, and make it better
d. Reflect on where you did not achieve, analyze, create an alternative plan, and implement
e. In the end, both these points are where you will experience the most significant personal growth
f. Do not focus negatively, be inspired that you have room to improve, act and enjoy

3. Celebrate and review all the positives and negatives and learn to from them.

WHO DO I WANT TO BE?

I am not sure; I have not written this part of my life yet. I will tell you that it involves my dear family, friends, an island, a boat, a plane, an 11-ft dinghy, a golf cart, and incredible dreams that I'll make reality.

Time to follow my own advice and planning for success.

Would you like to join me?

I will see you at the finish line.

www.RiseUpAndExcel.ca

DOUG PFLUG'S INFLUENTIAL LEADERS' WALL OF HONOUR

www.RiseUpAndExcel.ca

I dedicate this wall of honour to all of the great leaders that I worked for and worked with in my life. I post each name below in tribute because each person took the time to coach, counsel and mentor me and as such are placed in with respect on this wall for all to see.

Aaron Hanaka	Harry Schnurr	Paul Hebert
Alexis Pflug	James Gross	Paul Pflug
Andrea Ninacs	James Hosapien	Paul Schmidt
Attila Korga	Jeff Jackson	Paul Turner
Bryan Larkin	Jim Rooney	Paul Wright-
Cam Guthrie	Joan Gross	Pierre Chamberland
Carol Crowe	Joan Pflug	Reg McKeen
Carol Higgins	John Cater	Reighan Pflug
Colleen Fawcett	John Musselman	Richard Stewart
Cornelius Gronendyk	Kevin McCord	Rick Walker
Dave Barr	Kyle Walters	Robert Davis
David Grossman	Larry Lacey	Robert W. Allan
David Morrow	Laura Pflug	Ryan Sheahan
David Pringle	Leanne Piper	Sara Chamberland
Don Pflug	Lena Bradburn	Scott Green
Doug Cox	Lilian Pflug	Scott Grover
Doug Cummings	Lottie Kerr	Scott McRoberts
Ed Goddard	Louis Chamberland	Scott Raso
EJ McGuire	Maurice Obergan	Shawn Camp
Gary Boag	Michael Barnhart	Shelagh Morris
George Burnett	Michael Souliere	Steve Gill
Gord Hunter	Mike Gobeil	Steve Tanner
Gord Mason	Mike Kelly	Stuart Lang
Gord Mitchell	Neal Young	Thomas Gill
Gordon Kerr	Neil Widmeyer	Tom Arnott
Gregory Zinger	Patrick Martin	

And, my loving wife and best friend,
Michelle Pflug

Index

Printed in the United States
by Baker & Taylor Publisher Services